COMPLETE
CROCHET
COURSE

COMPLETE CROCHET COURSE

The Ultimate Reference Guide

SHANNON & JASON MULLETT-BOWLSBY

LARK
New York

New York

An Imprint of Sterling Publishing Co., Inc.
1166 Avenue of the Americas
New York, NY 10036

ISBN 978-1-4547-1052-3

Distributed in Canada by Sterling Publishing Co., Inc.
c/o Canadian Manda Group, 664 Annette Street
Toronto, Ontario M6S 2C8, Canada
Distributed in the United Kingdom by GMC Distribution Services
Castle Place, 166 High Street, Lewes, East Sussex BN7 1XU, England
Distributed in Australia by NewSouth Books
45 Beach Street, Coogee NSW 2034, Australia

For information about custom editions, special sales, and premium and corporate purchases,
please contact Sterling Special Sales at 800-805-5489 or specialsales@sterlingpublishing.com.

Manufactured in China

2 4 6 8 10 9 7 5 3 1

sterlingpublishing.com

Cover Design by Elizabeth Lindy
Interior Design by Jason Mullett-Bowlsby and Sharon Jacobs
Photography by Jason Mullett-Bowlsby

The authors would like to dedicate this book to all the women and men who continue to pick up hooks, learn new techniques, and make beautiful objects for themselves and the world around them.

To Anoree Kay Bowlsby, aka Mom.

Four words from you launched this wonderful journey
we've been on the past several years. Thank you for all
the conversations about the craft, fit, style, and teaching.
And most of all, thank you for always believing in us.
We know you would have been proud of this book.

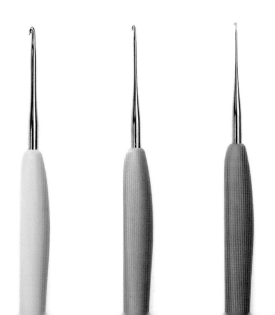

Contents

Introduction

As teachers, we love to ask our students when and why they became interested in learning crochet. What we've learned is that some of us come by crochet naturally as a result of being around family who wielded hooks to make afghans, cozy sweaters, and toys. Others are spurred to pick up the hook by the birth of a baby or upon seeing the latest crochet garments walk down the runway at Fashion Week. Still others come to crochet as a therapeutic way to keep their hands active and their minds calm. Whatever your reason, or however far along the path you are, we are thrilled that your crochet journey has led you here to our book.

Crochet is this wonderfully intriguing and often mesmerizing activity in which we use a hook to pull loops of yarn, string, wire (or any other material we can grab with that hook) through other loops. This simple repetition of pulling loops through loops results in the creation of beautiful fabrics and holds limitless possibilities for expressions both artistic and practical.

Historically, crochet has largely been a skill passed along through oral tradition: one craftsperson passing along their knowledge of the craft to the next through generations of family members and friends. As with all crafts passed along orally, we have been witness to regional and even family-specific terminology and techniques that are not always accessible universally. While this leads to a rich sense of heritage, it also lends itself to many problems, since we have transitioned within the last century to more formally written patterns and increasingly complex projects, requiring a universal language across the entire craft of crochet. This means that if we want to recreate a pattern from a magazine and have it look identical to the item photographed, then we all must speak the same language!

Designers must be able to tell you in written language where to put your hook and how to pull up loops so you can recreate the designs I have made here in my studio. You must be able to understand that written language exactly as intended so you can reproduce the results. No longer can you just assume that what your grandma called a "shell stitch" is the same thing your uncle calls a "shell stitch." Odds are high that they are two very different things that will produce dramatically different fabrics.

In addition to teaching you new techniques and improving upon your existing crochet skills, one of the purposes of this book is to solidify that universal language, and to give greater definition to our existing language. Using a clear and consistent crochet language ensures that we have a uniform way of passing on the skills of our craft. Those skills can be embellished upon with time and practice.

Jason and I have put all of our passion for teaching and the art of crochet into the book you are now holding in your hands. We fervently hope you will digest the information we give you, use the step-by-step instructions, photos, and illustrations to make the practice swatches and projects in this book, and learn how to create FAB crochet fabric for yourself.

Whether you come to the *Complete Crochet Course* as an absolute beginner or as an experienced crocheter looking to upgrade your hooking skills, we hope you take away a passion for crochet that is all your own, which you can share with your family, friends, and the fiber arts community.

STITCH ON!
S & J

"**The joy derived from the act of grabbing yarn with your hook and pulling that yarn through loops to make a new loop and thus creating fabric; this is, in the purest sense, the essence of crochet.**"

How to Use This Book

This book was created not only for new crocheters but also as the go-to reference book for crocheters who have more experience with a hook. We have organized *Complete Crochet Course* so you can start at the beginning and work your way through to the end, gaining more knowledge and developing your skills as you go, or you can turn to a specific page or section to see a technique or stitch you are curious about.

Both of us are, by nature, teachers, which means we want you to succeed at learning to crochet and at upping your crochet skills! To that end, the crochet stitches and techniques within *Complete Crochet Course* are organized as if you were taking a live class from us, and the layout of each section is designed to optimize your learning experience.

We start with the basic skills needed to make stitches with a hook and yarn, then progress to the next layer of stitches and skills based on your knowledge of those basics. We continue in this manner, building each new skill upon the last, until you are making more complex stitches and stitch patterns, and are then ready to apply them to the projects we have created for you.

Here are some of the special features you'll find throughout *Complete Crochet Course*.

Before You Stitch

This section is full of all the information you need to know even before you pick up a hook and yarn. We start off by introducing you to the larger focus of this book, which is making fabric. Then, we describe the tools you will use to crochet—including a quick primer on the makeup of yarns—before we get down to the nitty-gritty of picking up your hook and yarn. Next, we describe the parts of a crochet stitch and walk you through how to make stitches by inserting your hook into different parts of a stitch. Finally, we dive into pattern reading, ensuring you can understand the instructions in this book for the tutorials and projects. You will also find information about swatching, blocking, and how to tension your yarn to achieve proper gauge.

This first section of the book is designed both to set you up for success as you make your first crochet stitches and as a reference once you do actually start making stitches. Much of the information will make more sense the further you work through this book.

Making Stitches!

This is it! This is the moment you have been waiting for —when you put hook to yarn and make your very first crochet stitches. This is where the skill-building begins with the basic stitches you will need to make your first crochet fabrics and to build upon to develop more complex stitches later. These lessons are the basis for every crochet stitch you will ever make. Once you learn to make these basic stitches, we will lead you through a logical progression of new stitches and techniques stacking new skills on top of previously learned skills taught just as if you were taking a series of crochet classes from us in person. If you are new to crocheting, you will find it easy to work from the beginning to the end of this section acquiring new skills and creating more complex and interesting crochet stitches and fabrics as you go. If you are a more experienced crocheter, you will enjoy being able to start at any point in this section of the book and jump into a new technique or stitch while also being able to look back through previous sections for any clarification you might want.

Beyond the Basics

Next, we take your crochet skills to a whole new level by working on individual families of special stitches and pattern stitches that combine all of the skills you have learned so far in the book. This is where you really get to strut your stuff and play with new stitches and colorwork techniques that will keep you inspired and push your crochet skills to even higher levels.

Finishing

We wrap up the technical aspects of *Complete Crochet Course* with a section on finishing that will teach you the skills to put professional-looking finishing touches on your crochet projects, allowing you to really show off your new skills and crochet fabrics. Here, we have included everything from blocking and weaving in ends to our special techniques for sewing seams. We've also made sure to include some of the techniques we have developed over the years in our garment design studio that will help give your projects a polished and clean look. This section concludes with Jason's most requested tutorial: setting in a zipper.

The Projects

This is where it all comes together! "The Projects" section contains patterns designed for the application of all the stitches and techniques you have worked on throughout *Complete Crochet Course*. As with the rest of the book, we have added elements to these patterns to help you work through them with the best chances for success. This includes a special section at the beginning of each pattern that lists the specific skills and stitches used and where to find them in the book. In time, you will be better able to search through a pattern yourself and identify these points, but, for now, we'll help you out with references to each stitch and technique to ensure that you can complete your projects successfully. All you have to do is look through this "Skills Used" section and see which stitches and skills you need to learn or brush up on before you start; then you're ready to go!

As we said, each pattern is designed to give you a practical application of the stitches and techniques in this book, ensuring that your newfound crochet skills are engrained in your brain and muscle memory. But, to be completely honest, we also designed these patterns to give you maximum impact for showing off your FAB new crochet skills! From practical garments to showstoppers, you'll be proud to wear these designs or even to give them as gifts to some lucky person.

Resources

This final guide sources all of the products we featured here in our book. These are the folks who helped us out with products so we could bring this book to you. Each of them are listed along with their company website so you can check them out for yourself.

"The Resources" section includes the worksheets we use for calculating stitches and rows per inch and for working out stitch multiples for when you start making your own projects inspired by the stitch patterns you are learning. I mean, really, when you are cramming your brain full of all of this crochet knowledge, who has room in there for math? These easy-to-follow, step-by-step worksheets will be there for you when you are ready.

Also in this section you will find a number of helpful charts and the master key for all of the stitch charts found in this book. This is one section you will definitely want to bookmark!

Special Features

Throughout *Complete Crochet Course* you will find some special features we have tucked in here and there to help you along the way. Here is what you can expect to find:

Foundation Row and First Stitches of a Row Options

Most of the stitch patterns and project patterns are written with two options for the "Foundation Row." One option is the traditional method of making a chain, then working a return row of stitches into that chain. A second uses foundation stitches (*page 102*). We also provide alternate ways to create the first stitch in a row, thus alleviating that dreaded "wonky edge" so many crocheters of all skill levels battle. Take the time to master each of these so you can use different Foundation Rows and First Stitches to create fabrics that fit each of your projects.

Special Insets

Throughout the book, look for special sections labeled "**STITCH ON!**" These provide tips for continuing on with the stitch you are working on to create larger projects such as scarves, afghans, hats, and accessories. Jump into these! The sooner you start thinking of what you are doing as creating textiles and fabrics for your projects, the better you will be at this amazing art of crochet.

Practice Swatches

With each of the stitches and techniques taught in the book, we have included practice swatches for you to work on to help solidify your learning. Especially in the "Making Stitches" section, we recommend you start by working each stitch in a worsted-weight or DK-weight yarn (you'll learn about those later) that is smoother and lighter in color. Yarns that have a lot of fuzz or texture actually get in your way when you are first learning to wield a hook. We also recommend avoiding 100% cotton yarns when you are first learning, as these can be stiff and difficult to work with. You can use whatever is readily available in your area, but we like Lion Brand Wool-Ease, Cascade 220 Superwash, and Valley Yarns Haydenville for our beginner classes. You'll find websites for those companies in the "Resource Guide" on page 328. Once you feel comfortable working your new stitches and skills, try them again using different weights of yarn to see what kinds of fabrics they create. You'll be surprised how changing up yarn weights will affect the outcome.

A final note from the authors . . . your teachers!

First, it cannot be stressed strongly enough:

While you are working your way through this book, make sure you take time to go back to the previous sections and use them as a reference guide. This will help you remember what was said and also help you apply the principles introduced in those earlier sections to your work. Something that might not have been entirely clear in the "First Stitches of a Row" section might click into place in your mind when you are way over in the section on "Seams and Joins." Keep your bookmarks handy, and don't be shy about taking notes as you go so you can go back and reference earlier thoughts and skills.

And finally (no, really!) the most-important, number-one, ultimately important, can't-do-without, won't-work-without thing you need to keep in mind while you are learning is this: be patient with yourself and give yourself the opportunity to learn. Whether you are holding a hook in your hand for the first time or you are brushing up on techniques you've learned and since forgotten, or whether you are learning new, advanced skills, you must be patient with yourself. Impatience is the enemy

"Impatience is the enemy of learning."

of learning and only leads to more frustration, and it all ends with a hook and a tangle of yarn being chucked into the corner of the room while you head to the cabinet to find that stash of chocolate. (Yes, we've all been there.)

Give yourself time to comprehend and internalize the techniques and skills as they are presented. In time, you will be creating beautiful projects and reveling in the satisfaction that comes with saying "I made this!" You will get there!

Crocheting is largely a muscle-memory skill, and muscle memory is learned only by repetition. So, to assist in helping your muscles memorize, we've included practice swatches for each of the stitches and stitch patterns in this book.

Learn the individual stitches, then work the practice swatches, then move on to the patterns to apply your skills to a larger project. Repeat this for each stitch and swatch and you'll find success as long as you are patient with yourself and allow yourself to make mistakes (and to sometimes really make a mess) without judging yourself harshly. Be patient with the learning process, and be patient with yourself.

BEFORE YOU STITCH

Making Fabric

Before we dive into putting hook to yarn . . .

There are a couple of important points to cover, including specifics about that hook and yarn. It probably goes without saying that the goal of this book is to teach you to be a better crocheter. However, there is a goal that goes hand-in-hand with that: to give you the skills and techniques necessary to create your own crochet fabrics.

The factors that go into making those crochet fabrics are the tools, yarn, and stitches you use, and how you use them. Change any one of these factors and you can end up with a completely different fabric. For those keeping track, that's a staggering number of possible fabrics we have to choose from as crocheters! Our goal within these pages is to give you a clear understanding of these factors so you can manipulate them to make your own crochet fabrics.

Welcome to the world of textile design. Yes, when we put hook to yarn, we are making textiles! Textile is defined by Merriam-Webster as: "a woven or knit cloth." We will, for now, excuse the folks at Merriam-Webster for leaving out crocheters and assume our rightful place in this amended definition that will read: "A woven, knit, or crocheted cloth." There. Much better! So yes, when you make crochet fabric you are creating textiles and choosing the colors, fibers, and patterns those fabrics are made from. That makes you a textile designer! Doesn't that feel fancy?

As you are working your way through this book, you will notice that our primary focus as we are teaching you techniques and stitches is to apply those to the overall craft of making fabrics for your projects. In fact, you will see the phrase *"the right fabric for the right project"* used quite often within these pages even before you pick up a hook.

"The right fabric for the right project" is going to be our mantra and focus throughout this book. Every choice you make, from the yarn you use to the hook size and stitch pattern you choose, will affect the resulting fabric for your project. Just because you are in love with that yarn you saw at the store doesn't mean it will be the perfect yarn for that cardigan or throw pillow. Likewise, that gorgeous lace stitch pattern just might not be what is called for if you are making a warm fall jacket. While the project patterns you encounter in this and our other books, as well as out there in the crochet universe, will tell you what yarn and stitches to use to create the right fabrics for those projects, there will be times when you will be able to take off and create fabrics for projects of your own.

Whether you decide to develop one of the stitches in the "Pattern Stitches" section into an afghan or a scarf, or whether you decide to make a cardigan or pullover of your own, you will need to make decisions about the makeup of the fabric you are creating, based on the project you are making. Crochet fabrics that are appropriate for home decor pieces are going to be different from the fabric for a light spring top, while yarn for baby blankets is different than yarn for outerwear, rugs, or placemats. Stitch patterns that are loose and lacy may not be appropriate for long garments that will sag and stretch out of shape, and tight stitches are great for rugs, toys, and purses, but not so great for garments.

In the end, the fabric you are making depends on three factors:

1. **Hook**

2. **Yarn**

3. **Stitch**

Change any of these three factors and you will end up with a different fabric. For those keeping track, that's a staggering number of possible fabrics we are able to choose from as crocheters! And, since you are textile designers, you can appreciate just how FAB it is to have so many choices for making crochet fabrics.

As you work through *Complete Crochet Course*, don't just learn the stitches and techniques, and don't just look at your yarn and hooks as beautiful, yummy, resources and tools you use to make your stitches. Instead, think about them all in the context of what types of fabrics they will create and how you could use them for future projects. Keeping these in mind as you progress through your learning will ensure you can make more informed decisions later on about your projects and will guarantee you are making the right fabric for the right project!

The Tools: The Toys

Beyond the obvious first tool you need—your hook—there are other tools you will use as a necessary part of your process. Some are essential, some are great to have if you can get your hands on them, and some are downright collectible. We'll give you an overview here of the basic tools needed, as well as some that are just plain fun to have.

The Product: The Yarn

Oh, the yarn! Beyond what feels good in your hand and your favorite colors (as if that's not enough!), there is quite a bit of information to take in about yarn. While we won't go into the minutia of all things yarn, we will break down the most important parts into easy-to-understand pieces so you can make the best decisions about the right yarn for the right project.

How You Hold Them: Yarn Holds & Hook Holds

How you hold your hook and yarn definitely affects your final fabric. This section will give you options so you can work with and adjust your tension as needed.

What You Do with Them: The Stitches

Finally, we reach the moment where the hook meets the yarn. The stitches you make are the smallest components of the crochet fabric you are creating for your project. We start with the base stitches you need to know, then build from there to more complex, swirling, gorgeous crochet stitches that will have your hooks and your heart humming.

One More Thing . . .

Remember: you are creating fabric. To that end, the way you hold your hook, the yarn you use, and the stitches you choose will all affect the final fabric. In the pages that follow, we will lead you through the process of discovery that will guide your mastery of crochet, so you can feel the joy and freedom of making your own crochet projects!

General Items for Your Crochet Kit

Yarn Needles and Tapestry Needles

Yarn needles and tapestry needles have larger eyes for use with yarn. Sometimes the tips are angled and are more blunt than sewing needles, but there are tapestry needles with sharp tips too, so choose carefully based on the type of project you are going to use them for. This type of needle is used for sewing with yarn, e.g., weaving in ends and seaming garments.

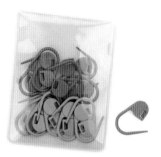

Stitch Markers

Used for keeping track of a stitch or a place in your work. Good for holding a stitch to keep it from coming undone when you put your project down, or for remembering your place within a complex stitch pattern.

Sewing Needles

Sharper points with smaller eyes for use with finer-weight threads. For sewing woven fabrics and items like buttons, clasps, and zippers to yarn.

Blocking Wires and Blocking Mats

Rustproof wires woven through finished fabrics to hold them in place for blocking (*see Blocking, page 240*). Depending on the thickness of the blocking wires, they will be more flexible for blocking curves or sturdier for holding more substantial pieces of fabric in place.

Blocking mats are surfaces used for pinning your fabric swatches and project components to while you are blocking them. Blocking mats can range from garage floor and playroom mats to an ironing board with a towel over it. The key functionality here is the ability to stick a pin through your crochet fabric and the blocking mat in order to hold the fabric securely in place while the fabric sets.

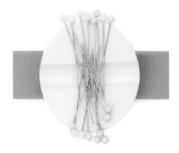

Pins

Used for holding your work in place on blocking mats or dress forms. Also used for holding zippers (*see Setting in a Zipper, page 268*) and trims in place for sewing.

- Straight pins
- T-pins
- Upholstery pins (U-pins)

Hang Tags

Great for keeping track of details of swatches and projects and for labeling yarn scraps for future use.

Scissors

Larger scissors for heavy-duty cutting or for cutting large pieces of woven fabric and trims. Small scissors for ease of transportation in project bags.

Measuring Tape

Used for taking measurements of projects and checking finished measurements of fabrics and project pieces.

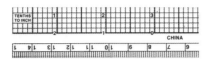

Ruler

Good for counting stitches and rows per inch to check gauge (*see Checking Tension and Gauge, page 74*).

Yarn Swift

Acts as an extra set of hands for holding hanks of yarn while you wind them into balls.

Hook and Needle Gauge

Used to determine the gauge of hooks that either don't have the gauge printed on them or for which the gauge information has worn off with use. Some come with a short ruler on the side for counting stitches and rows.

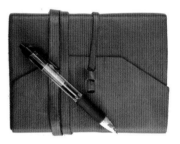

Notebook and Pen/Pencil

Not enough can be said about keeping track of thoughts that occur to you while you are learning new skills and techniques, or while you are working on projects. Record your thoughts and inspirations immediately or they tend to get lost in the task at hand.

Your hook is the tool you use to work directly with the yarn (or other materials you might be crocheting with) to make fabric, and will be your constant companion and creative partner in your future crochet endeavors.

Ball Winder

Great tool for winding hanks of yarn into usable balls. Some models have a hand crank but there are electric models on the market that do the cranking for you!

Crochet hooks come in all shapes, sizes, and colors, and are made from every material imaginable. Crochet hook designs range from the functional, to the quirky, to collectible works of art. Once you start exploring all of the different types of crochet hooks out there in the fiber arts universe, you will quickly discover that there is a hook for every type of crochet, and there is a hook to fit the mood and personal style of every crocheter. We recommend you experiment with a variety of hooks to see what works best for you. There are no right or wrong hooks! As long as it feels good in your hand and creates the fabric you want, you have the right hook for you.

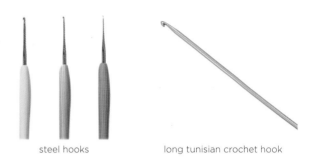

steel hooks   long tunisian crochet hook

interchangeable tunisian crochet hook with cord

crochet hooks on display

set of crochet hooks in standard sizes

Your hook is the tool you use to work directly with the yarn (or other materials you might be crocheing with) to make fabric, and will be your consistent companion and creative partner in future crochet endeavors.

Different sizes of hook are used with different weights of yarn to create different fabrics. Ensuring that this tool is the best it can be, and that it will do the best job for you, is of paramount importance to the success of your projects. That being said, every crocheter has their own preferences in their hooks, and just about every crocheter (the authors included!) will eagerly tell you what their favorite hooks are and why.

Some hooks are very specific to the type of crochet you are making.

For example: steel crochet hooks are very small gauge metal hooks (not always "steel" as the name implies) used for thread and very fine laceweight yarns. Tunisian crochet (or Afghan crochet) hooks have a long handle or cable attached to them so you can pick up a long row of stitches for working the unique two-pass rows of this particular style of crochet.

Then, of course, there is the standard set of crochet hooks you will be using for the majority of your learning.

There are hooks with shaped handles or special grips that can make them easier to use for crocheters with hand health issues. And there are fun hooks in different colors and materials.

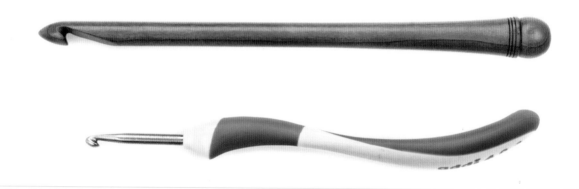

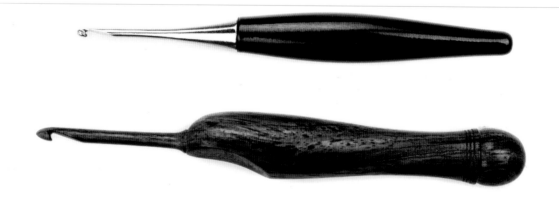

Anatomy of a Crochet Hook

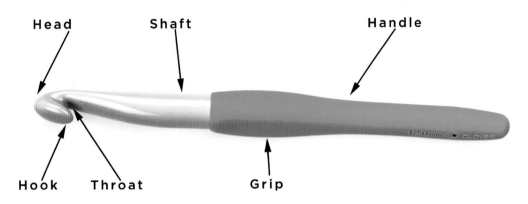

Head   Shaft   Handle

Hook   Throat   Grip

The hook can be further defined from the head as the actual curve and point

Important Things to Look For When Choosing a Hook

Does it feel comfortable in your hand?

After using a hook for an extended period of time, you will be able to tell if it causes or exacerbates hand or wrist pain. Having a hook that feels comfortable in your hand while you are crocheting is the most important factor in choosing a hook. If your hook causes you pain, you aren't going to enjoy crocheting, and you will not be successful at creating correct fabrics with that hook.

Does it help me achieve proper gauge?

The shape of the throat, head, and shaft of your hook should help ensure that you can achieve proper gauge if your tension is correct. If you have corrected your tension and still cannot achieve your gauge, you might need to explore other types of hooks. Also, what the hook is made of will also affect your tension and how you make your stitches, which will ultimately affect your final gauge.

Is it made correctly?

It is important to check the gauge of novelty and handmade hooks against standard measuring tools to ensure proper stitch and row gauge can be achieved. This is especially important when making garments and projects with precise measurements. If you are questioning the gauge of a novelty or handmade hook, you can check it against your commercially manufactured hooks or use a nail gauge from the hardware store.

Now let's break the hook down into its separate parts and see how the construction and materials used to make hooks can affect your stitches and, therefore, your final fabric.

Defining Characteristics of a Crochet Hook

Some differences in crochet hooks, like color, are simply aesthetic in that color doesn't usually affect the performance of the hook, unless the method for coloring the hook causes additional drag or pull along the surface of the hook. Others, like the shapes of the individual parts of the hook, or whether it is made from wood, metal, or plastic, are definitely functional and will affect both the way you make your stitches and, ultimately, the fabric you create.

Handle & Grip

Since how we hold our hook is key to how we create our crochet fabrics, the handle or grip of the hook is an important first consideration, as this is where the hook rests in our hand. Here are some important features to consider:

1. Length — Some hooks have handles that are shorter, while others have handles that are longer. This will vary due to the preferences of the hook manufacturer or maker. You should be sure the handle of the hook is not too long or too short to feel comfortable in your hand.

Depending on your hook hold, a handle that is too long can cause exaggerated movements, which will lead to fatigue and pain. Likewise, a handle that is too short will cause you to clench your fingers to secure your grip on the handle, also leading to fatigue and pain.

2. Grips — Some hooks come equipped or can be fitted with special grips to make your hook fit more comfortably in your hand. These special grips are made from a variety of materials—from hard to soft—and are often as decorative as they are functional.

Sometimes a grip is absolutely necessary, as in the case of arthritis or other degenerative joint conditions, or when prolonged hand tension around a thin hook handle causes joint pain and hand fatigue. Even in cases where there is no medical condition present, sometimes holding a grip is just more comfortable than holding a plain hook.

3. Shape — Many hooks come pre-made with shaped handles that are contoured to fit the hand more comfortably. Like grips, these are often as decorative as they are functional and can relieve a whole list of issues, from hand and joint pain to tension issues. That said, not all shaped handles fit all hands, and different hook holds can make these shaped handles downright painful.

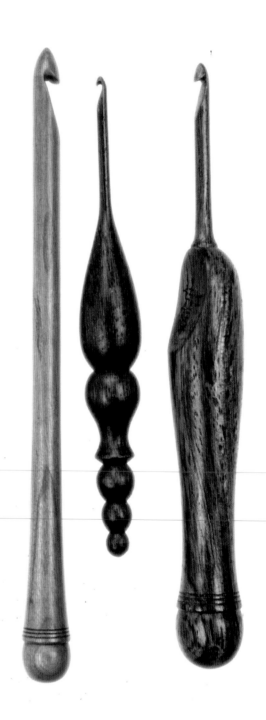

Shaft

The gauge of a crochet hook is given in millimeters, and is determined by measuring the width of the shaft of the hook. Like the handle, you should consider whether the shaft is long enough to allow for comfortable movement of the hook while making stitches. Sometimes, as in the case of hooks with special grips or shaped handles, the shaft can be shorter and feel less comfortable, depending on how you hold your hook and how you move the hook when you make your stitches.

Throat Types

The throat of a crochet hook is located right behind the head and under the hook. There are two basic types of throats on crochet hooks: tapered and inline.

The throat works with the hook to grab and secure the yarn so you can pull loops through loops and make crochet fabrics. If the throat is too wide, you might make looser stitches and have a difficult time making secure loops; if a throat is too narrow, you could end up making tighter stitches, resulting in fabric that is more dense than you intended. The reverse is also true: you can use the different types of crochet hook throats to help you obtain a more even tension to your stitches.

Head Types

How rounded or pointed the head of your hook is can have a definite effect on your crocheting. If the head is too pointed you might split the yarn you are working with or the stitches you are working into. If the head is too rounded you might not be able to get into the stitches of your crochet fabric, and more complex stitch patterns can be more difficult to work, causing you to slow down.

Hook

Yes, the entire tool is called a crochet hook, but the part of the head that comes down and over the yarn to grab it and pull the yarn to make loops is the hook. The hook and throat work together to grab and secure the yarn, allowing you to pull the loop through the other loops. Too shallow of a hook is definitely going to slow you down, since you could actually miss the yarn and won't be able to pull it through the loops on your hook.

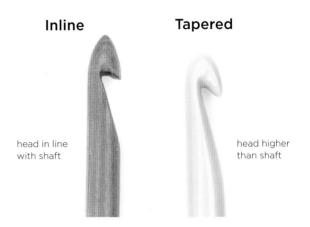

Inline

head in line with shaft

Tapered

head higher than shaft

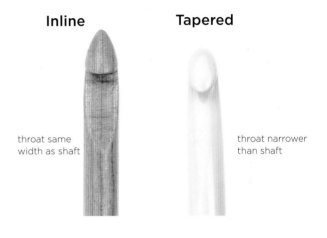

Inline

throat same width as shaft

Tapered

throat narrower than shaft

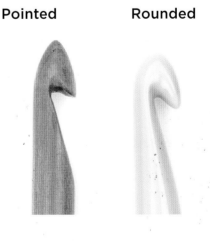

Pointed

Rounded

Composition

Yarn moves over the surface of a hook differently depending on what the hook is made from and, in the case of wooden hooks, the type of wood that is used and what kind of finish is on that wood. Often, crocheters will describe a hook as "fast" or "slow" depending on how quickly they can move the yarn over the hook while making stitches. While hooks can be made from virtually any material, there are three common types of hooks on the market:

Wood

There are as many types of wooden hooks as there are types of trees. These range from functional to creative and are often collector's items. With regard to functionality, how easily yarn moves over wooden hooks varies by the type of wood used to make the hook and by how polished the finish of the wood is. A more dense wood will naturally have a smoother surface, and any polish or finish on such a hook will make it that much smoother, making a faster hook.

Metal

Like wooden hooks, there is seemingly no limit to the types of metal hooks that can be created. Everything from aluminum to cast iron, precious metals, and steel can be found on the market with a quick internet search. Novelty hooks aside, metal hooks that are made by pouring molten material into molds are the most common of the metal hooks used. These metal hooks have smooth finishes and are, generally, "fast" since the metal allows yarn to move easily over the surface of the hook. However, as with wooden hooks, the finish used on the metal hooks can definitely affect how smoothly the yarn moves over the hook.

Plastic

Plastic hooks can be made from a vast array of materials that are molded or carved into shape. Plastic hooks have smooth surfaces but can be "slow" depending on the type of yarn you are working with, as well as on environmental factors such as humidity in the air that can cause moisture to work against you and your hook.

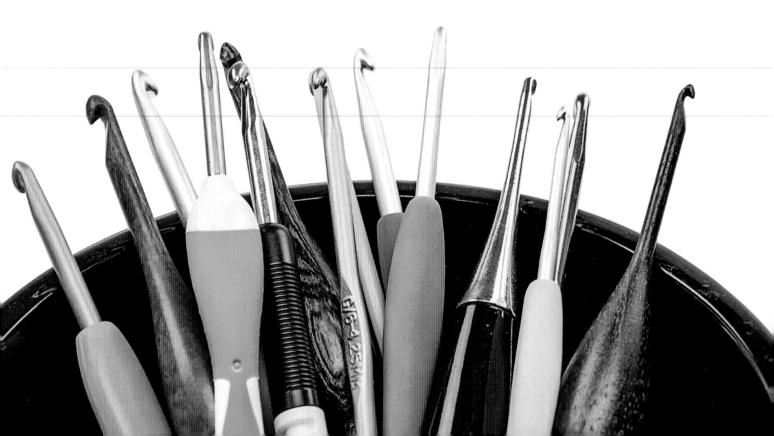

Hook Gauge

Hook gauges used in crochet patterns vary for different types of yarn and crochet materials, and for different choices made by the designer. The larger the yarn or other materials you might be crocheting with, the larger the hook gauge you will need. Most yarns will have the recommended hook gauge listed on the ball band (*see Ball Bands, page 36*).

How To Read the Gauge of a Crochet Hook

Hooks are sized based upon the diameter of the hook shaft in millimeters. Small changes in the gauge of the shaft can make drastic changes in the final fabric you create. Hook sizes are usually stamped on the handle of the hook in US, metric, or international size standards. The exception to this is a handcrafted hook that might not be labeled. You will need to use a needle/hook gauge (*see page 18*) to verify the size in this instance.

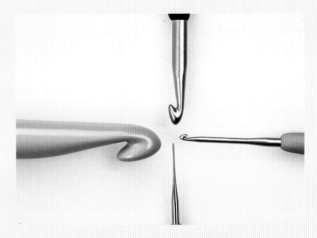

In addition to the standard set of crochet hooks, there are smaller hooks referred to as steel hooks. Steel hooks are used with fine laceweight yarns and threads, and their sizing is exactly the opposite of standard hooks.

For example, in steel hooks, the smallest size is a #14 (0.7mm) hook and the largest is a 00 (3.5mm) hook.

GO FORTH AND TRY DIFFERENT HOOKS!

The fun part of choosing a hook is holding it in your hand and, yes, making stitches with it. Do not jump into this lightly! Try different hooks with various handles, grips, throats, heads, and hook types. And definitely try hooks made from different materials. Each experience can be vastly different and even revelatory in nature. While one hook might feel awkward or even hurt your hands, another might feel like it was crafted just for your hand and your stitching styles leading to a lifetime of use. Personally, we have several sets of hooks, as well as individual hooks that we collect. That said, we do have our personal preference of hook style and composition and use a set of those hooks for all of our work projects. Be patient. Have fun trying hooks and explore everything out there. You'll soon have your own collection to use and admire for years to come.

FUN FACT: The smallest of the steel hooks are so small that they look like needles. In the past, lace made with the smallest of these hooks was called "cobweb lace."

Yarn

At this point you've probably perused the aisles of a yarn shop or craft store and are as enthralled as the rest of us by the endless array of colors and types of yarn available. The combination of fiber content, how the yarn is made, and the colors... Hand-dyed, kettle-dyed, space-dyed, factory-dyed... OH, the colors!

Bottom line: Crocheters love yarn in all of its combinations and for all of the possibilities we can imagine when we look at it and squeeze it in our hands. It is this exciting, seemingly endless combination that results in the parade of gorgeousness that can make picking the right yarn for your projects at once the most exciting and the most frustrating (but mostly exciting!) part of the whole making process.

With such a wide variety of yarn to choose from, the most important thing to keep in mind as you make your choices is that you are picking the right yarn for the right project. We cannot state this strongly enough! Just because you are in love with that alpaca/silk blend yarn and can't wait to get your hook into it doesn't make it the right yarn for your project. You are going to want to consider everything from yarn content and weight to how the yarn is made and know exactly what kind of fabric that yarn is going to create. Then, and only then should you give a yarn consideration for your project. Always ask: *Is this the right yarn for the right project?*

Having said that, we are strong proponents of buying yarn that you fall in love with keeping it until the right project comes along. We call it "Pet Yarn!" Everyone should have yarn that they have adopted just because it is beautiful and wonderful to hold and gloriously inspiring to have around. Then, one day, your Pet Yarn will merge perfectly with a project and become Project Yarn. Either that or you will create a project of your own especially for your Pet Yarn. Don't laugh... we currently have most of a wall full of inspiring, fabulous, Pet Yarn.

Believe us when we tell you we could go on for the entirety of this book talking only about what makes up this glorious wonder that is yarn and how the makeup of yarn gives it certain properties making different yarns appropriate for different projects. But since our goal is to put hook to yarn and actually get stitching, we will endeavor here to give you a primer with solid general guidelines to help you get started and to help you make good choices about which yarns to use to make the right fabrics for your projects.

The rest is up to you. Yes, you will have to go out and play with yarn, experiment for the good of your craft, and see which yarn combined with which hook size and which stitch pattern makes you happy and suits your project best. And, yes, there will be yarn that you buy just because it makes you happy even if you don't have the perfect project for it yet ("Pet Yarns"). So certainly learn the fundamentals of yarn in this section but then get out there, put your hands and hooks on all the yarn, and have fun exploring the wonders of it all.

So Much Yarn, So Little Time

Yarn Weights

In this context, when we refer to the "weight" of a yarn, we are not talking about how much the yarn registers in grams or ounces when you put it on a digital scale. The weight of the yarn as we are using the term here is actually the same way we talked about the gauge of a hook earlier. The weight of a particular yarn is determined by the width of the yarn as measured when it is lying flat and relaxed.

And naturally, different weights of yarn result in vastly different fabrics, even when using the same stitch pattern.

Here, for example, are three swatches made using a single crochet through the front loop only stitch (sc tfl) in three different weights of yarn:

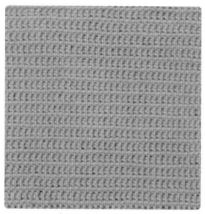

sc tfl in fingering weight

sc tfl in worsted weight

sc tfl in bulky weight

And here are three swatches made using a dc-shell stitch pattern in three different weights of yarn. It is easy: to see how each weight of yarn dramatically changes the finished crochet fabric.

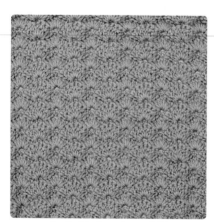

dc-shell in fingering weight

dc-shell in worsted weight

dc-shell in bulky weight

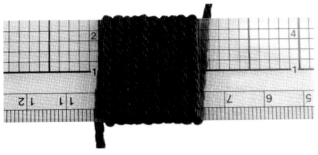

yarn wrapped around a ruler - 10 wpi = worsted weight

CYC - 0 Lace	CYC - 1 Super Fine	CYC - 2 Fine	CYC - 3 Light	CYC - 4 Medium	CYC - 5 Bulky	CYC - 6 Super Bulky	CYC - 7 Jumbo
0 LACE	1 SUPER FINE	2 FINE	3 LIGHT	4 MEDIUM	5 BULKY	6 SUPER BULKY	7 JUMBO
Lace, Light Fingering, #10 Crochet Thread	Sock, Fingering, Baby	Sport, Baby	DK, Light Worsted	Worsted, Afghan, Aran	Chunky, Craft, Rug	Bulky, Roving	Jumbo, Roving
35+ WPI	19–22 WPI	15–18 WPI	12–14 WPI	9–11 WPI	7–8 WPI	5–6 WPI	4 or less WPI

See page 319 for a larger version of this chart.

An even more specific way of determining a yarn's weight is by determining the wraps per inch (WPI) for that yarn. Here we have a worsted weight yarn that we have wrapped around a ruler. The yarn is wrapped lightly around the ruler so as not to stretch it out and, thereby, make it thinner. After the yarn is wrapped so that the wraps lie perfectly side by side, we count the number of wraps within one inch.

We have added a WPI section to the CYC chart so you can have both references. In our example, we can see we have 10 wraps per inch and, looking at the WPI section of our chart, we can confirm this is a worsted weight yarn.

The beauty of using this method to determine the weight of a yarn is that it works every single time. Regardless of whether the yarn is machine made or handspun, you will always know the exact WPI and be able to determine whether this yarn will match the yarn listed in your pattern.

WARNING: Just knowing the weight and even the WPI of a yarn does not guarantee that particular yarn will work for your project. Even if it is a worsted weight yarn at 10 WPI and the yarn content is the same, you must create a fabric swatch with the yarn to ensure that you have the right yarn to make the right fabric for your project. Not doing so would be like a cut-and-sew person blindly ordering a bolt of fabric without ever touching it . . . it just doesn't work like that. We have to test our fabric swatch and see if it fits our project, and then we can buy a project's worth of yarn.

The horror stories from crocheters who blindly chose a yarn and then ended up with something less than desirable could fill a dozen books of their own. But, since you are reading this, you won't have such a bone-chilling tale to tell in your future!

YARN WEIGHTS and WRAPS per INCH (WPI)

In this chart from the Craft Yarn Council (CYC) website, there are numbers and names assigned to each weight of yarn, from the lightest weight of yarn, which is called "Lace" and is given a "0" number designation, all the way up to the largest classification of yarn, which is called "Jumbo" and is assigned the number "7" as its signifier. This chart is useful as a starting point when determining which weight of yarn you will be using for your project.

Specifically, if a yarn company or pattern gives the number or name designation for a particular weight of yarn, you can start there when selecting your yarn, whether you are buying the yarn suggested in the pattern or substituting a yarn of your own preference. You will usually see this designation on the band or tag of the yarn (more on that in a minute) and at the beginning of a pattern where the yarn information is listed, *(see Parts of a Pattern, page 54)*.

Types of Fibers

Yarn will either be made exclusively from, or from a combination of, animal, plant, or synthetic materials. This is the main factor that contributes to the nearly endless variety of yarn available.

Picking the fiber your yarn is made from for your project fabric is the same as picking the fabrics for the clothes and accessories you wear and the home decor you use in your daily life. You must consider the form and function of the project you are making and apply that consideration to the type of fabric you are going to make, and, therefore, the type of yarn you will choose to make that fabric with.

For example, if you have a rough-and-tumble toddler (or adult) in the house, you probably aren't going to adorn your furniture with silk pillows and cashmere throws. Likewise, if that same toddler or perhaps a rowdy dog (or three!) is part of your household, you probably aren't going to use fine silks and cashmeres for your pillows and throws. On the other hand, if you are making a special home decor piece or a garment for a special occasion, those silk and cashmere yarns are exactly what you are going to reach for in the yarn aisle.

Current yarn manufacturing and processing allows for access to yarn that looks more high-end than it actually is. We can now create yarn that looks and feels luxurious without the luxury price. We are fortunate to have access to actual high-end fibers and blends with everything from camel and bison to rare sheep breeds to yarns blended with silk, bamboo, and even pearl dust and gold.

As you stand in the yarn aisle of your local store or peruse the stands at a specialty yarn market, always remember that you are using your hook to make fabrics with that yarn. Your focus is to pick the right yarn so you can make the right fabric for the right project. Fabrics for toys should be able to stand up to use, wear, and washing, while home decor and accessories should match your lifestyle, whether that be pastoral and genteel or wash and go. And, of course, garments should be appropriate to the occasion and to the individual who wears them, with some meant for running, jumping, and climbing trees, and others for lounging around the house or stepping out for a night on the town. That stunning camel/silk blend might get you excited in the store, but you have to ask yourself: *Will it stand up as fabric for a garment for someone who will wear it playing sports, working in the garden, or working at a rough job?*

Again, we could go on for an entire book about all the combinations and variations of yarn but, for our purposes here, let's take a look at some of the most common materials yarn is made from—and how that can affect your fabrics.

cashmere (goat)

angora (rabbit)

Animal

Wool, cashmere, camel, buffalo, mohair. . . if it comes from the coat of an animal

The blanket term "wool" has been used for years to describe yarn made from the coat of an animal such as a sheep or goat. It only takes a minute of searching your local yarn shop or online store to find that the traditional sheep and goat fibers have been joined by camel, buffalo, musk ox, rabbit, mink, possum, alpaca, llama, and vicuna . . . just to name a few. All of these wonderful beasts produce equally wonderful coats from which we can derive fiber for creating yarn. The naturally durable and even water-resistant nature of these fibers makes them suitable for everything from fine garments to children's clothing and toys to home decor and utilitarian accessories.

Our best advice is to wander out to fiber festivals and yarn shops or to let your fingers browse through an online store and sample a variety of these fabulous fibers. Work each one of them into fabrics and determine your preferences (obsessions?) for your projects both current and future. And don't forget what we said earlier about "Pet Yarns." More than a few spaces on our favored shelves are taken up by animal fibers and are just there for inspiration (and petting) from time to time.

merino wool (sheep)

Plant

Cotton, linen, bamboo . . . if it grew from the soil

There are a variety of processing methods required to refine and define plant fibers, making them available not only in their nearly raw forms as rustic and durable yarns, but also as smoother and more luxurious yarns. Everything from cotton and linen to hemp, thistle, bamboo, ramie, and sisal is available for working into fabrics with your crochet hooks. There is even a plant-based fiber created from seaweed called SeaCell.

For those with vegan preferences or allergies to animal fibers, yarns that come from plant fibers are not just a good substitute, but a FAB option. Do a quick internet search and you'll find a wide variety of these fibers available as single blends or in combination with other fibers, adding to the variety of options for your crochet fabrics. And, like animal fibers, these yarns are equally appropriate for home decor, toys, accessories, and garments.

linen yarn (plant)

Synthetic

Acrylic, metallic, plastic . . . if it came from a chemical process

Synthetic materials created for yarn are often made to emulate natural fibers but some do well on their own as durable, long-lasting yarns and crochet materials. There are storage closets and cedar chests around the world (including our own) holding afghans and throws made generations ago that are now cherished heirlooms. Plastic yarns make for great outdoor works of art and home decor accessories (think placemats for your patio set!), and metallic yarns and metallic threads make crisp, clean stitches that look great as home decor or shimmering garments. In addition to standing on their own, these fibers are often spun together with animal and plant fibers to create unique yarns that suit a variety of projects those fibers might not otherwise be suitable for on their own.

plastic yarn

Other Materials

Wire, fabric strips, leather, plastic, rope . . . these can come from anywhere and everywhere

If you can grab it with your hook and make a loop, you can use it to crochet with. Everything—from jewelry wire and strips of plastic shopping bags, rope, leather, to even old VCR tapes—has its place in the world of crochet.

Imagine outdoor placemats or rugs made from strips of plastic shopping bags or rope. How about a hammock for your back yard or a shopping bag made from . . . well, shopping bags? Why not a vest made from strips of old t-shirts or VCR tapes? Placemats made from kitchen string or leather cord? Paper? Shoelaces or floral wire? Sure! The possibilities are endless if you let your mind and your hook wander a bit. And you should! Wander away and play with all the materials you can think of. You might become the next avant-garde clothing designer or create a stunning piece of art.

buffalo wool with 24 karat gold fiber

How Yarn Is Made

Yarn is made by twisting fibers together to make one long piece of yarn. This act of twisting fiber "fluff" into yarn is called spinning. Most of the yarn you see broadly available has been spun in a factory on massive industrial machines. There is also, however, a huge marketplace of handspun yarns made on drop spindles and spinning wheels. Hand spinners are an excellent source for wonderful yarns that have personalities of their own, making your projects even more unique.

Whether handspun or factory made, your yarn will be described as having a certain number of plies or not plied at all. A basic understanding of how yarn is constructed will help you make an even more informed decision about choosing the right yarn to make the right fabric for your projects.

Let's do the twist!

Ply

Let's take a closer look at your yarn. Here we have close-up photos of lengths of different yarns laid side by side. In a close-up like this, it is easy to see that our yarn is made up of lengths of fiber that are spun and twisted into the final product. Some yarns have little or no twist at all. In this case, the yarn is close to its unprocessed form.

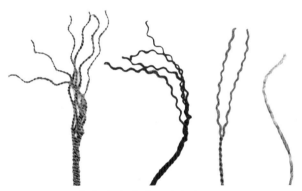

6-ply, 4-ply, 2-ply and single spun yarn

Roving

Roving is usually the base material a hand spinner uses to create yarn. Roving, pieces of loose fiber, are pulled off in long strips that is then spun with a drop spindle or wheel. In some cases, roving is used as yarn and some commercial yarns are produced that are called "roving yarns."

Roving can also be crocheted directly with no spinning at all by just pulling off lengths of the fiber as if you were going to spin it and then crocheting just like you normally would. This takes some practice, but does create fun and unique fabrics.

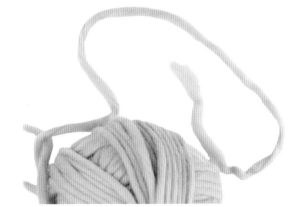

commercial roving

Single

One step from roving is single-ply yarn. Yarn made from a single ply is easy to see because it is one long strand of fiber that has been twisted or spun so that it adheres to itself and creates yarn. These yarns can be made with varying amounts of twist, depending on the length of the fiber used to spin with. If you had a length of spinning fiber (roving) in front of you, you could hold a length of the roving between your hands and pull it apart stretching the roving slightly. Then, by twisting the two ends between your fingers in opposite directions, you would see the yarn tighten up and twist. The tighter this twist, the more sturdy the resulting yarn becomes. The result is a single-ply yarn. Here are two examples of single-ply yarn: one a very fine weight, the other bulky. And here are two swatches of single crochet stitches made using those same yarns. Yarn spun this way retains more of the characteristics of the original roving and often has a more rustic appearance—even when using finer fibers.

On the right is an example of a single-ply yarn spun to be "thick and thin." That means the yarn has visible thick and thin spots along its length. You can see in this swatch made using a single-ply thick and thin yarn that the resulting fabric has a gorgeous texture and character.

Multiple Plies

From here we move on to yarn that is made up of multiple single-ply strands of yarn. Yes, it really is that simple! Take a single ply of yarn, spin that together with other singles, and you get 2-ply, 4-ply, and even 10-ply yarn. Generally, the more singles that are spun together, the stronger the resulting yarn and the smoother the surface texture of the yarn.

On page 33, we have taken apart the plies of a length of yarn so you can easily see the individual strands of singles. In the early stages of your crochet journey, you won't often seek out a certain ply of yarn. But, as your skills increase and your understanding of creating fabric becomes more refined, you will appreciate the subtleties of using a two-ply versus a four-ply yarn. And, if you should happen to venture into spinning your own yarn (something many of us find ourselves doing), you will definitely become more well-versed in certain yarns' plying techniques and how those result in different fabrics. Until then, this general understanding that yarn is made up of lengths of fibers twisted together, then twisted together again, is enough.

single crochet swatches in fine and bulky weight yarn

single crochet swatch in thick and thin yarn

plied yarn

Thus ends your primer on the basics of yarn. This is enough information at this point for you to go out into the universe and explore the different types of yarns available to you and to evaluate them based on your own preferences and on their appropriateness for your projects. It can't be said often enough so we'll say it again here: when you are selecting yarn, you are picking the right yarn that will create the right fabric for the right project.

Ball, Skein, or Hank?

Commercial yarn is usually packaged ("put-up") in one of three ways:

Ball

A ball of yarn is the most obvious of the three yarn put ups, because of the round ball shape. Yarn purchased in a ball can be used right away, with the working yarn pulled from either the outside of the ball or from the center.

Skein

A skein of yarn functions like a ball in that the yarn can be used right away, and yarn is worked from the outside or the inside of the skein. A skein of yarn can be identified by the oblong cylindrical shape.

"Pet Yarn"

Hank

A hank of yarn is yarn that is wound into a loose loop then twisted until the loop is tightened, and then one end is pulled through the other loop, securing the twist. Yarn purchased in a hank must be wound into a ball before it can be used.

NOTE: THE SECRET LANGUAGE OF CROCHETERS You will hear crocheters talk about the yarn they have as their "Stash" or "Yarn Stash." We prefer to think of our yarn as necessary inventory and have what we call "Pet Yarn." This is yarn that we keep around just because it is beautiful and the texture or color (or both!) inspires us. This "Pet Yarn" doesn't necessarily have to have a purpose other than to exist and inspire and, generally, to make you happy.

Ball Bands

The majority of the information you will need to know about the yarn you are about to use can be found on the packaging of the yarn, usually in the form of a ball band or tag. The ball band will have information such as the weight of the yarn, the stitched gauge of the yarn, the color information, and sometimes care information for the finished fabric. Here is an example of common ball band information in detail:

Yarn Weight

If a yarn company is a member of the Craft Yarn Council, their ball bands will include the CYC number (*see page 319*), as well as whether the yarn is lace, worsted, bulky weight, etc.

Knit and Crochet Gauges

This is neither the gauge you will get when working in a pattern stitch, nor is it the gauge you will match to the gauge given in your project patterns. This is the gauge made when working a panel of single crochet stitches with the specified hook size. The gauge as given here is only for the purpose of substituting yarn. That means if you can find another yarn that states it creates the same stitches and rows per inch with the same hook size, you might be able to use it as a suitable substitute for this yarn. Remember, this is only a starting point. You will always need to check your own gauge in pattern stitch before starting a project! Look for more on gauge in "The Swatch" section on page 72.

Color

In addition to the color name, this information often includes the number associated with the color and the dye lot this particular skein of yarn came from. This information is vital to ensure proper color matching, should you need to purchase additional yarn for your project. Using yarn from two different dye lots will almost always result in a slight color difference that will show in your finished fabrics. For information on what to do if you have to work with different dye lots, see "Colorwork," on page 194.

Fabric Care

Just like the tags inside your clothes, the ball band will often include care instructions that tell you about water and heat tolerance. These care instructions will help tell you whether the yarn you are choosing will create the fabric you need for your project.

For example, a yarn that creates a fabric that can only be hand washed in warm water probably isn't your best choice for that gardening jacket that is going to be covered in soil and compost. For a project like that, you're going to want to look for a yarn that is more sturdy and that can stand up to being exposed to the elements and then thrown in the washer and dryer. Again, remember our mantra: The right yarn makes the right fabric for the right project!

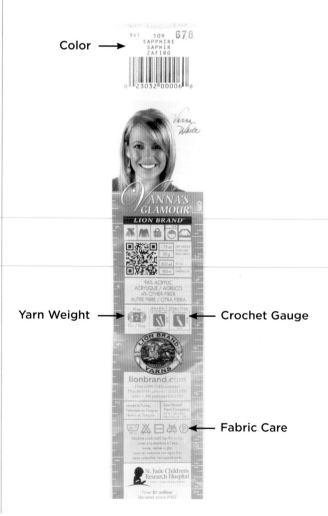

Color →

Yarn Weight → ← Crochet Gauge

← Fabric Care

SUBSTITUTING YARN

**"What if I can't get the yarn named in a pattern,
 or I don't want to use that particular yarn?"**

Looking for a yarn to substitute in your pattern is a matter of matching the fiber content and the weight of the yarn used in the original pattern. This can be as easy as looking at the yarn symbols on the ball band, checking the wraps per inch (WPI), and swatching with the new yarn to make sure you can achieve the desired stitch and row gauge. And, ultimately, remember that your new yarn must create the right fabric for your project.

Picking Up Hook and Yarn

Whether you are left-handed, right-handed, or ambidextrous, you will need to decide which hand you will hold your hook and yarn with. Whichever hand you hold your yarn with, be it the left or the right, that hand is your "yarn hand." Likewise, whichever hand you hold your hook with, be it the left or the right, that hand is your "hook hand." Since crochet requires the most amount of dexterity with the hook hand, your dominant hand is the one you should probably begin working with as your hook hand. That said, we have met people who are left-handed but who hold their hook in their right hand, and vice versa. Upon making your first stitches, you will know almost immediately which is your hook hand and which is your yarn hand.

Hook Holds

Every crocheter has their favorite way of holding a hook. Put a dozen of us in a room, and all of us can describe our hook holds and why we hold them that way. Some of us hold our hooks a certain way because that's the way we have always done it and can't remember ever doing it another way. Others have adapted hook holds that accommodate hand comfort, such as in the case of injuries or arthritis. The good thing about these different ways of holding a hook is that all of them are slight variations on two different basic holds, and all of them are "the right way," as long as you are able to work efficiently and make stitches without hurting yourself. In fact, in our classes we (half) jokingly say: "As long as you don't poke out your eye or the eyes of people around you, and you aren't hurting yourself, you'll be okay." Bottom line: All of these variations for how to hold a hook are "the right way." Especially when you are first learning to work with a hook, you might switch up holds until you settle on the one that works best for you and your hands. Here are the two basic hook holds; they are shown to the right.

As we said, there are many slight variations on how crocheters hold their hooks. You might even change your hold as you become more comfortable using a hook. All that really matters is that you are able to comfortably and efficiently use your hook to grab the yarn and make stitches. If you are experiencing wrist, hand, or shoulder pain while working, you might want to consider changing up your hook hold. You will see in the demonstration photos that Shannon holds his hook in a modified overhand position, with the end of the hook held between his third and fourth fingers. This is a perfect example of the slight adaptations that happen as we crochet more.

overhand (knife) hook hold for right-handed crocheter

underhand (pen) hook hold for right-handed crocheter

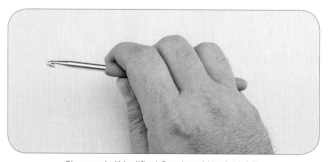

Shannon's "Modified Overhand Hook Hold"

Left-Handed Crocheters

underhand (pen) hook hold for left-handed crocheter

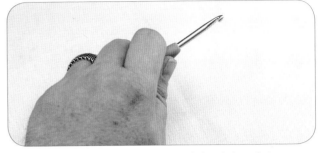

overhand (knife) hook hold for left-handed crocheter

The action of creating crochet stitches works the same for left-handed crocheters as it does for right-handed crocheters. However, because left-handed crocheters will be creating the stitching in essentially a backward order from the way their pattern reads, here are a couple of tips to use for keeping things straight in your head.

Special tips for left-handed crocheters

When teaching left-handed folks to crochet, we have them sit face to face with us and mirror our actions. We have been told by left-handed crocheters that they will set a book in front of a mirror to see how the tutorials look from a left- handed perspective.

When pattern instructions read in a certain direction, left-handed crocheters will need to translate them to read in the opposite direction. In other words, left-handed crocheters will always work from left to right rather than from right to left as shown in photos and some written instructions.

If a pattern says this stitch will skew or create a bias in your fabric to the left, it will, in fact, skew or create a bias to the right (and vice versa).

Especially in the case of more complicated stitches like those that cross or twist, left-handed crocheters will find that their stitches will twist or cross in the opposite direction from what the written pattern says.

For example, a left-handed crocheter reading the written pattern for a 2x2 double crochet left cross will end up with a stitch pattern that crosses to the right. In an overall stitch pattern like a cable, this means the left-handed crocheter will have stitches that cross in the opposite direction from those of a right-handed crocheter. This is not the end of the world. As long as the stitch pattern is consistent overall and produces the same overall design, nothing needs to be done. However, if you really want your crossed stitches to cross in the same direction as they do for a right-handed crocheter, you will need to learn both types of crosses, a 2x2 double crochet left cross and a 2x2 double crochet right cross, and switch those around when you get to that part of the pattern.

The surest way to keep track of this is to cross out "Left" and write in "Right." If that seems like too much of a fuss, the sure-fire way to keep your stitches crossing the same as for a right-handed crocheter is to read the stitch chart. On the stitch chart, left is left and right is right, no matter what the written instructions say. We have taught many left-handed crocheters this way and brought them successfully through crossed stitches and cable stitches.

Yarn Holds

While hook size is very important in determining your finished fabric, how you hold your yarn as you are crocheting will affect the way you make your stitches and, therefore, your fabric. How the yarn moves through the fingers of your yarn hand will determine how even your stitches are compared to the stitches around them, as well as your stitch and row gauge.

This will be most easily measured in the amount of yarn you use and in the stitches and rows per inch you achieve (*see Stitches and Rows per Inch Worksheet, page 315*). The tighter your tension, the more dense your fabric will be, and the more stitches and rows per inch you will have in your finished gauge.

The looser your tension, the less dense your fabric will be, and there will be fewer stitches and rows per inch in your finished gauge. Neither of these is preferable and are, in fact, subjective relative to the fabric you need to make for your project.

The main idea is to hold the yarn snug enough to maintain good tension as the yarn moves over your hand and your hook, while at the same time keeping the yarn out of the way of the hook until you want to use it. Being able to adjust how the yarn flows through your yarn hand is important so you can make adjustments to your stitch and row gauge and, therefore, to your finished fabrics.

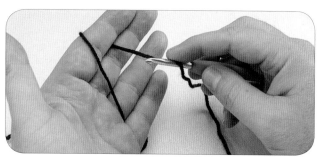

basic yarn hold right-handed

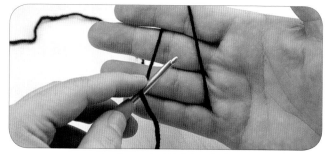

basic yarn hold left-handed

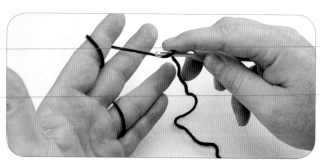

wrapping through fingers right-handed

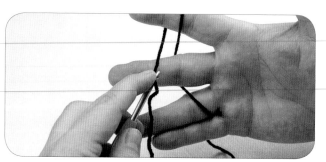

wrapping through fingers left-handed

NOTE: The more wraps through the fingers of your yarn hand, the more snug your stitches will be. For more tension, wrap or loop the yarn through your fingers more. For less tension, use fewer wraps to allow the yarn to move more freely through your fingers while you are making your stitches.

Parts of a Stitch

Every stitch has the same basic parts: the base, the post, and the head. Being able to identify the parts of a stitch is the first step to correctly making crochet stitches and to successfully reading crochet patterns.

The front loop and back loop of a stitch are identified by which side of the fabric is facing you as you are working a row of stitches. When looking at the fabric the loop that is closest to you is always the front loop, and the loop farthest from you is always the back loop.

Head

The head of the stitch is created when you make the last yarn over and draw through all the loops on your hook, leaving just the one active loop. The head of the stitch is broken down into two parts: the front loop and the back loop. To create different stitch variations, you will insert your hook under both loops of the head or under only the front loop, or under only the back loop of the head of a stitch.

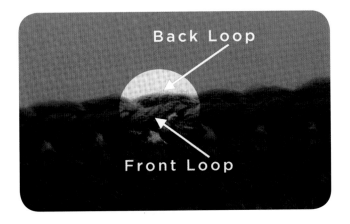

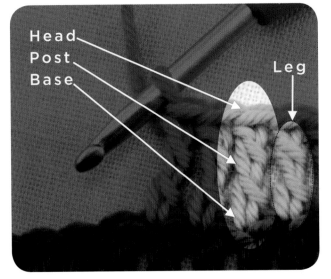

Post

The post is the part of the stitch from the bottom of the head to the base. The post is created by the yarn over made before you insert your hook into the crochet fabric to make a new stitch. Taking a closer look at the post of the stitch, we can see the number of wraps we made when the stitch instructions read to yarn over. To the right is a double crochet (dc) stitch, for which the instructions read to yarn over once before inserting the hook to make the stitch, resulting in one wrap.

To the right is a treble crochet (tr) stitch, for which the instructions read to yarn over twice before inserting the hook to make the stitch.

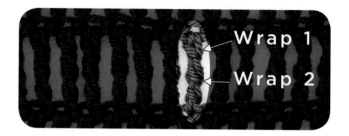

Base

The base of the stitch is created when the hook is inserted into the head of the indicated stitch or space and the first loop is drawn up. Making the base wraps the yarn around the stitch where you inserted your hook to make your new stitch, and anchors the stitch into place.

Leg

The post and base of a crochet stitch are often referred to collectively as the leg of a stitch. This will become particularly relevant when you are counting the legs of a compound stitch such as a decrease or a cluster stitch, and for the loopy legs of pulled stitches.

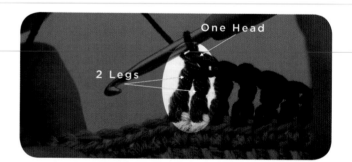

Parts of a chain

The chain stitch stands on its own, without inserting your hook into another stitch. This creates a stitch that floats out in space on its own, connected only to the previously made stitch. Chain stitches are made up of a front loop, a back loop, and a bump. As with other stitches, the front loop of a chain stitch is always the loop closest to you and the back loop is always the loop farthest from you.

Being able to recognize the parts of a stitch will become easier as you start making stitches, so be sure to check back here when you get to the "First Stitches" section on page 78.

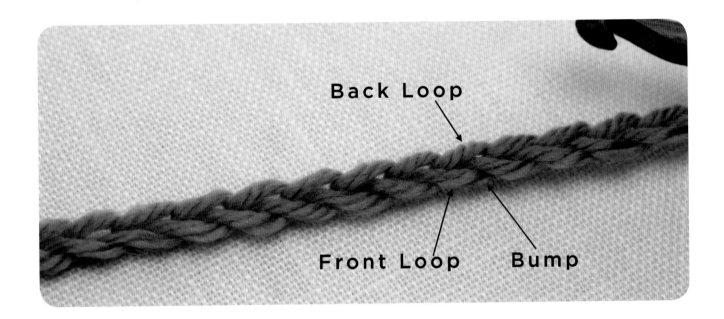

Where to Put Your Hook

Where you put your hook as you make your crochet stitches determines the type of fabric you will make as much as the stitch pattern you are using, your hook size, and the yarn you are working with. Fabric made using a simple single crochet stitch is transformed dramatically depending on whether you insert your hook under both loops, the front loops, or the back loops of the stitches in the row you are working into. (Likewise, fabric made using half double crochet stitches looks very different depending on whether you insert your hook under both loops of the stitch you are working into, between the stitches of the row you are working into, or around the posts of the stitches in the row. Remembering the Parts of a Stitch from page 41, we are going to make several fabrics using different parts of the stitch, as well as the spaces between stitches.

hook under both loops of stitch head

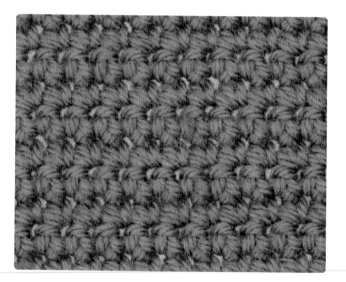

Inserting Your Hook Under Both Loops

Unless otherwise indicated in the written pattern, when instructed to make a stitch, you will insert your hook under both loops of the stitch you are working into. There is no special designation or terminology for this method for making a stitch, since it is just assumed that you will insert your hook under both loops unless otherwise prompted.

if a pattern says to single crochet in the next stitch and in each stitch to the end of the row, you will insert your hook from front to back under both loops of each stitch you are working into.

Worked every row as shown here, this creates a solid fabric that can be used for everything from garments to home decor, toys, and outerwear. Because of the way crochet stitches are formed, fabric made this way will have a double thickness because the loop that makes up the base of the stitch is drawn through the two loops of the head of the stitch you are working into.

hook under front loop only

BOOKMARK HERE: Be sure to come back to review this section after you have learned to make a few rows of stitches so you can apply what you have read here. This practical application of the words will ensure you develop a working knowledge of the information.

Inserting Your Hook Under Only the Front Loop (tfl)

When a lighter fabric is desired, the pattern will instruct you to make your stitch by inserting your hook under only the front loop (tfl) of the stitch you are working into.

For example, single crochet through the front loop (sc tfl) or half double crochet through the front loop (hdc tfl) are created by inserting your hook from front to back under only the front loop of the stitch you are working into.

An important point to keep in mind as you work through the stitches and patterns in this book is that the front loop is always the loop on the front of the fabric and is the loop closest to you as you are holding your work in your hand and making your current row of stitches.

Worked every row as shown here, working tfl creates a thinner, lighter fabric that is appropriate for everything from home decor to fashion fabrics for garments. The fabric is lighter weight because the base of the stitch you are making is wrapped around only one strand of yarn— the front loop of the stitch you are working into.

NOTE: Working through the front loop only results in a visible line on the surface of the fabric every other row. This visible line is the unused loop of the stitch you are working into.

Inserting Your Hook Under Only the Back Loops (tbl)

A very special kind of texture stitch is created when the pattern instructs you to insert your hook under only the back loop (tbl) of the stitch you are working into. Logically, inserting your hook under only the back loop of the stitch you are working into would create a similar fabric to front loop only (tfl) stitches, since you are still working under only one loop of the stitch. However, because of the way crochet stitches are constructed, making your new stitch by inserting your hook under only the back loop creates troughs and pronounced ridges of varying degrees, depending on the height of the stitch you are making.

Worked every row as shown here, working single crochet through the back loop (sc tbl) creates a distinct set of ridges. The resulting fabric is more compact and dense, and is most often used as a textural element in the middle of a fabric, or on its own as single crochet ribbing.

hook under back loop only

Why So Different?

Why does sc tfl fabric vary so greatly from sc tbl fabric? When you are making a row of crochet stitches, take a close look at the row you have just made and notice how the tops of the stitches you are making tilt slightly toward you. This tilt is more obvious in the shorter stitches like single crochet, but can be seen in all crochet stitches. Since these stitches are tilted toward us, we can look at the front loop of each stitch as the "low side" of the stitch and the back loop of each stitch as the "high side" of the stitch. We learned earlier that the designation of "front loop" and "back loop" changes as we turn our work, with the front loop always being closest to us and the back loop always being furthest away from us. However, the "high side" and "low side" of a stitch always stay the same, because the tilt of the stitches does not change as you turn your work. This persistence in the tilt of crochet stitches is what makes tfl and tbl fabric so different, despite the fact they both are made through only one loop of the stitch from the previous row.

When you turn your work and make a new stitch by inserting your crochet hook under only the front loop of the stitch in the previous row, you are inserting your hook into the "high side" of the stitch. Working consecutive rows of tfl stitches means you are always working into the loop on the "high side" of the stitch from the previous row, and therefore are stacking one "high side" on top of another "high side." This creates a more lightweight fabric that is flatter and less textured. Once this type of fabric is blocked, it will have fewer rows per inch than fabrics created with stitches made under both loops or tbl.

When you turn your work and make a new stitch by inserting your crochet hook under only the back loop of the stitch in the previous row, you are inserting your hook into the "low side" of the stitch. Working consecutive rows of tbl stitches means you are always working into the loop on the "low side" of the stitch from the previous row. This sets the new stitch onto the low side of the fabric, and subsequent rows all tilt inward toward each other. This creates a deeper set of troughs between the "high side" of the stitches, creating highly defined ridges. This type of fabric is suitable as a general fabric but is most often used in the form of single crochet ribbing (*see page 226, Single Crochet Reversible Ribbing*).

sc tbl fabric seen from the side

Inserting Your Hook Between the Stitches

This method for creating stitches involves inserting your hook between the posts of the stitches of the previous row. While the posts and heads of these stitches are the same thickness as regular stitches, the bases are plumper since they are created by yarning over and pulling up a loop around all of the loops of the head of one of the two stitches you are working between. This creates a beautifully textured fabric in which the stitches have a nested look and the finished fabrics have a woven appearance.

Patterns for this type of fabric will very specifically tell you to insert your hook between two stitches.

For example: hdc in space between next two stitches.

Following these instructions, we yarn over (yo), then insert our hook from front to back between the posts of the next two hdc stitches. (*See photo 1 for example.*)

Another example: dc in space between next two stitches.

Here, we yarn over (yo), then insert our hook from front to back between the posts of the next two double crochet (dc) stitches. (*See Photo 2 for example.*)

Note here that the shorter the stitches used, the more dense the resulting fabric, while taller stitches create more of a woven mesh fabric.

This fabric is great for everything from garments to home decor, depending on the weight of the yarn and the height of the stitch you are using. You will see more of these types of stitches when you make offset stitches (*see Offset Stitches, page 114*).

Photo 1. inserting hook between posts of hdc stitches

offset hdc fabric

Photo 2. inserting hook between posts of dc stitches

offset dc fabric

Working Around the Post of the Stitch

Stitches made around the posts of stitches are called . . . yes, you guessed it: post stitches. Post stitches are made by working your hook around the post of the indicated stitch. Making stitches by working around the post of the indicated stitch creates a highly textured fabric because the base of a post stitch wraps around the post of the indicated stitch and the finished stitch either stands out on the front (Front Post stitch) or the back (Back Post stitch) of the fabric. In addition, Front Post stitches will show the front of the post stitch you made on the front of the fabric, and Back Post stitches will show the back of the post stitch you made on the front of the fabric.

Written instructions for these stitches indicate first whether the stitch will stand out on the front (Front Post) or back (Back Post) of the fabric, then the height of the stitch (double crochet, treble crochet, etc.)

For example, if the pattern called for a double crochet stitch that is to stand out on the front of the fabric as you are working it, the written instruction will tell you to make a Front Post double crochet (FPdc). A treble crochet stitch that is to stand out on the back of the fabric as you are working it will be called a Back Post treble crochet (BPtr).

Front Post and Back Post stitches are usually used in combination with other stitches to create surface features and textures such as ribbing, crossed stitches, and cables.

Front Post Stitches

Front Post stitches stand out on the front of the row of the fabric as you are making it, and are made by inserting your hook around the post of the indicated stitch, starting from the front of the fabric.

For example, if the pattern calls for the next stitch to be a Front Post double crochet (FPdc), you will yarn over (yo) just as you normally would for a double crochet stitch, then you will insert your hook from the front to the back of the fabric around the post of the indicated stitch, then to the front again.

Here is a swatch of Front Post double crochet (FPdc) stitches worked every other stitch and every other row to create raised stitches on the front of the fabric, resulting in Front Post double crochet ribbing (FPdc ribbing).

hook ready for FPdc

FPdc ribbing

Back Post Stitches

Back Post stitches stand out on the back of the row of the fabric as you are making it, and are made by inserting your hook around the post of the indicated stitch starting from the back of the fabric.

For example, if the pattern calls for the next stitch to be a Back Post double crochet (BPdc), you will yarn over (yo) just as you normally would for a double crochet stitch, then you will insert your hook from the back of the fabric to the front around the post of the indicated stitch, then to the back again.

Here is a swatch of Back Post double crochet (BPdc) stitches worked every other stitch, alternating with Front Post double crochet (FPdc) stitches every other row to create vertical post stitch ribbing.

hook ready for BPdc

FPdc/BPdc vertical ribbing

Inserting Hook XX Rows Below

Some pattern stitches will require that you work into a row other than the last row made. In these cases, the written pattern will read to insert your hook or to work around a stitch a certain number of rows below the working row.

For example, when the pattern instructions read to work in a stitch "2 rows below," you will count one unworked stitch over and then insert your hook in the indicated stitch in the row numbered 2 less than the row you are making. When working "2 rows below," the stitch of the current row will remain unworked, meaning you will not insert your hook into that stitch to make another stitch.

For example, if you are making Row 5, a stitch worked "2 rows below" is worked in Row 3. Row 5 – 2 = Row 3.

Example:

Front Post double crochet around next stitch 2 rows below.

In this example, you would make a Front Post double crochet stitch by counting one unworked stitch over and then working around the post of the stitch two rows below the row you are currently working. You will encounter this most often in cables (*see Cables, page 174*).

1 Row Below

2 Rows Below

FPdc in next stitch 2 rows below

Example:

If you are making Row 8 of a swatch of single crochet stitches and the pattern reads to insert your hook into the next stitch 5 rows below and pull up a loop to the height of the working row, you will count one unworked stitch over and 5 rows down to Row 3. This makes a pulled stitch (*see Pulled Stitches, page 220*).

This type of pattern instruction applies to nearly every type of stitch and can add stunning graphics to any fabric, from home decor to fine garments.

Spike Wedge pattern stitch made using pulled stitches

NOTE: Front and **Back** refers to the front and back of a stitch or a row, or, more generally, to the front and back of the fabric you are making as you are looking at the stitch or row while you are working on it. As you turn your work, the side facing you is ALWAYS the front side of your work. The loops on this side of your work are the front loops.

In Front of or Behind Stitches

There will be a whole family of exciting stitches you will learn called Crossed Stitches (*see page 177*) and Cables (*see page 174*). These stitches require that you work in front of or behind a stitch or stitches previously worked. This can be done with any height of stitch and with any combination of regular, post, or pulled stitches. Instructions will tell you to make a stitch by "... working in front of stitches just made ..." or "... working behind stitches just made ..." This does require some dexterity with your hook but can be learned and mastered with a little practice so you can make projects like the cabled version of our Signature Vests in the "Projects" section on page 287.

cable from Signature Vests pattern In this book

Around Stitches

Working around a stitch or stitches results in Wrapped Stitches. Wrapped stitches are a hybrid stitch that use crossed and pulled stitch techniques to create a stitch that is made around previously worked stitches. The base of a wrapped stitch completely encompasses one or more stitches and creates a double-sided fabric. This is where the pulled stitches technique comes into play, since you need to pull up the loops of the yarn over (yo) and the base of your stitch around the previously worked stitches, then up to the height of the current stitches of your current working row.

For example, in this book you will learn to make a double crochet stitch that wraps around two other double crochet stitches, called a wrapped double crochet (wrapped dc) stitch (*see page 224*).

The wrapped stitch is made by inserting your hook into a skipped stitch, then pulling the loops of your yarn over (yo) and base up to the height of the working row. Wrapped stitches can be made using any height of stitch and add a new dimension of texture to your crochet fabrics.

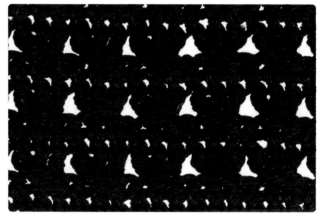

wrapped dc

NOTE: RIGHT SIDE (RS) AND WRONG SIDE (WS) refer to the right and wrong sides of the finished fabric. **For example,** if you are working a stitch pattern that highlights the stitches on only one side of the fabric, that fabric will have a right side (RS) and a wrong side (WS). The right side and wrong side of the work do not change. More broadly, the right side of your work is the side that looks the best on the right side of your finished project.

Pattern Reading

The pattern is how we, the designers, communicate to you, the makers, how to reproduce the project we have designed here in our studios. In fact, the best way to think of a pattern is to imagine the designer right there next to you, talking you through each step of the process. To better communicate what we need you to do to complete your project successfully, we use a combination of written words, abbreviations, symbols, and charts.

Properly deciphering and understanding this method of communication is the key to successfully completing your project. With a little information, what might at first seem like a jumble of words, abbreviations, symbols, and numbers quickly becomes a well-organized system of communication between you and the designer, so you can successfully complete your project. All it takes is understanding the parts of the pattern and having a key for deciphering the meaning of those words, abbreviations, symbols, and numbers that make up a pattern. In this chapter we'll break down each of the elements that comprise a crochet pattern is the key to unlocking every project you can possibly dream of.

Breaking It Down

When you first look at a written pattern, start by looking through the entire pattern from beginning to end to get a broad overview of the project. At this point, you are simply seeing how long the pattern is, what pieces you will be making, how many pieces (if more than one) you will be making, and generally getting a feel for the language of the pattern, to identify the designer's writing style or the style of the magazine or book publisher. This is also when you will identify whether the pattern includes more than the written text and has features like schematics, charts, and even tutorials.

Next, take a deeper look at the individual lines of stitch instructions and establish your working order, as well as what stitches, stitch patterns, and techniques you will be using in this particular pattern.

Finally, look at any tools and supplies you will need for completing your project, such as hook sizes, buttons, zippers, or other fasteners or trims. This is where you will also see what yarn this project calls for and will decide if it's time to go shopping!

This initial assessment of the parts of a crochet pattern gives you a quick overview of the big picture of the piece you are about to make, and helps you identify any potential trouble spots for which you might need to brush up on a technique or learn a new skill. Following that same method of overview, in this section we will start with the big picture and break down the parts of a pattern, then we'll take a closer look at the details of how a pattern is written.

To see all the charts full size, go to the "Projects" section beginning on page 271.

My First Cardi

My First Cardi features easy-to-follow instructions, with minimal shaping from the cuffs to the tops of the sleeves. That's it . . . no other shaping! After making your fabric panels, all that's left is simple construction: sewing straight seams on the sides and shoulders, then setting the straight-edged sleeves into the armholes.

You'll love being able to show off your first handmade crochet garment project, and, once you develop into a crochet master, you will love making this easy project that you can whip up in no time.

SKILLS USED

Knotless Starting Chain *(see page 79)* Blocking *(see page 240)*
Foundation Single Crochet *(see page 104)* Locking Mattress Stitch *(see page 257)*
Increases *(see page 138)* Setting in a Sleeve *(see page 253)*

SKILL LEVEL

EASY

SIZES S (M, L, XL, 2X, 3X, 4X, 5X)
Sample shown in size Medium

FINISHED MEASUREMENTS

To Fit Bust: 32.5 (36, 40, 44, 48.5, 52.5, 56.5, 60.5)"/82.5 (91.5, 101.5, 111.75, 123.25, 133.25, 143.5, 153.75) cm

Finished Bust: 36.5 (40, 44, 48, 52.5, 56.5, 60.5, 64.5)"/92.75 (101.5, 111.75, 122, 133.25, 143.5, 153.75, 163.75) cm

Finished Length from Shoulder: 28 (28, 28, 29, 29, 29, 30, 30)"/71 (71, 71, 73.75, 73.75, 73.75, 76.25, 76.25) cm

MATERIALS AND TOOLS

Sample uses Valley Yarns Valley Superwash Worsted (100% Extra Fine Merino; 1.75 ounces/50g = 97 yards/88.75 m): 21 (22, 24, 26, 28, 29, 32, 33) balls in color Periwinkle #342—2037 (2134, 2328, 2522, 2716, 2813, 3104, 3201) yards/1863.75 (1952.5, 2130, 2307.5, 2485, 2573.75, 2840, 2928.75) m of medium weight yarn

MEDIUM

Crochet hook: 5.00mm (size H-8) or size to obtain gauge

Yarn needle

Parts of a Pattern

Starting with the big overview of our pattern, let's identify the parts of a pattern. These are the sections a pattern will be broken down into from beginning to end. Not all patterns contain all of these sections, but most will include a majority of them, and the more information you have, the more likely you are to be able to successfully complete your project.

Parts of a Written Pattern

1. Clear photo of the finished project

The main photo of the project should give you a clear idea of what you will be making if you follow the directions of the pattern.

2. Name of the project

Sometimes the name given to a project is descriptive of the actual project, but more often it is a fanciful title given to set the tone of the project, much like the romance text.

3. Pattern Description

This block of text sets the tone for the project with descriptive language that sometimes includes the designer's inspiration for creating this particular piece. Often, romance text will also give you details about the project so you have an at-a-glance idea of the features of the project or pattern that might not be evident from the main photo. These details might include descriptive text indicating a garment that is made in one piece or an afghan that is made from the center out.

4. Skill Level

This can be somewhat subjective, and different language is often used to describe skill levels. Always be sure to check for a skill level chart to see if this pattern really fits your level of experience. If no information about skill level listed in the pattern is available, or if the skill level information is not descriptive enough, be sure to do a close examination of the entire pattern to see if you have the skills and experience necessary to successfully complete this project (*see Skill Level Chart, page 318*). If no skill level is given, you can do a thorough look through of the pattern to see if you have the skills needed to complete the project successfully or if you need to brush up on or learn new skills.

5. Sizes

This section lets you know if the pattern is written in one size or in multiple sizes and, if multiple sizes, what those sizes are. If a pattern is written in one size, this section will either not be in the pattern or will read "One size." If a pattern is written for multiple sizes, the individual sizes will be listed and broken down, with the first size written before a set of parentheses and the larger sizes listed inside the parentheses in order from smallest to largest.

For example, a pattern for an afghan might be written in just one size, so this section will either not be in the pattern or it will read "One size." If that same afghan is written to fit different sizes of beds, they might be listed as "Twin (Full, Queen, King)," with the smallest size listed first outside the parentheses, and the larger sizes listed in order inside the parentheses.

In the case of garments, if there is only one size, this section will say "One size" or "One size fits most." If a garment pattern is written for multiple sizes, this section will show a breakdown of those individual sizes as Small (Medium, Large, 1X, 2X, 3X, 4X, 5X) or S (M, L, 1X, 2X, 3X, 4X, 5X). Again, the smallest size is listed first, with the larger sizes listed inside the parentheses from smallest to largest.

Keep in mind that these indicators are subjective. While the fiber industry has a set of guidelines regarding garment sizing, everyone has their own guidelines for what the designations small, medium, large, 1X, etc., represent. Especially in the case of garments and wearable accessories, this section must be accompanied by a sizing guide or a section of Finished Measurements with physical measurements in inches or centimeters, or it actually means very little beyond telling you that a pattern is written in multiple sizes.

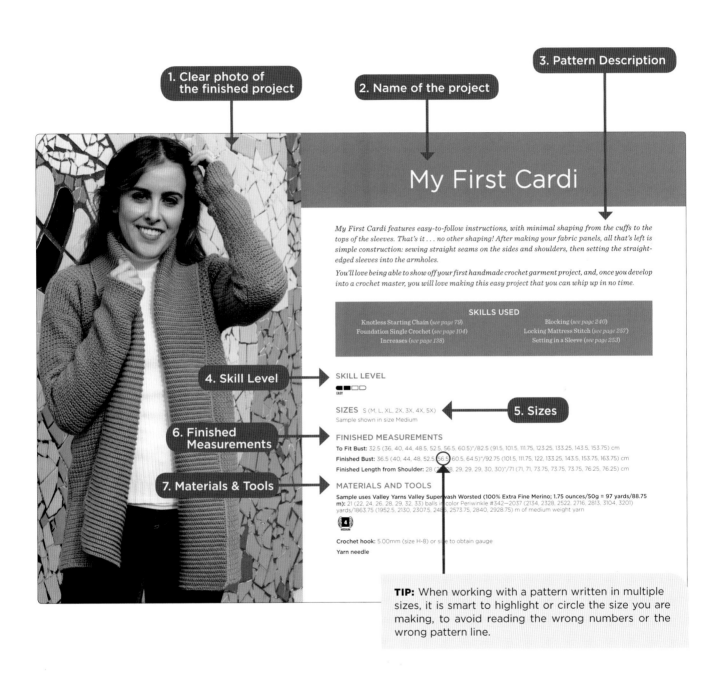

1. Clear photo of the finished project

2. Name of the project

3. Pattern Description

My First Cardi

My First Cardi features easy-to-follow instructions, with minimal shaping from the cuffs to the tops of the sleeves. That's it ... no other shaping! After making your fabric panels, all that's left is simple construction: sewing straight seams on the sides and shoulders, then setting the straight-edged sleeves into the armholes.

You'll love being able to show off your first handmade crochet garment project, and, once you develop into a crochet master, you will love making this easy project that you can whip up in no time.

SKILLS USED

Knotless Starting Chain (*see page 79*)
Foundation Single Crochet (*see page 104*)
Increases (*see page 138*)

Blocking (*see page 240*)
Locking Mattress Stitch (*see page 257*)
Setting in a Sleeve (*see page 253*)

4. Skill Level

SKILL LEVEL
■■□□ EASY

SIZES S (M, L, XL, 2X, 3X, 4X, 5X)
Sample shown in size Medium

5. Sizes

6. Finished Measurements

FINISHED MEASUREMENTS
To Fit Bust: 32.5 (36, 40, 44, 48.5, 52.5, 56.5, 60.5)"/82.5 (91.5, 101.5, 111.75, 123.25, 133.25, 143.5, 153.75) cm
Finished Bust: 36.5 (40, 44, 48, 52.5, 56.5, 60.5, 64.5)"/92.75 (101.5, 111.75, 122, 133.25, 143.5, 153.75, 163.75) cm
Finished Length from Shoulder: 28 (28, 28, 29, 29, 29, 30, 30)"/71 (71, 71, 73.75, 73.75, 73.75, 76.25, 76.25) cm

7. Materials & Tools

MATERIALS AND TOOLS
Sample uses Valley Yarns Valley Superwash Worsted (100% Extra Fine Merino; 1.75 ounces/50g = 97 yards/88.75 m): 21 (22, 24, 26, 28, 29, 32, 33) balls in color Periwinkle #342—2037 (2134, 2328, 2522, 2716, 2813, 3104, 3201) yards/1863.75 (1952.5, 2130, 2307.5, 2485, 2573.75, 2840, 2928.75) m of medium weight yarn

4 MEDIUM

Crochet hook: 5.00mm (size H-8) or size to obtain gauge
Yarn needle

TIP: When working with a pattern written in multiple sizes, it is smart to highlight or circle the size you are making, to avoid reading the wrong numbers or the wrong pattern line.

To see all the charts full size, go to the "Projects" section beginning on page 271.

6. Finished Measurements

This section should provide you with enough information to give you an idea of whether or not this project is the size you need, or if it will fit you. If you are making an accessory or a piece of home decor, you should be able to tell if the size is right for the space you are using it in. If the pattern is for a garment, you should be able to look at these numbers and know if the garment will fit. As with the Sizes section, if a pattern is written for multiple sizes, the individual finished measurements will be given, with the first size written before a set of parentheses and the larger sizes listed inside the parentheses in order from smallest to largest.

For example, a pattern for an afghan sized Twin (Full, Queen, King) will list the finished measurements as 69 (84, 90, 110) x 90 (90, 90, 110) inches/175.25 (213.25, 228.5, 279.5) x 228.5 (228.5, 228.5, 279.5) cm.

A garment pattern sized S (M, L, 1X, 2X, 3X, 4X, 5X) will list both the To Fit and the Finished measurements, as well as any other significant measurements the designer feels you should know in order to make a good choice about the fit of this particular garment.

For example, our To Fit Bust is 32.5 (36, 40, 44, 48.5, 52.5, 56.5, 60.5)"/82.5 (91.5, 102, 111.75, 123.25, 133.25, 143.5, 153.75) cm. This tells us that the smallest size is meant to fit a 32.5 inch bust, and that a 52.5 inch bust is classified as a 3X size for this pattern. Regardless of your off-the-rack size, you should go by the To Fit measurement.

Also, this garment pattern shows Finished Bust measurements of 36.5 (40, 44, 48, 52.5, 56.5, 60.5, 64.5)"/92.75 (101.5, 112, 122, 133.25, 143.5, 153.75, 163.75) cm. This shows that the size small is meant to fit a 32.5 inch but the finished garment will measure 36.5 inches at the bust. This means that size will have 4 inches of ease at the bust.

Other To Fit and Finished measurements listed in patterns, such as hip circumference or sleeve length, depend on the design of the garment. If any fit element isn't readily evident from looking at the photo, this is where the designer will list that information so you can make your best choice about which size to make to fit your body. Remember, the pattern is just like the designer standing there next to you, telling you what do to so you can successfully complete your project.

7. Materials and Tools

Yarn name—the name of the company that sells the yarn, as well as the name that company has given to the yarn.

Yarn content—what the yarn is made from.

Yarn put up—how many ounces/grams and yards/meters are included in each ball, hank, or skein of the yarn used to make this project.

Yarn color—name and color number (if available) of the yarn used to make this project.

Yarn amounts—total ounces/grams and yards/meters of the yarn used to make this project. For projects made in different sizes, yarn amounts should be listed for each size.

Hook size needed—US, international, and metric hook size measurements for the hook size used to make this project (*see Hook Size Charts, page 318*).

8. Gauge/Blocked Gauge/Tension

This section includes the stitches and rows per inch in the pattern stitch used to create the finished fabric for this project. Multiple gauges will be given for projects using multiple pattern stitches. The additional designation of "Blocked Gauge" indicates the gauge of a certain number of stitches and rows per inch that will be achieved after blocking the fabric. This is the stitch gauge and row gauge you must attain in order to create the same fabric the designer did when they created the project this pattern is written for.

9. Stitch Guide

This is like a mini stitch dictionary for all of the stitches used to create the fabric for this project. Often, common stitches like single crochet, half double crochet, and double crochet are not listed in this section, because it is assumed the crocheter already knows these. The stitch guide is where you should look first to see if there are any stitches you aren't familiar with or techniques you need to brush up on before beginning this project.

10. Notes

Think of this as a note someone leaves for you on your desk or on a message board. This is where the designer and/or pattern writer will clue you in to anything other than stitches and techniques that will help you complete your project successfully. Notes included here might be specifics about how a garment is constructed, or unusual details about your project that might not be readily evident.

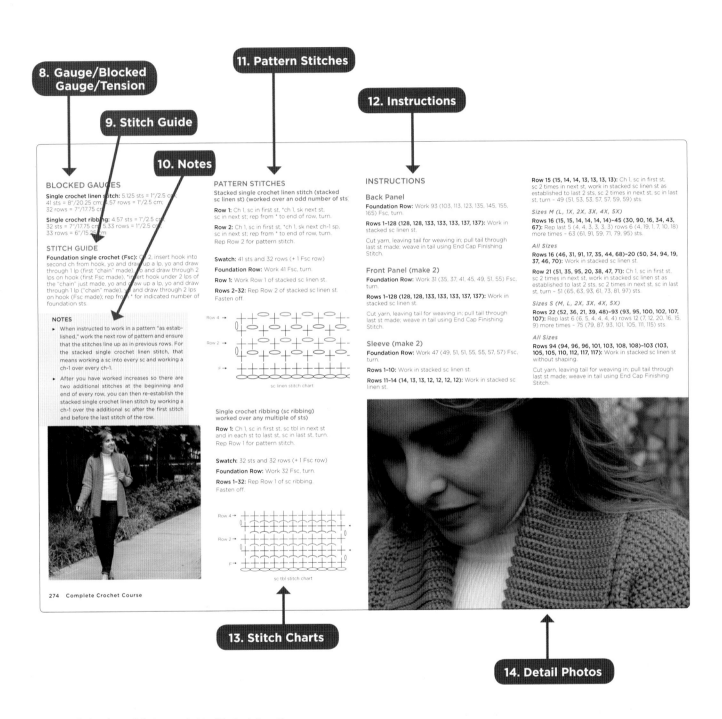

8. Gauge/Blocked Gauge/Tension

9. Stitch Guide

10. Notes

11. Pattern Stitches

12. Instructions

13. Stitch Charts

14. Detail Photos

BLOCKED GAUGES

Single crochet linen stitch: 5.125 sts = 1"/2.5 cm; 41 sts = 8"/20.25 cm; 4.57 rows = 1"/2.5 cm; 32 rows = 7"/17.75 cm

Single crochet ribbing: 4.57 sts = 1"/2.5 cm; 32 sts = 7"/17.75 cm; 5.33 rows = 1"/2.5 cm; 33 rows = 6"/15.25 cm

STITCH GUIDE

Foundation single crochet (Fsc): Ch 2, insert hook into second ch from hook, yo and draw up a lp, yo and draw through 1 lp (first "chain" made), yo and draw through 2 lps on hook (first Fsc made), *insert hook under 2 lps of the "chain" just made, yo and draw up a lp, yo and draw through 1 lp ("chain" made), yo and draw through 2 lps on hook (Fsc made); rep from * for indicated number of foundation sts.

NOTES

► When instructed to work in a pattern "as established," work the next row of pattern and ensure that the stitches line up as in previous rows. For the stacked single crochet linen stitch, that means working a sc into every sc and working a ch-1 over every ch-1.

► After you have worked increases so there are two additional stitches at the beginning and end of every row, you can then re-establish the stacked single crochet linen stitch by working a ch-1 over the additional sc after the first stitch and before the last stitch of the row.

PATTERN STITCHES

Stacked single crochet linen stitch (stacked sc linen st) (worked over an odd number of sts)

Row 1: Ch 1, sc in first st, *ch 1, sk next st, sc in next st; rep from * to end of row, turn.

Row 2: Ch 1, sc in first st, *ch 1, sk next ch-1 sp, sc in next st; rep from * to end of row, turn. Rep Row 2 for pattern stitch.

Swatch: 41 sts and 32 rows (+ 1 Fsc row)

Foundation Row: Work 41 Fsc, turn.

Row 1: Work Row 1 of stacked sc linen st.

Rows 2–32: Rep Row 2 of stacked sc linen st. Fasten off.

Row 4 →
Row 2 →
F →

sc linen stitch chart

Single crochet ribbing (sc ribbing) worked over any multiple of sts)

Row 1: Ch 1, sc in first st, sc tbl in next st and in each st to last st, sc in last st, turn. Rep Row 1 for pattern stitch.

Swatch: 32 sts and 32 rows (+ 1 Fsc row)

Foundation Row: Work 32 Fsc, turn.

Rows 1–32: Rep Row 1 of sc ribbing. Fasten off.

Row 4 →
Row 2 →
F →

sc tbl stitch chart

274 Complete Crochet Course

INSTRUCTIONS

Back Panel

Foundation Row: Work 93 (103, 113, 123, 135, 145, 155, 165) Fsc, turn.

Rows 1–128 (128, 128, 133, 133, 133, 137, 137): Work in stacked sc linen st.

Cut yarn, leaving tail for weaving in; pull tail through last st made; weave in tail using End Cap Finishing Stitch.

Front Panel (make 2)

Foundation Row: Work 31 (35, 37, 41, 45, 49, 51, 55) Fsc, turn.

Rows 1–128 (128, 128, 133, 133, 133, 137, 137): Work in stacked sc linen st.

Cut yarn, leaving tail for weaving in; pull tail through last st made; weave in tail using End Cap Finishing Stitch.

Sleeve (make 2)

Foundation Row: Work 47 (49, 51, 51, 55, 55, 57, 57) Fsc, turn.

Rows 1–10: Work in stacked sc linen st.

Rows 11–14 (14, 13, 13, 12, 12, 12, 12): Work in stacked sc linen st.

Row 15 (15, 14, 14, 13, 13, 13, 13): Ch 1, sc in first st, sc 2 times in next st, work in stacked sc linen st as established to last 2 sts, sc 2 times in next st, sc in last st, turn – 49 (51, 53, 53, 57, 57, 59, 59) sts.

Sizes M (L, 1X, 2X, 3X, 4X, 5X)

Rows 16 (15, 15, 14, 14, 14, 14)–45 (30, 90, 16, 34, 43, 67): Rep last 5 (4, 4, 3, 3, 3, 3) rows 6 (4, 19, 1, 7, 10, 18) more times – 63 (61, 91, 59, 71, 79, 95) sts.

All Sizes

Rows 16 (46, 31, 91, 17, 35, 44, 68)–20 (50, 34, 94, 19, 37, 46, 70): Work in stacked sc linen st.

Row 21 (51, 35, 95, 20, 38, 47, 71): Ch 1, sc in first st, sc 2 times in next st, work in stacked sc linen st as established to last 2 sts, sc 2 times in next st, sc in last st, turn – 51 (65, 63, 93, 61, 73, 81, 97) sts.

Sizes S (M, L, 2X, 3X, 4X, 5X)

Rows 22 (52, 36, 21, 39, 48)–93 (93, 95, 100, 102, 107, 107): Rep last 6 (6, 5, 4, 4, 4, 4) rows 12 (7, 12, 20, 16, 15, 9) more times – 75 (79, 87, 93, 101, 105, 111, 115) sts.

All Sizes

Rows 94 (94, 96, 96, 101, 103, 108, 108)–103 (103, 105, 105, 110, 112, 117, 117): Work in stacked sc linen st without shaping.

Cut yarn, leaving tail for weaving in; pull tail through last st made; weave in tail using End Cap Finishing Stitch.

To see all the charts full size, go to the "Projects" section beginning on page 271.

11. Pattern Stitches

Like the Stitch Guide, the Pattern Stitches section is a mini stitch dictionary for the pattern. The difference is that the Pattern Stitches section describes the combination of stitches and stitch repeats used to create the fabric for your project, rather than just the individual stitches listed in the Stitch Guide. This is the section you will work from to make your fabric test swatch.

12. Instructions

The actual line-by-line instructions you must follow in order to complete the project created using this pattern.

13. Stitch Charts

Crochet stitch charts are the visual representation of the stitches you are making with your yarn and hook. These can be as simple as a chart of the pattern stitches for a project or as complex as a chart of a tricky shaping or colorwork section of your project. When used hand in hand with the written text of a pattern, stitch charts are a valuable tool for ensuring the success of your project (*see Chart Reading, page 71*).

14. Detail Photos

These are close-up photos of the stitches or sections of your project that help you see what you are making. These are good references to check if you are unsure of what your stitches or a project detail should look like. Often these photos will include flat photos of the fabric you are making, or a border stitch, or finishing details like seams, buttons, or edgings. These are another valuable communication tool for the designer since this is where fine details can be pointed out that aren't necessarily easy to see in the main project photos.

15. Finishing

After all of the main stitching is over, the "Finishing" section includes any final steps you must take to complete your project. This section will often give you instructions for blocking, sewing seams, adding buttons or zippers, setting in sleeves, and sometimes, a friendly reminder to weave in those ends!

16. Schematic

Think of this as the blueprint for your project. A schematic includes the specific technical measurements for every part of your completed project pieces. This is where you will find the most information about size and, in the case of wearables, the fit for your project, since the numbers given here are the finished measurements for your project. The lines next to the larger shapes of the pieces indicate the areas the measurement numbers refer to.

For example, if there is a long line drawn from the top of a garment panel to the bottom, the numbers on that line will indicate the length of that piece of fabric. Smaller lines are drawn over the areas they represent, such as cuffs, armholes, and necklines, and their corresponding numbers represent the inches and/or centimeters those lines indicate. If a pattern is written in various sizes, the numbers here will follow the same system as the written pattern, with the smallest size written first and additional sizes listed inside parentheses, from smallest to largest.

Also, just like a blueprint, the schematic gives you a good visual of the individual project pieces you are making, ensuring you aren't constructing a component backward or missing pieces . . . Hey . . . it happens!

17. Alternate Project View Photos

These are included when space permits and are designed to give you a better look at the project you are making. These might include a garment or accessory made in a different size, or styled differently, or a piece of home decor in a stylized setting. These are an extension of the romance language in that they set the mood for the garment, and often express the designer's creativity intended with the pattern.

18. Special Techniques

This section lists all of the special techniques and skills other than actual stitches and pattern stitches you will need to know to successfully complete your project. This is a particularly valuable section to look for when determining if this is a project that matches your skill level or if you will need to learn a new technique or skill before starting. Working a swatch in which you practice these techniques is advisable if you encounter an unfamiliar or altogether new technique.

Not all patterns will contain all of these sections. How much of this information is included in a pattern is, largely, decided by the amount of space available in the book or magazine the pattern is published in. That said, if a pattern does not include enough information for you to feel confident that you can complete the project successfully, it is best to move on and find another project to spend your valuable time on.

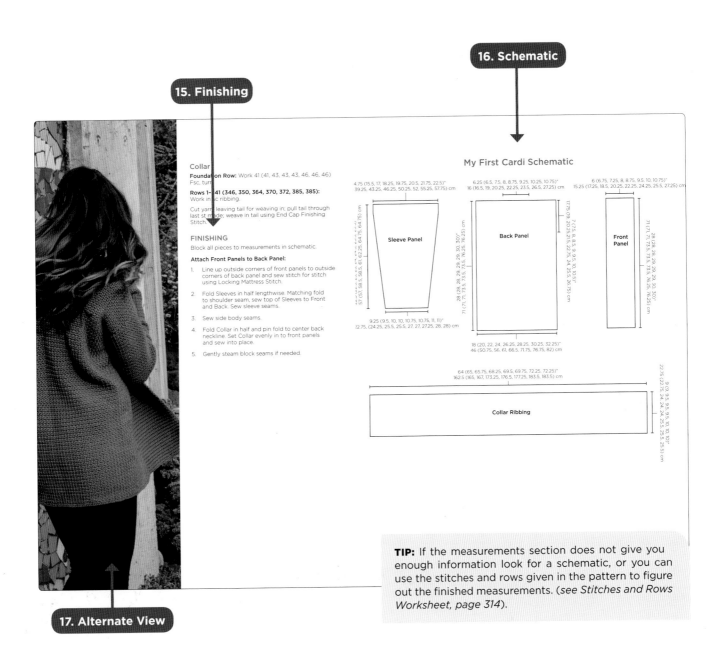

15. Finishing

Collar

Foundation Row: Work 41 (41, 43, 43, 43, 46, 46) Fsc, turn.

Rows 1–41 (346, 350, 364, 370, 372, 385, 385): Work in sc ribbing.

Cut yarn leaving tail for weaving in; pull tail through last st made; weave in tail using End Cap Finishing Stitch.

FINISHING

Block all pieces to measurements in schematic.

Attach Front Panels to Back Panel:

1. Line up outside corners of front panels to outside corners of back panel and sew stitch for stitch using Locking Mattress Stitch.

2. Fold Sleeves in half lengthwise. Matching fold to shoulder seam, sew top of Sleeves to Front and Back. Sew sleeve seams.

3. Sew side body seams.

4. Fold Collar in half and pin fold to center back neckline. Set Collar evenly in to front panels and sew into place.

5. Gently steam block seams if needed.

16. Schematic

My First Cardi Schematic

Sleeve Panel

4.75 (15.5, 17, 18.25, 19.75, 20.5, 21.75, 22.5)"
39.25, 43.25, 46.25, 50.25, 52, 55.25, 57.75) cm

57 (57, 58.5, 58.5, 61, 62.25, 64.75, 64.75) cm

9.25 (9.5, 10, 10, 10.75, 10.75, 11, 11)"
22.75, (24.25, 25.5, 25.5, 27, 27, 27.25, 28, 28) cm

Back Panel

6.25 (6.5, 7.5, 8, 8.75, 9.25, 10.25, 10.75)"
16 (16.5, 19, 20.25, 22.25, 23.5, 26.5, 27.25) cm

17.75 (19, 20.25, 21.5, 22.75, 24, 25.5, 26.75) cm

28 (28, 28, 29, 29, 29.5, 30, 30)"
71 (71, 71, 73.5, 73.5, 76.25, 76.25) cm

18 (20, 22, 24, 26.25, 28.25, 30.25, 32.25)"
46 (50.75, 56, 61, 66.5, 71.75, 76.75, 82) cm

Front Panel

6 (6.75, 7.25, 8, 8.75, 9.5, 10, 10.75)"
15.25 (17.25, 18.5, 20.25, 22.25, 24.25, 25.5, 27.25) cm

7 (7.25, 8.5, 9.5, 10, 10.5)"
71 (71, 73.5, 73.5, 73.5, 76.25, 76.25) cm

Collar Ribbing

64 (65, 65.75, 68.25, 69.5, 69.75, 72.25, 72.25)"
162.5 (165, 167, 173.25, 176.5, 177.25, 183.5, 183.5) cm

9 (9, 9.5, 9.5, 9.5, 10, 10, 10)"
22.75 (22.75, 24, 24, 24, 25.5, 25.5, 25.5) cm

17. Alternate View

TIP: If the measurements section does not give you enough information look for a schematic, or you can use the stitches and rows given in the pattern to figure out the finished measurements. (*see Stitches and Rows Worksheet, page 314*).

To see all the charts full size, go to the "Projects" section beginning on page 271.

Anatomy of a Line of Pattern Text

After first looking at the big picture of the pattern, next you will look at the individual lines of text to see if there is anything you don't understand yet or need to brush up on before beginning your project. This might be a stitch called for in the pattern that you haven't seen before and need to learn, or a finishing technique you haven't used in a while and should brush up on before you get started. Also, is this a stitch pattern you can see yourself working on for the entire time it takes you to complete this project? All of these decisions should be made before you put hook to yarn, to ensure you don't end up with partially finished projects sitting in your project bag that you can't stand to pick back up.

We often compare lines of crochet pattern text to recipes or to a line of computer code. And in a way, that's not too far off since both contain instructions, commands, and information that result in a final output. In the case of a crochet pattern, you are reading lines of instruction and information that will result in your finished project. Just as with a recipe or computer coding, if you are patient, follow a few simple guidelines, and look at each element of a line of pattern text one step at a time, you will find yourself able to read even the most complex patterns with ease.

> **Row 1 (RS):** Ch 1, sl st in each of first 7 (8, 11, 15, 17, 20, 20, 22) sts, ch 1, sc in next st, work in pattern st to end of row, turn – 49 (52, 52, 51, 50, 49, 49, 49) sts.

As you look at a line of pattern text, there are some readily identifiable features we will analyze here:

1. Row or round number

2. Number for the size you are making (it is a good idea to highlight this throughout the pattern to stay on track with the correct stitches for the correct size)

3. Stitches you are going to make, written using words and abbreviations

4. Repeat indicators: asterisk, semicolon, parentheses "(. . .)" and brackets "[. . .]"

5. Number of stitches given at the ends of rows or rounds in which the number of stitches changes (increases or decreases); this is the number of stitches you should have after you work this row or round of the pattern

Now let's go deeper with explanations for these individual lines of text and symbols that communicate the designer's instructions to you.

The Secret Language of Crocheters

WIP, FO, and UFO are three abbreviations you will see used in the crochet community (and, indeed, the entire maker community) that you won't find in any abbreviations chart.

WIP = Work In Progress • FO = Finished Object • UFO = Unfinished Object

Numbers

The first thing most people see when they look at a block of pattern text is all the numbers. These can be confusing if you try to take them in all at once, but taken individually, their meanings become clearer. Here are the most commonly occurring instances of numbers in pattern text:

1. Row or round number—This number is given after the word "Row" or "Round" to indicate the order the lines of text are to be worked in. These follow a logical progression of 1, 2, 3, etc.

   For example, if you are looking at a line of pattern instruction and it begins with Row 12, you know you are reading the 12th row of pattern instructions for a pattern that is written in rows. If you are looking at a line of pattern instruction and it begins with Round 2, you know you are reading the second round of pattern instructions for a pattern that is written in rounds.

2. Stitch and pattern stitch counts and repeats—this number occurs in conjunction with an individual stitch or a set of stitch instructions, and tells you how many times a stitch or stitch pattern is to be repeated.

   For example, a section of pattern text that reads "dc 5 times in next stitch" is telling you to work 5 double crochet stitches in the next st. These become more complex with compound lines of text, and we cover those in detail in the section on Repeats (*see page 62*).

3. Total stitches—Any time there is a change in the total number of stitches in a row or round, there will be a number at the end of that written line of instruction indicating how many stitches you should now have in your row or round. This is used in the case of increases or decreases.

   For example, if you have been working in rows of 30 stitches and the next line of pattern text makes a decrease of 2 stitches, that line of pattern text would end with 28 sts, indicating that, after working that row, you should have 28 stitches remaining. The same is true for increases: if you started with 30 stitches and the next line of pattern text makes an increase of 2 stitches, that line of pattern text would end with 32 sts, indicating that, after working that row, you should have 32 stitches.

4. Stitch multiples—when you are reading a pattern, there will often be a line of text written in the Pattern Stitches section that talks about the number of stitches you need in order to work an even repeat of that pattern stitch. This is called the Stitch Multiple, and we give you a detailed breakdown of how this works in the Shaping section on page 136.

Written Words and Abbreviations

The next features you will notice in a line of crochet pattern text are the stitch instructions and general working instructions that are necessary to create the actual row of crochet fabric. Even without charts and schematics, every crochet pattern will have written lines of text that guide you stitch by stitch and line by line through the process of making your project. Rather than writing out the full names of stitches, stitch patterns, and some instructions, abbreviations are used to save space and to make the patterns easier to read and follow.

In the "Resources" section (*see page 313*) you will find a list of common abbreviations you will encounter. If you ever encounter an abbreviation you aren't sure of, check the pattern's "Stitch Guide" or "Pattern Stitches" sections for clarification.

Repeats

Often, when you are reading a written pattern, you will be asked to repeat a particular stitch, a specific section of stitches, or a certain row or set of rows. As with abbreviations, this is a space-saving feature of pattern writing and avoids having to repeatedly write out long sections of patterning, making the pattern less cluttered looking and easier to read and follow.

If a pattern calls for making a single stitch multiple times, the patterning shorthand will simply state the name of the stitch, then give you the number of times to make the stitch and where the stitch is to be made. This will be done all in one short section of patterning, rather than writing the instruction out over and over again.

Here are examples of several types of repeats you will encounter as you read through a pattern.

Repeating a Single Stitch Multiple Times

Example:

Dc in each of next 5 sts

Here, you are going to work a double crochet stitch in each of the next five stitches. You will have made five double crochets over five stitches at the end of this instruction.

dc in each of next 5 stitches

Example:

Dc 5 times in next st

Here, you are going to work five double crochet stitches in one stitch. You will have made five double crochet stitches in one stitch at the end of this instruction.

dc 5 times in next stitch

Repeating a Section of Stitches

This is used when a section of stitches is to be repeated multiple times. This can be written differently in the pattern, depending on how the repeats are indicated.

Parentheses and Brackets

Work all stitch instructions inside the parentheses or brackets, then look for the number following the parentheses or brackets to tell you how many times to repeat the sequence of stitches inside them.

Example 1:

[Ch 1, sk next ch-1 sp, dc in next st] 5 times

For this repeat, you are going to work everything inside the brackets five times. This line breaks down as:

1. Chain 1.
2. Skip next chain-1 space.
3. Double crochet in the next stitch.
4. Work Steps 1–3 a total of 5 times

In cases of parentheses within brackets, work stitches from the inside out—work the stitch sequence inside the innermost set of parentheses the indicated number of times first, then work the rest of the stitch sequence inside the brackets, then repeat the whole sequence the indicated number of times given after the outermost bracket.

Example 2:

[Ch 1, sk next ch-1 sp, (work dc-v in next st, sk next ch-1 sp) 3 times] 4 times

In this example you will work as follows:

First Repeat

Step 1: Ch 1, sk next ch-1 sp.

Step 2: Work dc-v in next st, sk next ch-1 sp.

Step 3: Work dc-v in next st, sk next ch-1 sp.

Step 4: Work dc-v in next st, sk next ch-1 sp.

Second Repeat

Step 1: Ch 1, sk next ch-1 sp.

Step 2:. Work dc-v in next st, sk next ch-1 sp.

Step 3: Work dc-v in next st, sk next ch-1 sp.

Step 4: Work dc-v in next st, sk next ch-1 sp.

Third Repeat

Step 1: Ch 1, sk next ch-1 sp.

Step 2: Work dc-v in next st, sk next ch-1 sp.

Step 3: Work dc-v in next st, sk next ch-1 sp.

Step 4: Work dc-v in next st, sk next ch-1 sp.

Fourth Repeat

Step 1: Ch 1, sk next ch-1 sp.

Step 2: Work dc-v in next st, sk next ch-1 sp.

Step 3: Work dc-v in next st, sk next ch-1 sp.

Step 4: Work dc-v in next st, sk next ch-1 sp.

Example 1: (ch 1, skip next ch 1 space, dc in next stitch) 5 times

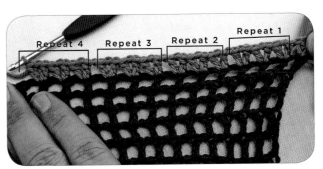

Example 2: 4 sequence repeats

Asterisk and Semicolon "*" and ";"

These repeat indicators work much like parentheses and brackets, with the exception that you will not be given a specific number of times to work the repeat. This is often used when there is a repeat of the stitch pattern to the end of the row or to a clearly defined section in the pattern.

Example 1:

*Ch 1, sk next st, dc in next st; repeat from * to end of row, turn.

Here, you are going to repeat everything after the "*" (asterisk) and before the ";" (semicolon) until you come to the end of the row and turn your work.

Example 1

Example 2:

*Ch 1, sk next st, dc in next st; repeat from * to last 2 sts, dc in each of last 2 sts, turn.

Here, you are going to repeat everything after the "*" (asterisk) and before the ";" (semicolon) until you come to the last 2 stitches of the row, then you will double crochet in each of the last 2 stitches and turn your work.

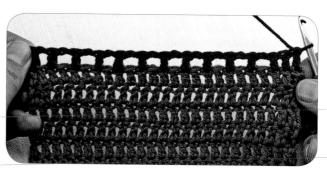

Example 2

Repeating Rows

Just like stitch repeats, the patterning shorthand for row repeats gives you the row or rows to repeat and the number of times you are to repeat them.

Repeating a Single Row Once

Example:

Row 6: Repeat Row 2.

This is telling you that, when you make Row 6, you will make the stitches exactly as you did in Row 2.

repeating a single row once

Repeating a Single Row Multiple Times

Example:

Rows 6-9: Rep Row 2.

For Row 6 through Row 9, you will make the stitches exactly as you did in Row 2.

repeating a single row multiple times

Repeating a Section of Rows

Example:

Rows 6-9: Rep Rows 2-5.

For Row 6 through Row 9, you will make the stitches exactly as you did for Row 2 through Row 5.

repeating a section of rows

Rows 2-5 and Rows 6-9 are shown in contrasting color to show same stitches being made.

Other Commonly Used Phrases

Aside from specific instructions for what to do with your hook and yarn, there are a few other instructions you are likely to encounter:

Fasten Off

This instruction will appear at the end of a section of patterning, where you have either finished the project or finished a section of fabric and are starting with new yarn on a different section of fabric. When you see this instruction, you should cut your yarn, leaving approximately 8″–10″ for weaving in, then pull the tail of the yarn through the last stitch you made. This will make a nice, clean finish without making a knot at the end of your work. You can then proceed to finish off the last stitch with the End Cap Finishing Stitch (*see page 250*).

Work in Pattern Stitch as Established or Work as Established

This instruction will appear in a written pattern as a way of saying "keep doing what you have been doing up to this point" without repeating every line of text. When you see this instruction, you should maintain the stitch as it has been worked up to this point, ensuring that each stitch you make lines up with the stitches from previous stitch pattern rows.

Working Row

The working row is the row you are working into with your hook. This is usually the top row, but sometimes patterns say to work into a row that is below the top row.

Work as for . . .

This line of instruction will appear as "work as for back" or "work" as for first side or "work as for first sleeve," etc., and the "as for" can be read "like you did for the." If this instruction is written by itself, it means to work another panel of fabric just like you did for the back/first side/first sleeve/etc. In the Drape Front Cardigan pattern in this book (*see page 303*), this phrase appears as "Work as for back to armhole shaping." This means you are to work exactly the same number of stitches and exactly the same number of rows that you did for the section of the pattern labeled Back, up to but not including the armhole shaping. This tells you that the fabric panel you are making for the section where this text appears is exactly the same as the fabric panel in the Back section until you reach the armhole shaping.

With RS facing; with WS facing

As listed in our abbreviations section, RS = right side and WS = wrong side. Sometimes a pattern will break off and come back to a specific section, requiring you to identify the RS or WS before starting again. This is often true when adding a new section of a garment, or when adding trims and finishing to projects.

Left Side, Right Side, Left Front, Right Front

In garment patterns, any reference to a part of the garment as left and right refers to left and right as worn.

For example, Left Front refers to the left front part of a garment as the garment is worn.

First Side, Second/Next Side

There are times in a garment pattern when it is not necessary to specify the Left Side and Right Side, but two "sides" must be made. In these cases, left and right sides might be interchangeable, or whether the left or the right might be made first, depending on the size you are making. In cases like these, the pattern will read "First Side" and "Second Side" or "Next Side."

Direction of Work

Another important piece of information gleaned from looking at a crochet pattern is your direction of work. When you create crochet fabric you can work in rows, rounds, turned rounds, and spirals. These are referred to as your direction of work—that is, the direction you work the stitches as you make your fabric.

Crochet stitches look different when they are worked in rows versus when they are worked in rounds or spirals. This sometimes (but certainly not always) determines the "Right Side" (RS) and "Wrong Side" (WS) of your work.

Working in Rows

If a pattern is worked in rows, each line of instruction will start with the word Row followed by the number of the row that line of text represents.

For example: Row 1, Row 2, Row 23, etc. Patterns worked in rows create flat fabrics that have at least two distinct edges created by the first and last stitch of each row.

Because you are turning at the end of every row, working in rows creates fabric where the fronts and backs of the stitches alternate each row. The front of the stitch on one row alternates with the back of the stitch on the next row.

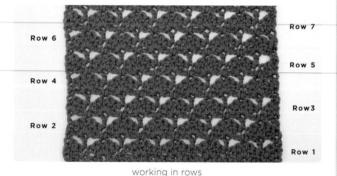

working in rows

> **TIP:** When working in the round, it is smart to place a stitch marker in the first stitch of the round, to keep track of where the round starts and ends. This starting and ending point might be obvious with some stitches, but with others it is easy to get carried away and lose track of where you are, resulting in a spiral instead of a round . . . Better safe than sorry!

Working in the Round

If a pattern is worked in rounds, each line of instruction will start with the word Round followed by the number of the round that line of text represents.

For example: Round 1, Round 2, Round 23, etc. When a pattern is worked in the round, the last stitch of the round is joined to the first stitch of the round (usually with a slip stitch), then a chain up or first stitch is worked to come up to the height of the new round, just like when working in rows. As you start your next round, you will work in the same direction as the previous round, without turning your work.

Working in the round creates a joined tube or circle of fabric, and ensures that all of the stitches you make have their fronts facing to one side of the fabric and their backs to the other. This can create a distinct "Right Side" and "Wrong Side" of your work, depending on the project you are working on.

Use a stitch marker to keep track of rounds

working in the round

Working in Turned Rounds

If a pattern is worked in turned rounds, the lines of instruction will start with the word Round followed by the number of the round that line of text represents.

For example: Round 1, Round 2, Round 23, etc. This is the same as for working in the round.

The difference when working in turned rounds is that the last stitch of the round is joined to the first stitch of the round (just as for working in the round) and then, after the chain up or first stitch is worked to come up to the height of the new round, you will turn your work and crochet in the opposite direction, just as you would for working flat in rows. Crocheting in turned rounds is a hybrid technique, since it creates the look of flat crochet fabric (the stitches alternate front and back each turned round, creating a double-sided fabric) while creating a joined tube or circle.

As with working in the round, you can use a stitch marker to keep track of the first stitch of your round, so you don't get carried away and start a spiral.

Working in a Spiral

If a pattern is worked in a spiral, the lines of instruction will begin with the word Round followed by the number of the round that line of text represents, just like when you are working in the round.

When a pattern is worked in a spiral, the last stitch of the round is not joined to the first stitch of that round with a slip stitch. Instead, the first stitch of the next spiral round is worked directly into the first stitch of the previous round, without a step up. This creates a true spiral, with the beginning of one round overlapping the end of the previous round.

Working in a spiral creates a circle or tube of fabric with all of the fronts of the stitches facing one side of the fabric, and all of the backs facing the other side. This can create a distinct Right Side and Wrong Side, depending on the project you are working on.

Once a spiral direction of work is established, you will definitely need to place a stitch marker in the first stitch of your spiral round, to keep track of your rounds.

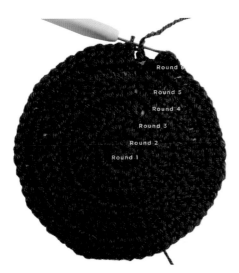

working in turned rounds

working in a spiral

Chart Reading

Crochet charts are a visual representation of the stitches you are about to make. They are a wonderful tool by themselves, because they give you an at-a-glance-picture of what you are about to make with your hook and yarn, without reading multiple lines of text over and over again. Stitch charts are also handy to use as a reference tool when you are trying to decipher a particularly complicated written stitch pattern, since they will show you exactly what stitches are made where, and when.

To demonstrate exactly how crochet charts are a visual representation of the stitches you are making, here is a stitch chart and the swatch made from that stitch chart.

Just like reading the written text of a pattern, the way to read stitch charts is to first look at the larger picture to see what the overall pattern stitch and resulting fabric will look like. Then, after you have a good understanding of the big picture, break the chart down into smaller pieces (the stitches) and look at each of those pieces one at a time. Just like a written pattern, you read a chart one stitch at a time, with an understanding of how that stitch works into the whole fabric.

When you are looking at the chart, you are looking at the visual representation of the FRONT, or RIGHT SIDE of your work.

Parts of a Crochet Chart

Key

With every chart, there should be a key as shown here. This is, in fact, the key for the stitch pattern shown at left. In the case of one-off patterns, there will be a simple key like this that will allow you to interpret just the stitch symbols used in that particular pattern.

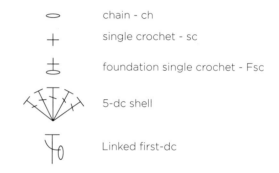

Master Key

The "Master Key" is used to interpret the most common stitch symbols used in most crochet stitch charts. This is not as specific as the key for an individual stitch pattern or project pattern, but it is a valuable reference guide for you to keep around for reading future crochet charts. We have provided you with a "Master Key" in the Resources section of this book on page 324.

Here are a few examples of the most common stitch symbols you will encounter. Don't worry, these are all included in your "Master Key"—no need to memorize them.

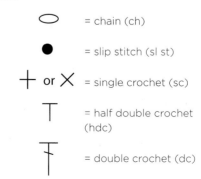

Reading a Crochet Chart

Once you have the key for interpreting the symbols, it is very easy to know which stitch to work when, what kind of stitch you are going to make, and where you are going to put your hook to make that stitch. Let's take a look at the elements that allow you to "read" a stitch chart the same way you read a written pattern.

1. Direction of work

Look for row numbers on the sides of the charts to tell you which line of symbols to "read" next. Some charts have an arrow next to the row showing the direction you will read the chart. Remember: When you are looking at the chart, you are looking at the visual representation of the FRONT or RIGHT SIDE of your work.

2. Follow the "heads"

The cross bar on top of the stitch symbol represents the head of the stitch. The stitches in a crochet chart are worked in the order of the heads of the stitches. Regardless of where the post of the symbol points to, the next stitch to be worked is the next stitch head in line.

3. Hash marks

The number of hash marks on the body of the chart symbol represents the number of times you will yarn over to make your stitch. The cross bar on top of the stitch represents the head of the stitch. You only count the hash marks on the body of the stitch.

For example, if we see one hash mark across the body of the symbol, that means we are going to yarn over once. Likewise, if the symbol has two hash marks, we are going to yarn over twice. You don't have to memorize what all of the symbols mean! All you need to do is remember to count the number of hash marks and make a yarn over for each of them.

4. Where to put the hook to make the stitch

After determining which stitch is worked next, the next thing we will do is follow the post of the stitch symbol to see where we are going to put the hook. The post of the stitch symbol will point directly to the stitch where you will insert your hook to make the stitch the symbol represents. Just follow the post!

And that's all there is to it! Just remember to think of a crochet stitch chart as the visual representation of the stitches you are about to make with your hook and yarn, follow the stitches one at a time just like you would for a written pattern, and make your stitches.

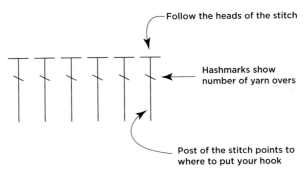

arrows indicating direction of work

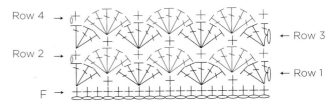

Row 4 →   ← Row 3

Row 2 →   ← Row 1

F →

The crochet chart symbol tells you how to make your stitch.

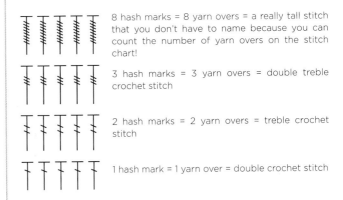

8 hash marks = 8 yarn overs = a really tall stitch that you don't have to name because you can count the number of yarn overs on the stitch chart!

3 hash marks = 3 yarn overs = double treble crochet stitch

2 hash marks = 2 yarn overs = treble crochet stitch

1 hash mark = 1 yarn over = double crochet stitch

The Swatch

A swatch is a piece of fabric you make as the first step in your creative process. Whether you are following a written pattern and need to match your tension to achieve a certain gauge, or if you are playing around with a new yarn, stitch pattern, or technique, swatching is how you make sure you are making the right fabric for your project. There are a number of different reasons for making a swatch ... and all of them are good ones!

1. Checking Tension for Stitch and Row Gauge

This is the swatch you will make to check your stitching tension, to see if you can match the stitch and row gauge for a written pattern—to find out if you are able to duplicate the stitches and rows per inch that the designer of the pattern you are following used. Once you make your gauge swatch and block it (*see Blocking, page 240*), you should have the same stitches and rows per inch given in the pattern (*see Checking Tension and Gauge, page 74*).

2. Stitches and Techniques Swatch

Making a practice swatch of the stitches and techniques you are going to be making in your project is an easy way to find out if you have the necessary skills to finish the project successfully, or if you need to brush up on a technique or add some new skills to your crochet repertoire. A practice swatch like this might include the main stitch pattern and any increases or decreases and specialty stitches you see in the written pattern, as well as buttonholes and seaming techniques. Not to be overlooked in your assessment of this swatch is whether or not you want to work this particular set of skills with the yarn called for in the pattern. You might be familiar with the stitches and techniques, but working those stitches and techniques in the laceweight yarn the pattern calls for might not be something you are really eager to do. So this swatch represents decision-making time: put it down and move on to another project, or pull out your copy of *Complete Crochet Course* and up your crochet skills.

3. Fabric Test Swatch

"The right fabric for the right project!"

Making sure you have the right fabric for your project is key to the success of your finished piece. To ensure that you are, indeed, making the fabric you need for your project, you will need to make a large enough swatch to be able to tell if the finished fabric is suitable and, more to the point, something you will really like.

The size of your fabric test swatch depends on the type of project you are making and on how comfortable you are with the yarn and stitch pattern you are using to make your fabric.

For example, a project with a lot of drape and hang (like a skirt, a tunic, or a drape front cardigan) would require a larger fabric swatch so you can hang block the fabric, making sure it is going to hold up properly with wear and not sag or droop (*see Blocking, page 240*). Also, if you are using a yarn you are unfamiliar with, or a stitch pattern you have not used before, you might need to make a larger fabric swatch so you can get a good look at what your final fabric is going to look like in your project.

How big you make this type of swatch is up to you, but when we really need to get a good look at a new fabric, our fabric swatches are at least 12″ x 12″ or larger. If you are familiar with the yarn and the stitch pattern, you won't need to make such a large fabric swatch. In fact, we keep all of our swatches and label them so we can reference them for future use. If you do not make a fabric test swatch, you won't know what your finished fabric will be like, and you are stitching blind until you reach the end of your project. This has led to much wailing and gnashing of teeth for crocheters who finish their project, only to find that the fabric sags or pulls, and their pullover turns into a droopy tunic. Ugh . . .

> **Important Note:** Changing hook size, yarn weight, or yarn content will result in a different fabric. If any of these are changed, a new swatch should be made to test the finished fabric and to check for gauge accuracy. Tag each swatch so you can go back and see which one makes the right fabric for your project.

4. Experiment OR Just-for-the-Fun-of-It! Swatch

This type of swatching is a great way to play with a new yarn or a stitch pattern you've never worked with before. There are few crochet activities more fun than experimenting and playing with a new yarn, a different hook size (or shiny new hook!), or a new stitch pattern, to see what kind of fabric you can create.

Remember: you are creating fabrics! Play and have fun with it . . . Yes, there are enough patterns out there in the world to keep you busy until we run out of yarn (GASP!), but remember to stop and have fun and use some of your own creativity!

Making a just-for-the-fun-of-it swatch is the equivalent of finding inspiration by going to the fabric store and holding up lengths of different woven fabrics to see how they drape and hang, and then wrapping yourself in them and twirling around . . . What? Just me?!? This is the type of swatch we like to do when we don't particularly know what we want to do. It is like when you want to sketch, but need to just doodle to warm up your brain and see what jumps out at you. This is doodling with your hook and yarn! Keep these swatches and tag them, so you can build your own fabric and stitch library for future reference.

Here in the studio, we use hang tags from the office supply store to keep track of the information on our swatches. Each tag has the yarn used, the color, the hook size, and the stitch pattern. If you use a stitch dictionary or are swatching to practice a certain technique, it is a good idea to indicate the book you used and the page number from the book on the tag. For our design work, we also mark our tags with the stitch and row gauge, as well as the weight of the swatch, so we can calculate the amount of yarn we will need for the project. Also, if we work out a particular technique like an increase or decrease that we like, we will write as much of that out on the tag as possible.

Some of those kinds of tagged swatches have ended up being the basis for entire sections of this very book!

Bottom line: if you want to remember it, write it on the tag, and soon you will have your own visual reference library of swatches!

Blocking the Swatch

Next, after you make your swatch, you will block it. We cover everything you need to know about Blocking in the "Finishing" section on page 239, so be sure to jump ahead and read that section when you are ready to start swatching. In short, blocking is introducing moisture into your fabric to rejuvenate the fibers, and to make the swatch easier to pin into place for shaping. After your fabric swatch is dry, the stitch pattern will be set and the fabric will be more pliable, allowing it to drape and move. Without blocking, you have no way of assessing if your fabric will work for your project.

Checking Tension and Gauge

Once your swatch is blocked and dry, it is time to check to see if your working tension gave you the correct gauge for the fabric you are making. Your tension is how snug or how loose the yarn moves through your yarn hand and over your hook. Too loose, and your fabric can stretch and sag; too tight, and your fabric will be too stiff.

The tension at which you hold your yarn and work it over your hook is what determines your gauge. Gauge is the stitches and rows per inch of your swatch. Knowing your stitches and rows per inch is a vital part of swatching, and of your overall making process. The stitches and rows per inch is the gauge the designer gives you so you can duplicate the fabric they have created their design in. Generally, if you are using the same or similar yarn as called for in the design, and your stitches and rows per inch match the designer's stitches and rows per inch, you will be making the same fabric.

Before you measure your stitches and rows per inch, we suggest you allow time for your dry fabric to relax after removing the pins. If you measure your swatch while it is pinned, or immediately upon removal of the pins rather than waiting for it to relax, the fabric could contract and shrink up a bit, causing your gauge measurements to be off. This will result in a finished project that is not the size you expected and that will not fit. So: make, block, pin, dry, rest, measure. Now you are ready to check your gauge.

The blocked gauge of your fabric is the stitches and rows per inch after you have blocked your swatch. Every pattern you read will give you the stitches and rows per inch. Determining your stitches and rows per inch is a simple matter of measuring, counting, and basic math. We have provided you with a worksheet for calculating your stitches and rows per inch in the "Worksheets" section on page 314. To fill in that worksheet you will:

1. **Measure the total width of your swatch.**
2. **Measure the total height of your swatch.**
3. **Count the total number of stitches in one row.**
4. **Count the total number of rows.**

After the measuring and counting, it's a simple matter of filling in those numbers on your worksheet and you will have your stitches and rows per inch!

Now it's time to compare your gauge to the gauge given in the pattern. Are you on track? If so, you're good to stitch on. If not, it is best to make another swatch and make adjustments to ensure that you are making the same fabric the designer intended for the pattern they designed.

1. Measure the total width of your swatch.

2. Measure the total height of your swatch.

3. Count the total number of stitches in one row.

4. Count the total number of rows.

For example, if you have fewer stitches or rows per inch than the pattern calls for, that means you need to snug up your tension a bit. In other words, you will hold the working yarn a little more securely as you are making your stitches, and make sure your stitches aren't too loose. On the other hand, if you have more stitches or rows per inch than the pattern calls for, that means you can relax your tension a bit.

Tension changes under different circumstances. The swatch you make when you are learning a new stitch or working with a new yarn is *not* the swatch to use for checking your gauge. When we are learning a new stitch or working with a new yarn for the first time, we tend to be a little more tentative, which can result in an uneven tension and in a gauge that is not representative of how we would be stitching if we were more confident with the stitch and yarn.

Other factors like watching a movie or television show that is particularly engaging can cause us to tighten up or completely lose track of our tension altogether, which, again, will not be representative of our actual working stitches. Yelling at the contestants on a cooking reality show (because *why* would anyone put *that* in their sauce anyway?!?) or cheering on your favorite sports team is sure to result in some tight tension.

Other factors that affect our tension are mood, lack of sleep, the cat walking across your lap, and did you remember to take out the recycling? You get the picture. Distractions can cause our tension to vary and, therefore our gauge to be off. That said, life happens, and unfortunately it is not likely that we are always going to be able to focus entirely on our crochet. The good news is, the more you crochet, the better you will be at recognizing whether you are stitching too loosely or too tightly, and you will be able to make adjustments as you go. The bottom line is: be mindful of the tension you need to use to create the correct fabric for your project and, if your team is a little behind, or the monster was chasing the heroine, go back and give your work a glance and see if you need to make some adjustments.

MAKING STITCHES

First Stitches Made

In this section you will see the names of the stitches and how to make them by themselves. This is the part you will come back to as a reference when you can't remember exactly how many times to yarn over before you make a double treble crochet stitch, or how many turning chains to work for a half double crochet. Next, you will see a practice swatch so you can put your new stitch knowledge to work and acquire the muscle memory needed to make these stitches at will in the future. Finally, so you can actually make that practice swatch, we have given you a step-by-step tutorial for each swatch, with photos to help in the trickier spots.

The Stitches: What's in a Name?

Almost there . . . let's make sure we're all on the same page when we are talking about the names of stitches. The naming of crochet stitches is different depending on whether the pattern you are reading uses US or UK terminology. The patterns in this book are written using US terminology. Here is a handy conversation chart for you if the patterns you are reading use different terminology than you are used to in your home country.

For example:

▶ Single crochet (sc) = yarn over and draw through 2 loops 1 time

▶ Double crochet (dc) = yarn over and draw through 2 loops on hook 2 times

▶ Treble crochet (tr) = yarn over and draw through 2 loops on hook 3 times

US TERM	UK TERM	CHART SYMBOL
Slip Stitch	Slip	●
Single Crochet	Double Crochet	+
Half Double Crochet	Half Treble Crochet	⊤
Double Crochet	Treble Crochet	⊤
Treble Crochet	Double Treble Crochet	⊤
Double Treble Crochet	Triple Treble Crochet	⊤

NOTE: With the exception of the half double crochet (hdc) stitch, all stitches are given their US names according to the number of times you work the instruction to yo and **draw through 2 loops on the hook**.

A Stitch, By Any Other Name...

The only way we will ever come to a true consensus on all stitch and technique names is if the Intergalactic Council of Crochet Elders[1] assembles and engages in meaningful debate and consideration regarding all of the names of crochet stitches and techniques that have ever been used. In order to be as consistent as possible in terminology and stitch names, we have made our decisions based on scholarly review and after many hours of pacing, walking through the woods, eating chocolate and, generally, staying up too late extolling the virtues of using "mesh" rather than "grid." In the end, even without a final ruling from the Intergalactic Council of Crochet Elders, it's all about making FAB fabrics so it's all good.

---

[1] What? You've never heard of the Intergalactic Council of Crochet Elders? Okay, we might have made that part up . . . or did we? Either way, you understand our point: everyone isn't going to agree on the names for every little flip of the crochet hook.

Slip Knot

The slip knot is how you attach the yarn to your hook so you can make your first stitches.

1. Make a loop around your hook by passing the yarn tail (the end of the yarn not attached to the ball or skein) from front to back over your hook then over your working yarn (the yarn coming from the ball or skein).
2. Hold the point where the yarn crosses.
3. Wrap the working yarn from front to back over your hook.
4. Use your hook to pull a loop of the working yarn through the loop on your hook.
5. Gently tighten the knot to fit on the shaft of your hook.

Knotless Starting Chain

The knotless starting chain is an alternate way to start your first stitch without ending up with a knot on the end of your work.

1. Pass the yarn tail (the end of the yarn not attached to the ball or skein) from back to front over your hook with tail crossing the side of the working yarn closest to your hook hand.
2. Hold the point where the yarn crosses.
3. Yarn over and draw up a loop through the loop you are holding.
4. Continue to make desired number of chains.
5. Gently pull tail until length of loop you were holding is drawn through the first chain you made, being careful to tighten loop so it matches the gauge of the rest of the chains made.

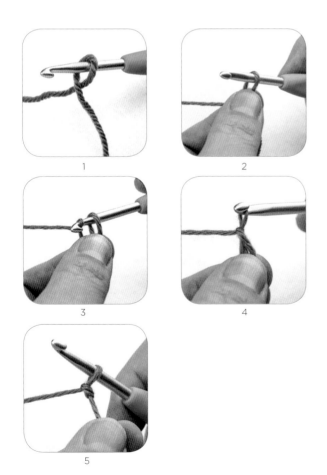

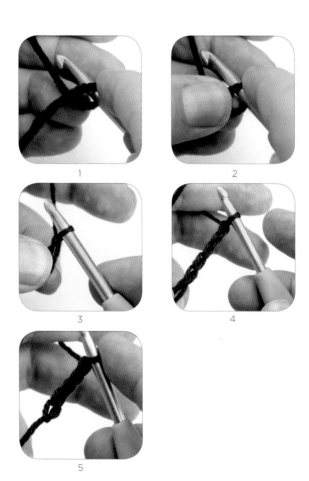

Yarn Over (yo)

A yarn over is made before starting a stitch that is taller than a single crochet. The yarn over gives the stitch added height by putting more wraps between the base of the stitch and the head.

To make a yarn over, wrap the working yarn from back to front over your hook. You can do this by either moving your hand to manipulate the yarn or by moving your hook.

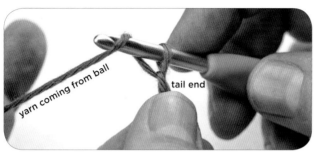

yarn over in correct direction

2 yarn overs

3 yarn overs

Yarn over "XX" times

If written instructions only read yo, it is assumed you are only going to yarn over once. This means the yarn will wrap from back to front over your hook one time, making one extra loop on your hook. Sometimes, however, the instructions for starting a stitch will tell you to yarn over (yo) a certain number of times. This is for the purpose of putting more loops on your hook so you can make taller stitches. The more yarn overs at the start of a stitch, the taller the resulting stitch will be!

Number of yarn overs needed before making a new stitch.

- Single crochet (sc) = no starting yarn over
- Half double crochet (hdc) = 1 starting yarn over
- Double crochet (dc) = 1 starting yarn over
- Treble crochet (tr) = 2 starting yarn overs
- Double treble crochet (dtr) = 3 starting yarn overs
- Triple treble crochet (trtr) = 4 starting yarn overs
- Quadruple treble crochet (qtr) = 5 starting yarn overs

⬭ Chain (ch)

Chain stitches are the first stitches you will see every beginner working, because chain stitches are used as the base for our very first row of stitches. Chain stitches are also used to make turning chains and are often used as the bridge between stitches when you are making lace. So, yes, chain stitches are the easiest of the stitches to make but they are also very important!

1. With a slip knot on your hook, tension the working yarn and secure the tail with your yarn hand.
2. Yarn over.
3. Pull up a loop through loop on hook.
4. Repeat Steps 1 and 2 to make as many chains as called for in pattern.

1

2

3

4

5

The Foundation Chain

One of the methods for starting your crochet fabric is to use a foundation chain. The foundation chain is, very simply, a series of chain stitches into which you will then insert your hook in order to make your first row of stitches.

When using a foundation chain to start your fabric, you will make as many chains as needed for the first row of stitches AND the number of chains needed for your turning chain (*see The Turning Chain, page 82*) to "step up" to the next row. The number of chains you need to step up depends on the height of the stitches in your working row.

foundation chain

stitch marker in top chain

Working Row 1 into the Foundation Chain

After you make a foundation chain row, the pattern will tell you to insert hook into "XX" ch from hook to begin Row 1 of your stitch pattern. When you are counting the chains, it is important to only count the chains that are not on the hook. The loop on the hook does not count as a chain.

In our example, we made 21 chains, and we will make our first single crochet stitch in the second chain from the hook.

For taller stitches, you will be instructed to make more chains and to begin working into a chain that is further from the hook. In these cases, it will be helpful to put a stitch marker in the top chain of the turning chain that counts as your first stitch of the row (bottom left photo). This will help remind you where to insert your hook when you work the last stitch of your next row.

In the practice swatches that follow, the instructions will say to work a Foundation Row of chains, then to work Row 1, Row 2, etc. To work the first row of stitches, you will insert your hook into the foundation chain, under either one or two loops of the foundation chains. Which loop or loops you insert your hook under will dramatically change how the starting edge of your work looks and how firm or stretchy the edge of your fabric is. Depending on the project you are making, you will need to experiment and see where you prefer to insert your hook, both aesthetically and functionally. In the stitch tutorials that follow, you will see us work into one or two of the loops of the foundation chain. Once you have the hang of it, try reworking your first rows using different parts of the foundation chain to see how the look and feel of the edge changes.

There are other foundation stitches that offer more flexibility and are more decorative than the foundation chain. Once you feel comfortable using the foundation chain method of starting your crochet fabric, try the other Foundation Stitches found on page 102.

The Turning Chain

To make a second row (and each row following) you will need to "chain up" to the height of the new row. We do this with a turning chain. Think of the turning chain as building a ladder where each chain represents a rung. How high your ladder reaches depends on the height of the row you are about to make.

For example, you will need a higher ladder (turning chain) to climb up to the height of a row of double crochet stitches than you will for a row of single crochet stitches.

For example, if your first row of stitches has 28 single crochet stitches, you will make 28 foundation chains plus 1 chain, for a total of 29 chains.

Most patterns call for the turning chain to be counted as the first stitch of the row.

For example, if you are about to make a row of double crochet stitches, the pattern will read: "ch 3, count as first dc." Then you will skip the first stitch of the row you are working into and make your next double crochet stitch into the second stitch of the row.

As mentioned earlier, if you are using this method of counting a chain as your first stitch of a row, you should use a stitch marker placed in the last chain of the turning chain so you know where to insert your hook to make the last stitch of the following row. The more you practice, the easier it will be for you to see where to insert your hook, but until then, the marker will be a lifesaver.

Common Problems

One of the most common question we address with newer crocheters (and some who have been crocheting for longer) is the issue of accidentally decreasing the number of stitches in a row. This happens one of two ways:

1. Missing the top of the turning chain when you work the last stitch of the row. If you are using the turning chain method for the first stitch of your row, be sure you are inserting your hook into the top chain of the previous row's turning chain to make the last stitch of the row you are making. Missing this last stitch will shorten your row by one stitch.

2. Turning your work and missing the first stitch of the row. Be sure to work into the actual first stitch of the row to prevent decreasing the number of stitches as you work. This happens most often when using First Stitches (*see page 96*) or when making single crochet stitches. Missing this first stitch will shorten your row by one stitch. Until you are proficient at eyeing the number of stitches in a row and recognizing a skipped stitch or a missed stitch, count your stitches at the end of every row. Even when you are an accomplished crocheter, counting stitches is still an excellent idea when working more complicated stitch patterns.

Here is a guide for the number of chains needed for the turning chain for each stitch height:

- ▶ Single crochet (sc) = 1 chain
- ▶ Half double crochet (hdc) = 2 chains
- ▶ Double crochet (dc) = 3 chains
- ▶ Treble crochet (tr) = 4 chains
- ▶ Double treble crochet (dtr) = 5 chains

+ or ✕ Single Crochet (sc)(UK Double Crochet)

Single Crochet (sc)

Insert hook into indicated st, yo and draw up a lp (2 lps on hook), yo and draw through 2 lps on hook.

1. Insert hook into indicated stitch or space.

2. Yarn over.

3. Draw up a loop (2 loops on hook).

4. Yarn over.

5. Draw through 2 loops on hook.

6. Repeat Steps 1–5 to make as many single crochet stitches as called for in the pattern.

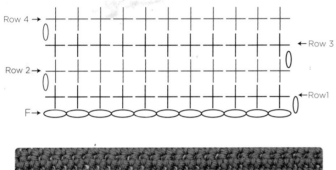

1

2

3

4

5

6

Single Crochet Practice Swatch

Foundation Row: Ch 21.

Row 1: Sc in second ch from hook and in each ch to end of row, turn - 20 sc.

Row 2: Ch 1, sc in first st and in each st to end of row, turn.

Rows 3–10: Repeat Row 2.

Fasten off.

Foundation Row

Make 21 foundation chains.

Row 1

1. Insert hook into the second foundation chain from the hook.
2. Yarn over and draw up a loop (2 loops on hook).
3. Yarn over and draw through both loops on hook (single crochet made).
4. Insert hook under 2 loops of the next foundation chain.
5. Repeat Steps 3–4 until you reach the end of the row, turn (20 single crochet stitches made).

Row 2

1. Chain 1.
2. Insert hook under both loops of the first stitch of the row.
3. Yarn over and draw up a loop (2 loops on hook).
4. Yarn over and draw through both loops on hook (single crochet made).
5. Insert hook under both loops of the next stitch.
6. Repeat Steps 3–5 until you reach the end of the row, turn (20 single crochet stitches made).

Subsequent Rows

Repeat Row 2 until you have made a total of 10 rows.

Fasten off.

Row 1

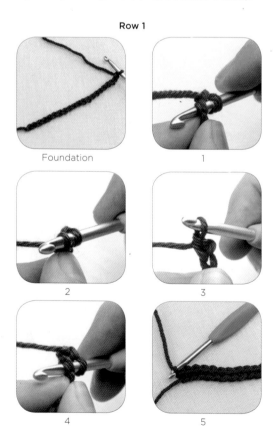

Foundation   1

2   3

4   5

Row 2

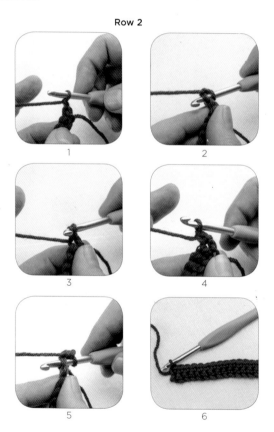

1   2

3   4

5   6

Double Crochet
(UK Treble Crochet)

Double Crochet (dc)

Yo, insert hook into indicated st, yo and draw up a lp (3 lps on hook), [yo and draw through 2 lps on hook] 2 times.

1. Yarn over.
2. Insert hook into indicated stitch or space.
3. Yarn over.
4. Draw up a loop (3 loops on hook).
5. Yarn over.
6. Draw through 2 loops on hook (2 loops on hook).
7. Yarn over.
8. Draw through 2 loops on hook.
9. Repeat Steps 1–8 to make as many double crochet stitches as called for in the pattern.

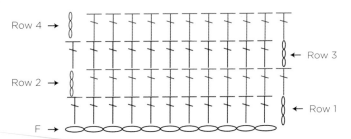

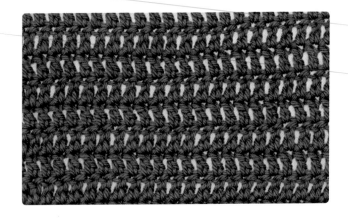

1

2

3

4

5

6

7

8

9

Double Crochet Practice Swatch

Foundation Row: Ch 22.

Row 1: Dc in fourth ch from hook (first 3 chains count as first dc of row), dc in next ch and in each ch to end of row, turn - 20 dc.

Row 2: Ch 3 (count as first dc), dc in second st and in each st to end of row, turn.

Rows 3–10: Repeat Row 2.

Fasten off.

Foundation Row

Make 22 foundation chains

Row 1

1. Yarn over and insert hook into the fourth foundation chain from the hook.
2. Yarn over and draw up a loop (3 loops on hook).
3. Yarn over and draw through 2 loops on hook (2 loops on hook).
4. Yarn over and draw through 2 loops on hook (double crochet made).
5. Yarn over and insert hook into the next foundation chain.
6. Repeat Steps 2–5 until you reach the end of the row, turn (20 double crochet stitches made).

Row 2

1. Chain 3 (count as first dc of row).
2. Yarn over and insert hook under both loops of the second stitch of the row.
3. Yarn over and draw up a loop (3 loops on hook).
4. Yarn over and draw through 2 loops on hook (2 loops on hook).
5. Yarn over and draw through 2 loops on hook (double crochet made).
6. Yarn over and insert hook under both loops of the next stitch.
7. Repeat Steps 3–6 until you reach the end of the row, turn (20 double crochet stitches made).

Subsequent Rows

Repeat Row 2 until you have made a total of 10 rows.

Fasten off.

Row 2

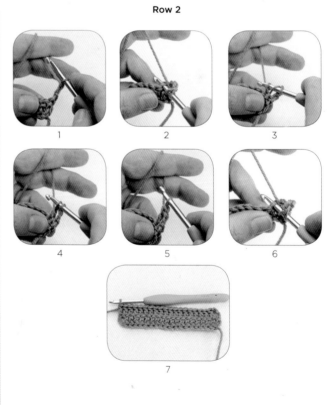

Row 1

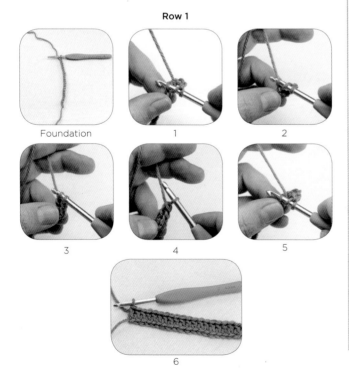

Treble Crochet (tr)(UK Double Treble Crochet)

Treble Crochet (tr)

Yo 2 times, insert hook into indicated st, yo and draw up a lp, (yo and draw through 2 lps on hook) 3 times.

1. Yarn over 2 times.
2. Insert hook into indicated stitch or space.
3. Yarn over.
4. Draw up a loop (4 loops on hook).
5. Yarn over and draw through 2 loops on hook (3 loops on hook).
6. Yarn over and draw through 2 loops on hook (2 loops on hook).
7. Yarn over and draw through 2 loops on hook.
8. Repeat Steps 1–7 to make as many treble crochet stitches as called for in pattern.

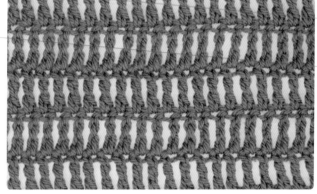

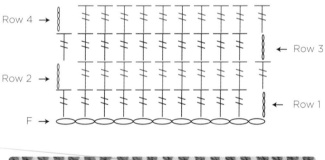

1

2

3

4

5

6

7

8

Treble Crochet Practice Swatch

Foundation Row: Ch 23.

Row 1: Tr in fifth ch from hook (first 4 chains count as first tr of row), tr in next ch and in each ch to end of row, turn - 20 tr.

Row 2: Ch 4 (count as first tr), tr in second st and in each st to end of row, turn.

Rows 3–10: Repeat Row 2.

Fasten off.

Foundation Row

Make 23 foundation chains.

Row 1

1. Yarn over 2 times and insert hook into the fifth foundation chain from the hook.
2. Yarn over and draw up a loop (4 loops on hook).
3. Yarn over and draw through 2 loops on hook (3 loops on hook).
4. Yarn over and draw through 2 loops on hook (2 loops on hook).
5. Yarn over and draw through 2 loops on hook (treble crochet made).
6. Yarn over 2 times and insert hook into the next foundation chain.
7. Repeat Steps 2–6 until you reach the end of the row, turn (20 treble crochet stitches made).

Row 2

1. Chain 4 (count as first tr).
2. Yarn over 2 times and insert hook under both loops of the second stitch of the row.
3. Yarn over and draw up a loop (4 loops on hook).
4. Yarn over and draw through 2 loops on hook (3 loops on hook).
5. Yarn over and draw through 2 loops on hook (2 loops on hook).
6. Yarn over and draw through 2 loops on hook (treble crochet made).
7. Yarn over 2 times and insert hook under both loops of the next stitch.
8. Repeat Steps 3–7 until you reach the end of the row, turn (20 treble crochet stitches made).

Subsequent Rows

Repeat Row 2 until you have made a total of 10 rows.

Fasten off.

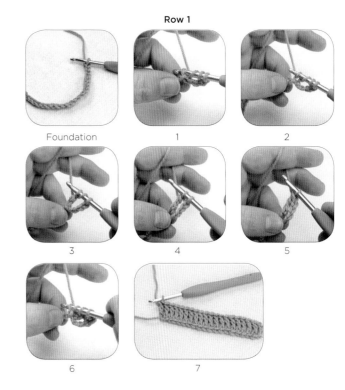

Row 1

Foundation

1

2

3

4

5

6

7

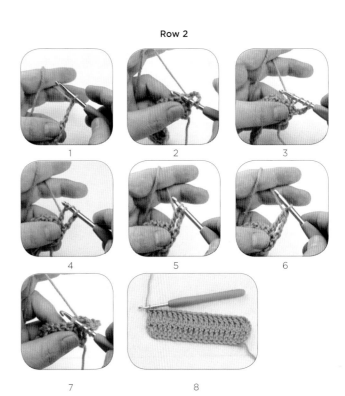

Row 2

1

2

3

4

5

6

7

8

Double Treble Crochet (dtr) (UK Triple Treble Crochet)

Double Treble Crochet (dtr)

Yo 3 times, insert hook into indicated st, yo and draw up a lp, (yo and draw through 2 lps on hook) 4 times.

1. Yarn over 3 times.
2. Insert hook into indicated stitch or space.
3. Yarn over and draw up a loop (5 loops on hook).
4. Yarn over and draw through 2 loops on hook (4 loops on hook).
5. Yarn over and draw through 2 loops on hook (3 loops on hook).
6. Yarn over and draw through 2 loops on hook (2 loops on hook).
7. Yarn over and draw through 2 loops on hook.
8. Repeat Steps 1–7 to make as many double treble crochet stitches as called for in pattern.

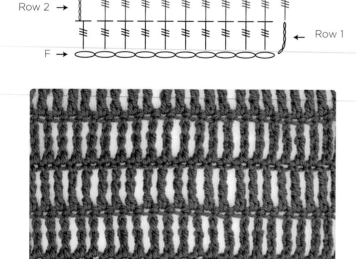

Double Treble Crochet Practice Swatch

Foundation Row: Ch 24.

Row 1: Dtr in sixth ch from hook (first 5 chains count as first dtr of row), dtr in next ch and in each ch to end of row, turn - 20 dtr.

Row 2: Ch 5 (count as first dtr), dtr in second st and in each st to end of row, turn.

Rows 3–10: Repeat Row 2.

Fasten off.

Foundation Row

Make 24 foundation chains.

Row 1

1. Yarn over 3 times and insert hook into the sixth foundation chain from the hook.
2. Yarn over and draw up a loop (5 loops on hook).
3. Yarn over and draw through 2 loops on hook (4 loops on hook).
4. Yarn over and draw through 2 loops on hook (3 loops on hook).
5. Yarn over and draw through 2 loops on hook (2 loops on hook).
6. Yarn over and draw through 2 loops on hook (double treble crochet made).
7. Yarn over 3 times and insert hook into the next foundation chain.
8. Repeat Steps 2–7 until you reach the end of the row, turn (20 double treble crochet stitches made).

Row 2

1. Chain 4 (count as first tr).
2. Yarn over 3 times and insert hook into the second stitch of the row.
3. Yarn over and draw up a loop (5 loops on hook).
4. Yarn over and draw through 2 loops on hook (4 loops on hook).
5. Yarn over and draw through 2 loops on hook (3 loops on hook).
6. Yarn over and draw through 2 loops on hook (2 loops on hook).
7. Yarn over and draw through 2 loops on hook (double treble crochet made).
8. Yarn over 3 times and insert hook under two loops of the next stitch.
9. Repeat Steps 2–8 until you reach the end of the row, turn (20 double treble crochet stitches made).

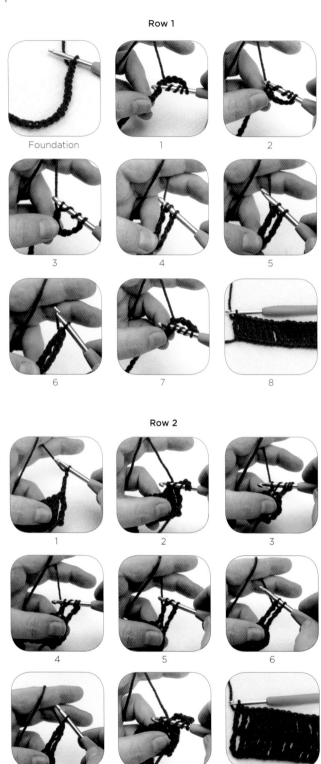

Row 1

Foundation

1

2

3

4

5

6

7

8

Row 2

1

2

3

4

5

6

7

8

9

⊤ Half Double Crochet (hdc) (UK Half Treble Crochet)

Half Double Crochet (hdc)

Yo, insert hook into indicated st, yo and draw up a lp (3 lps on hook), yo and draw through all 3 lps on hook.

1. Yarn over.
2. Insert hook into indicated stitch or space.
3. Yarn over.
4. Draw up a loop (3 loops on hook).
5. Yarn over.
6. Draw through all 3 loops on hook.
7. Repeat Steps 1–6 to make as many half double crochet stitches as called for in pattern.

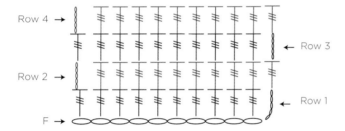

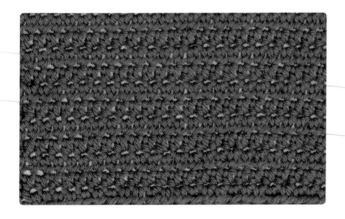

Half Double Crochet Practice Swatch

Foundation Row: Ch 21.

Row 1: Hdc in third ch from hook (first 2 chains count as first hdc of row), hdc in next ch and in each ch to end of row, turn - 20 hdc.

Row 2: Ch 2 (count as first hdc), hdc in second st and in each st to end of row, turn.

Rows 3–10: Repeat Row 2.

Fasten off.

Foundation Row
Make 21 foundation chains.

Row 1
1. Yarn over and insert hook into the third foundation chain from the hook.
2. Yarn over and draw up a loop (3 loops on hook).
3. Yarn over and draw through all 3 loops on hook (half double crochet made).
4. Yarn over and insert hook into the next foundation chain.
5. Repeat Steps 3–4 until you reach the end of the row, turn (20 half double crochet stitches made).

Row 2
1. Chain 2 (count as first hdc of row).
2. Yarn over and insert hook into the second stitch of the row.
3. Yarn over and draw up a loop (3 loops on hook).
4. Yarn over and draw through all 3 loops on hook (half double crochet made).
5. Yarn over and insert hook under both loops of the next stitch.
6. Repeat Steps 3–5 until you reach the end of the row, turn (20 half double crochet stitches made).

Subsequent Rows
Repeat Row 2 until you have made a total of 10 rows.

Fasten off.

Row 1

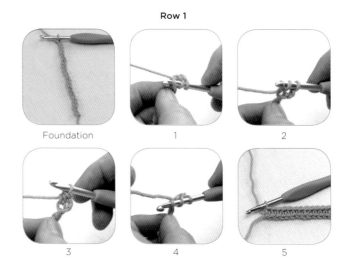

Foundation   1   2

3   4   5

Row 2

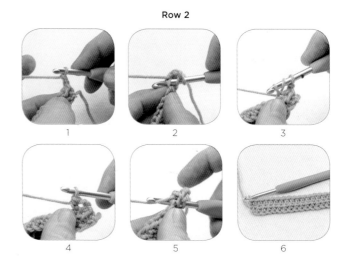

1   2   3

4   5   6

● Slip Stitch (sl st)

Slip Stitch (sl st)

Insert hook into indicated st, yo and draw up a lp through st AND lp on hook at the same time.

1. Insert hook into indicated stitch or space.

2. Yarn over.

3. Draw up a loop through stitch AND loop on hook at the same time.

4. Repeat Steps 1–3 to make as many slip stitch stitches as called for in the pattern.

The slip stitch is the shortest in height of the crochet stitches because it sits low, right up against the stitch it is made into. This makes the slip stitch great for joining chains (when working projects made from the center out, like motifs or top-down hats) and for joining stitches (when working in the round or in turned rounds). Slip stitches are also perfect for working decreases at the beginning of a row, like on the edge of an armhole or where you need a quickly stepped decrease (we'll get to those in the Shaping section on page 136).

Although often overlooked as a fabric stitch, a quick search for Bosnian Crochet, Pjoning, or Shepherd's Knitting will show you a vast array of intricate stitches and patterns that can be created by utilizing the slip stitch.

For our practice swatch, we are going to work slip stitches through the back loop (tbl) of each row. I encourage you to play and experiment by alternating working through the back loops and front loops of your stitches, under both loops, and even working in the round to truly discover all of the fabulous textures the slip stitch can create.

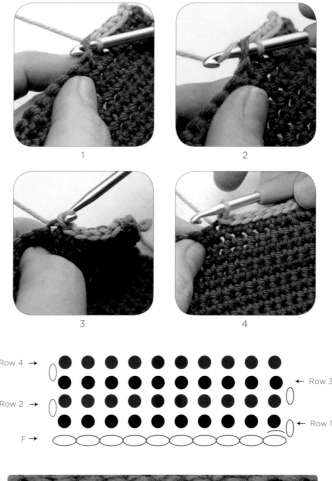

Slip Stitch Practice Swatch

Foundation Row: Ch 21.

Row 1: Sl st tbl of second ch from hook and in each ch to end of row, turn - 20 sl sts.

Row 2: Ch 1, sl st in first st and in each st to end of row, turn.

Rows 3-20: Repeat Row 2.

Fasten off.

Foundation Row

Make 21 foundation chains

Row 1

1. Insert hook under the back loop only of the second foundation chain from the hook.
2. Yarn over and draw up a loop through the chain AND the loop on the hook (slip stitch made).
3. Insert hook under the back loop only of the next foundation chain.
4. Repeat Steps 2-3 until you reach the end of the row, turn (20 slip stitches made).

Row 2

1. Chain 1.
2. Insert hook under the back loop only of the first stitch of the row.
3. Yarn over and draw up a loop through the chain AND the loop on the hook (slip stitch made).
4. Insert hook under the back loop only of the next stitch.
5. Repeat Steps 3-4 until you reach the end of the row, turn (20 slip stitches made).

Subsequent Rows

Repeat Row 2 until you have made a total of 20 rows.

Fasten off.

Row 1

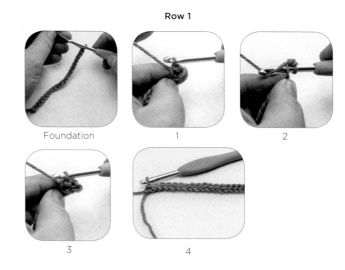

Foundation

1

2

3

4

Row 2

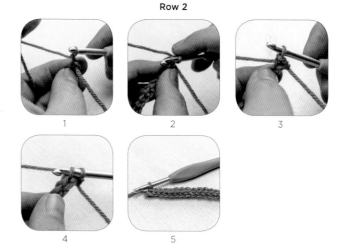

1

2

3

4

5

First Stitches of a Row

Especially in the case of taller stitches, turning chains can leave a large gap in the sides of your work. This happens when a row of pattern instruction starts with a chain up that is meant to be counted as the first stitch of the row. These chains have a tendency to sit on the outside of the fabric and leave an unsightly gap where the first stitch should be.

To prevent this from happening, there are a number of techniques for making First Stitches at your disposal. Each one is a great tool for different circumstances of stitch pattern, yarn weight, fabric, and project, and each one has its own set of strengths and weaknesses depending on the circumstances it's they are used in.

As you are making your practice swatches, try all of them with different stitch heights and in different yarn weights to see which one you prefer in each instance. Then, when you are making your fabric swatch before you start your project, try these first stitch techniques to see which works best for your specific project.

All of the first stitches in this section are interchangeable and can be used any time there is a dc, tr, dtr, etc., to be worked as the first stitch of a row.

For example, if you see a row of instruction that starts with "ch 3 (count as first dc of row,)" you can use a linked first-dc or wrapped first-dc instead.

Throughout the practice swatches in this book, you will see "work first-dc in first st" or "work first-hdc in first st." When you see this, pick your favorite version of these stitches and see which one works best with that particular stitch.

1 2

3 4

Stacked First Stitches

Stacked first stitches use chains stacked on top of a "tilted" single crochet stitch to achieve the height needed to step up to the new row. This lessens the large gap you'll see at the end of the row when using a chain-up. To prevent the gap we make a single crochet stitch in the first stitch of the row, without making a chain-up first. This tilts the head of the sc stitch slightly outward giving it the look of the base of a taller stitch. ,

1. Without chaining up to the height of the new row, insert your hook into the first stitch of the row.

2. Yarn over and draw up a loop.

3. Yarn over and draw through both loops on your hook.

4. Chain up to the height of the stitches in your working row.

| CORRECT | INCORRECT |

A good general rule when you are building your stacked first stitches is that the tilted single crochet counts as the base of the stitch and one yarn over, and the chain stitches on top of that sc are the remaining yarn overs and head of the stitch you need.

For example, if you are making a double crochet, you "yo and draw through 2 loops on your hook" 2 times. Your tilted single crochet is the base and one "yo and draw through 2 loops on hooks," so you would work one more chain for the second "yo and draw through 2 loops on hook," and one more chain for the head of the stacked double crochet.

For a treble crochet, the instructions read to [yo and draw through 2 loops on hook] 3 times. So, for a treble crochet, you need your tilted sc for the base and one "yo and draw through 2 loops on hook," on hook two more chains for the second and third "yo and draw through 2 loops on hook" instructions. Finally, you will need one more chain for the head of your stacked treble crochet.

You should definitely test this with different yarn sizes and different types of crochet fabric. We find these work particularly well for double and treble stitches, but can leave a gap at the end of the row for the taller stitches. In addition, there will be times with heavier weight yarns that you may not need to work as many chains to get to the height of your working row. As with all stitches and techniques, the key is to swatch and see what works best for the fabric you are making for your project.

With stacked first stitches, it is important to remember to insert your hook into the top chain of the stacked first stitch when you are making the last stitch of the following row.

For example, if you worked a stacked first-tr at the beginning of Row 3, when you come to the last stitch of Row 4, you have to insert your hook into the last chain of the stacked first-tr at the beginning of row 3. If you miss and make your stitch into the space made by the chains, you will have another hole in the end of your fabric and it will not look as neat and tidy as you would like.

Three types of Stacked First Stitches

Stacked first half double crochet (stacked first-hdc)

Sc in first st, ch 1.

Stacked first double crochet (stacked first-dc)

Sc in first st, ch 2.

Stacked first treble crochet (stacked first-tr)

Sc in first st, ch 3.

stacked first-dc st

stacked first-tr st

Linked First Stitches

Linked first stitches use a combination of chains and the technique from linked stitches (*see page 130*) to step up to the height of the working row. Linked first stitches make a neat and tidy border on your crochet fabrics that look FAB when left as a raw edge and are perfect for working into when sewing seams or picking up stitches for a border.

The rule for making linked first stitches is that you need to make a chain for every yarn over you would make before inserting your hook to make a stitch.

For example, a linked first-dc would have one chain because you would do one yarn over before inserting your hook into your working row to make a double crochet stitch; a linked first-tr would have 3 chains to account for the two yarn overs done before working a treble crochet stitch; and a linked first-dtr would have 4 chains . . . you get the picture. The higher the stitch, the more chains you make to accommodate the number of yarn overs you would make for that stitch.

After you have made the correct number of chains, you will then insert your hook into each chain and then into the first stitch, giving you the loops you need on your hook to complete the stitch. The key to working a successful linked first stitch is to keep your chains at the right tension so they do not close up before you can insert your hook into them. This is the same mindfulness you must exhibit when working a foundation chain to work your first row into, so this should not be a problem for you at all by now!

Here, we give you the instructions for working linked first-hdc, dc, and tr stitches but you can work linked stitches to any height. In fact, linked first stitches work better for taller stitches than most other first stitch techniques. Just remember to make a chain for every yarn over you would do before you start your stitch. And, yes, as always, use your fabric swatches to see which technique works best with your fabric for your project.

Linked First Half Double Crochet

Linked first half double crochet (Linked first-hdc)

Pull loop on hook up to slightly taller than normal loop, ch 1, insert hook in first ch from hook, yo and draw up a loop (2 loops on hook), insert hook into first st, yo and draw up a loop (3 loops on hook), yo and draw through all 3 loops on hook.

1. Pull loop on hook up to slightly taller than a normal loop and chain 1.
2. Insert your hook into the bottom bump of the first chain from your hook.
3. Yarn over and draw up a loop (2 loops on hook).
4. Insert your hook into the first stitch of the row, yo and draw up a loop (3 loops on hook).
5. Yarn over and draw through all 3 loops on hook.

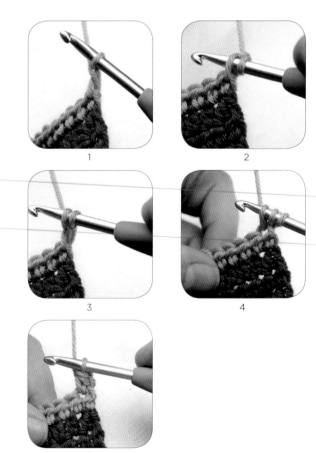

Linked First Double Crochet

Linked first double crochet (Linked first-dc)

Pull loop on hook up to slightly taller than normal loop, ch 1, insert hook in first ch from hook, yo and draw up a loop (2 loops on hook), insert hook into first st, yo and draw up a loop (3 loops on hook), [yo and draw through 2 loops on hook] 2 times.

1. Pull loop on hook up to slightly taller than a normal loop and chain 1.

2. Insert your hook into the bottom bump of the first chain from your hook, yarn over and draw up a loop (2 loops on hook).

3. Insert your hook into the first stitch of the row, yo and draw up a loop (3 loops on hook).

4. [Yo and draw through 2 loops on hook] 2 times.

1

2

3

4

Linked First Treble Crochet

Linked first treble crochet (Linked first-tr)

Ch 2, insert hook in first ch from hook, yo and draw up a loop (2 loops on hook), insert hook in next ch from hook, yo and draw up a loop (3 loops on hook), insert hook into first st, yo and draw up a loop (4 loops on hook), [yo and draw through 2 loops on hook] 3 times.

1. Pull loop on hook up to slightly taller than a normal loop and chain 2.

2. Insert your hook into the bottom bump of the first chain from your hook, yarn over and draw up a loop (2 loops on hook).

3. Insert your hook into the bottom bump of the next chain from your hook, yarn over and draw up a loop (3 loops on hook).

4. Insert your hook into the first stitch of the row, yo and draw up a loop (4 loops on hook).

5. [Yo and draw through 2 loops on hook] 3 times.

1

2

3

4

5

Wrapped First Stitches

Wrapped first stitches start by using chain-ups to achieve the height needed for the working row of stitches. Then, because of the way the hook is wrapped around those chains, a yarn under is used to grab the yarn and bring it back around to the front of the working row. While a yarn under is rarely called for in a pattern, you will see how it is necessary here to make this stitch work correctly.

Here, the guideline for the number of chains used for making a wrapped stitch is the same as if you were working a turning chain for that particular stitch.

For example, if you are making an hdc you would chain up once; for a dc, you would chain up 2 times; for a tr, you would chain up 3 times (*see The Turning Chain, page 82*).

That said, be sure to test your wrapped first stitches in the fabric swatch you make and decide what works best for your fabric and your project, and don't be afraid to adjust the number of chain ups to match the height of your row. Since the chain ups are only used to achieve the height needed and do not show on the outside of the stitch, use as many or as few as you need for your yarn to make your fabric look correct for your project. Use your test swatch!

Making a successful wrapped first stitch involves keeping the loop on your hook and your yarn overs from sliding around your hook and becoming twisted. This slippage is easily prevented by simply holding the loop down tightly against your hook with your finger. This holds true for all wrapped first stitches and we will demonstrate here with a wrapped first-dc.

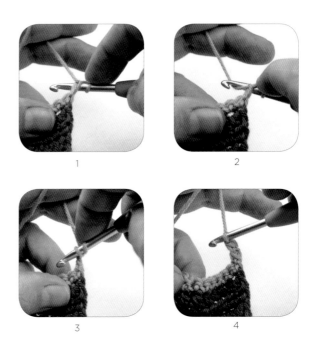

1   2

3   4

1. Ch 1, being careful not to twist the loop on your hook (to keep the loop from twisting, hold the loop down tightly against the hook with your finger), wrap your hook from front to back around the right-hand side of the chain you just made (for left-handed crocheters, you will wrap around the left-hand side of the chain you just made).

2. Yarn under. Note here that the yarn is coming under the hook rather than over the hook as in a yarn over.

3. Again, being careful to not twist the loop on your hook, bring the yarn back around the chain to the front of the work (2 loops on hook).

4. Insert your hook into the first st of the row and complete the dc as usual.

Three Types of Wrapped First Stitches

Wrapped first half double crochet (wrapped first-hdc)

Ch 1, being careful not to twist loop on hook, wrap hook from front to back around right-hand side of ch just made, yarn under, bring yarn to front of work (2 loops on hook), insert hook into first st, yo and draw up a loop (3 loops on hook), yo and draw through all 3 loops on hook.

Wrapped first double crochet (wrapped first-dc)

(Ch 2, being careful to not twist loop on hook, wrap hook from front to back around right-hand side of ch just made, yarn under, bring yarn to front of work (2 loops on hook), insert hook into first st, yo and draw up a loop (3 loops on hook), [yo and draw through 2 loops on hook] 2 times.

Wrapped first treble crochet (wrapped first-tr)

Ch 3, yo, being careful not to twist loops on hook, wrap hook from front to back around right-hand side of chs just made, yarn under and bring yarn to front of work (3 loops on hook), insert hook into first st, yo and draw up a loop (4 loops on hook), [yo and draw through 2 loops on hook] 3 times.

Foundation Stitches

As mentioned previously, there are foundation stitches other than the foundation chain that make a more decorative and flexible starting row than the foundation chain. Once you feel comfortable using the foundation chain method of starting your crochet fabrics, these other foundation stitches are great options to have in your crochet toolkit.

These foundation stitches are perfect for the hems of garments, sleeve cuffs, necklines of top-down construction garments, and, generally, any place you will need a little more flexibility to the edge of your fabric. They are also decorative and have a unique look that can make your fabric edges stand out beautifully.

Foundation stitches create a row of stitches that can best be compared to making the foundation chain and the first row of stitches at the same time. In fact, what you are creating is a sideways chain (a completely unique stitch) and another stitch on top of that sideways chain before moving on to the next foundation stitch. The stitches are named according to the stitch created on top of the sideways chain: Foundation single crochet, Foundation double crochet, etc. After you are comfortable working these types of stitches, look carefully at what you are actually doing with your yarn and hook and you will see just how unique these types of stitches are.

In this section, we will show you how to use foundation stitches both as a starting point for your fabric and to create extensions to your existing fabric.

For example: a pattern that calls for 35 Foundation single crochet stitches would mean that you should chain 35 stitches, then chain one more to come up to the height of a single crochet row, for a total of 36 stitches.

For a complete breakdown of the number of chains you should work to come up to the height of your working row, see "The Turning Chain" on page 82.

Foundation Stitches as a Starting Point

Foundation Stitches are a perfect alternative to working a starting chain, then working your first row of stitches back into that chain. Using foundation stitches this way makes a more flexible base row that is vital at garment hems, sleeve cuffs, and necklines of top-down garments. Foundation stitches used as the starting point for your crochet fabrics also create an even edge that looks beautiful as a raw hem but is also perfect for sewing side seams if the garment is worked from side to side. Also, the even bottom of the foundation stitch hem makes a perfect base for working a lace border into for garments or home decor.

NOTE: Throughout this book, you will see practice swatches that start with a row of foundation stitches. If you would rather use foundation chains for your fabric, simply chain the number of foundation stitches called for in the foundation row, then add the number of chains needed to chain up to the height of your first row of stitches.

foundation chain with row of sc worked into it

foundation sc worked as one row

foundation chain with row of dc worked into it

foundation dc worked as one row

⊥ Foundation Single Crochet (Fsc)

Foundation single crochet (Fsc)

Ch 2, insert hook into second ch from hook, yo and draw up a lp, yo and draw through 1 lp (first "chain" made), yo and draw through 2 lps on hook (first Fsc made), *insert hook under 2 lps of the "chain" just made, yo and draw up a lp, yo and draw through 1 lp ("chain" made), yo and draw through 2 lps on hook (Fsc made); rep from * for indicated number of foundation sts.

1. Chain 2.
2. Insert hook into second chain from hook.
3. Yarn over and draw up a loop.
4. Yarn over and draw through 1 loop (first "chain" made).
5. Yarn over and draw through 2 loops on hook (first Fsc made).
6. Insert hook under 2 loops of the "chain" just made.
7. Yarn over and draw up a loop.
8. Yarn over and draw through 1 loop ("chain" made).
9. Yarn over and draw through 2 loops on hook (Fsc made).
10. Repeat Steps 6–9 for indicated number of Foundation Single Crochet stitches.

NOTE: There are times when we refer to a chain with quotation marks around it ("chain"). This is because what you are making is the equivalent of the foundation chain but, as described earlier, this is actually a sideways chain.

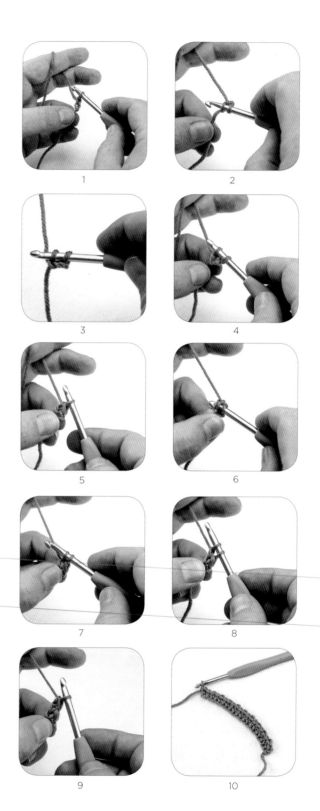

Foundation Half Double Crochet (Fhdc)

Foundation half double crochet (Fhdc)

Ch 2, yo, insert hook into second ch from hook, yo and draw up a lp, yo and draw through 1 lp (first "chain" made), yo and draw through all 3 lps on hook (first Fhdc made), *yo, insert hook under 2 lps of the "chain" just made, yo and draw up a lp, yo and draw through 1 lp on hook ("chain" made), yo and draw through all 3 lps on hook (Fhdc made); rep from * for indicated number of foundation sts.

1. Chain 2.
2. Yarn over and insert hook into second chain from hook.
3. Yarn over and draw up a loop.
4. Yarn over and draw through 1 loop (first "chain" made).
5. Yarn over and draw through all 3 loops on hook (first Fhdc made).
6. Yarn over and insert hook under 2 loops of the "chain" just made.
7. Yarn over and draw up a loop.
8. Yarn over and draw through 1 loop ("chain" made).
9. Yarn over and draw through all 3 loops on hook (Fhdc made).
10. Repeat Steps 6-9 for indicated number of Foundation half double crochet stitches.

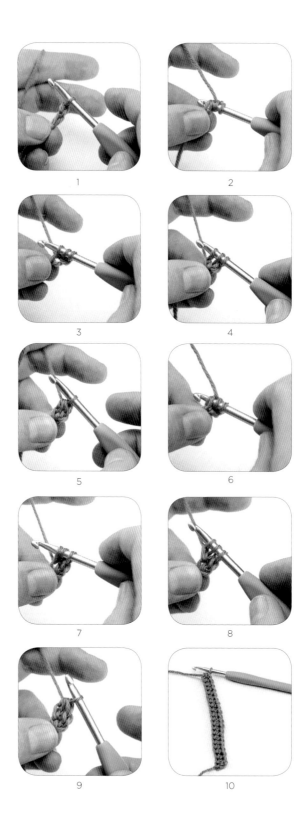

⊥ Foundation Double Crochet (Fdc)

Foundation double crochet (Fdc)

Ch 2, insert hook into second ch from hook, yo and draw up a lp, yo and draw through 1 lp (first "chain" made), yo and draw through 2 lps on hook, ch 2 (first Fdc made), *yo, insert hook under 2 lps of the "chain" just made, yo and draw up a lp, yo and draw through 1 lp ("chain" made), [yo and draw through 2 lps on hook] 2 times (Fdc made); rep from * for indicated number of foundation sts.

NOTE: There are two methods for making the first stitch of the Foundation double crochet. The difference between the two can be subtle, but can make a huge difference in the edge of your crochet fabric. Practice both and keep them in your crochet bag of skills so you can pick which one works best for the fabric you are creating for your project.

1. Chain 2.
2. Insert hook into second chain from hook.
3. Yarn over and draw up a loop.
4. Yarn over and draw through 1 loop (first "chain" made).
5. Yarn over and draw through 2 loops on hook.
6. Chain 2 (first Fdc made).
7. Yarn over and insert hook under 2 loops of the "chain" just made.
8. Yarn over and draw up a loop.
9. Yarn over and draw through 1 loop ("chain" made).
10. Yarn over and draw through 2 loops on hook.
11. Yarn over and draw through 2 loops on hook (Fdc made).
12. Repeat Steps 7–11 for indicated number of foundation double crochet stitches.

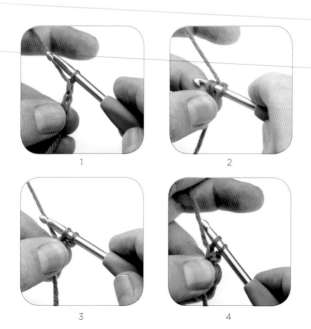

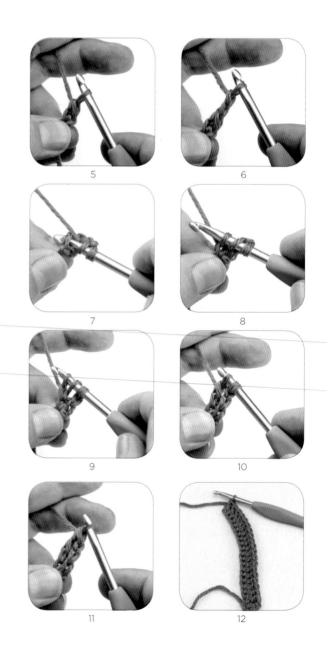

Fdc Made with Linked First-dc

Foundation double crochet made with Linked First-dc (Linked Fdc)

Ch 2, insert hook into first ch from hook, yo and draw up a lp, insert hook into next ch, yo and draw up a lp (3 lps on hook), yo and draw through 1 lp (first "chain" made), [yo and draw through 2 lps on hook] 2 times (first Linked-Fdc made), *yo, insert hook under 2 lps of the "chain" just made, yo and draw up a lp, yo and draw through 1 lp ("chain" made), [yo and draw through 2 lps on hook] 2 times (Fdc made); rep from * for indicated number of foundation sts.

1. Chain 2.
2. Insert hook into first chain from hook.
3. Yarn over and draw up a loop.
4. Insert hook into next chain.
5. Yarn over and draw up a loop (3 loops on hook).
6. Yarn over and draw through 1 loop (first "chain" made).
7. Yarn over and draw through 2 loops on hook.
8. Yarn over and draw through 2 loops on hook (first Linked-Fdc made).
9. Yarn over and insert hook under 2 loops of the "chain" just made.
10. Yarn over and draw up a loop ("chain" made).
11. Yarn over and draw through 1 loop.
12. Yarn over and draw through 2 loops on hook. Yarn over and draw through 2 loops on hook (Fdc made).
13. Repeat steps 9–12 for indicated number of foundation double crochet stitches.

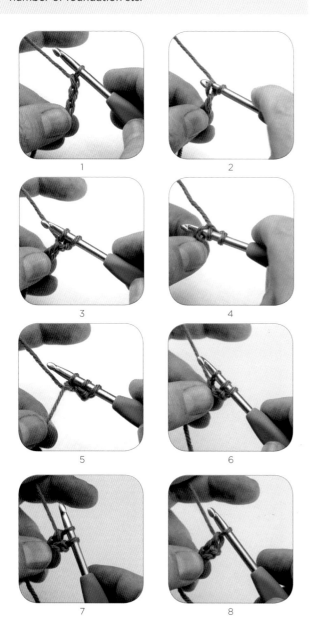

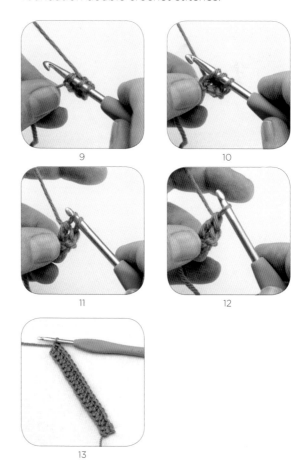

⌲ Foundation Treble Crochet (Ftr)

Foundation treble crochet (Ftr)

Ch 4, insert hook into second ch from hook, yo and draw up a lp, [insert hook into next ch, yo and draw up a lp] 2 times (4 lps on hook), yo and draw through 1 lp (first "chain" made), [yo and draw through 2 lps on hook] 3 times (first Linked-Ftr made), *yo 2 times, insert hook under 2 lps of the "chain" just made, yo and draw up a lp ("chain" made), yo and draw through 1 lp, [yo and draw through 2 lps on hook] 3 times (Ftr made); rep from * for indicated number of foundation sts.

1. Chain 4.
2. Insert hook into second chain from hook.
3. Yarn over and draw up a loop.
4. Insert hook into next chain.
5. Yarn over and draw up a loop.
6. Insert hook into next chain.
7. Yarn over and draw up a loop (4 loops on hook).
8. Yarn over and draw through 1 loop (first "chain" made).
9. [Yarn over and draw through 2 loops on hook] 3 times (first Linked-Ftr made).
10. Yarn over 2 times and insert hook under 2 loops of the "chain" just made.
11. Yarn over and draw up a loop ("chain" made).
12. Yarn over and draw through 1 loop.
13. [Yarn over and draw through 2 loops on hook] 3 times (Ftr made).
14. Repeat Steps 10–13 for indicated number of Foundation treble crochet stitches.

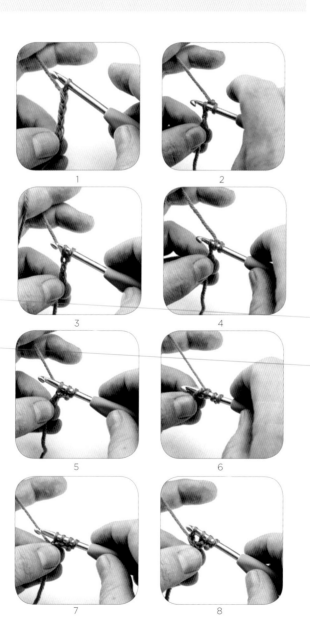

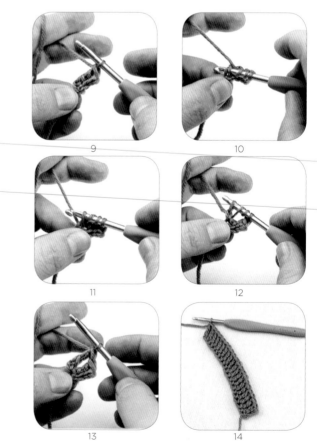

Foundation Slip Stitch

The Foundation slip stitch is the perfect alternative when you want the ease and flexibility of a foundation stitch row but don't want the foundation row to be as pronounced in the overall fabric. The Fslst creates a narrower band while still being decorative and more flexible than a foundation chain.

Foundation slip stitch (Fslst)

Ch 2, insert hook into second ch from hook, yo and draw up a lp (first "chain" made) (2 lps on hook), yo and draw through 2 lps on hook (first Fslst made), *insert hook under 2 lps of "chain" just made, yo and draw up a lp (2 lps on hook), yo and draw through 2 lps on hook (Fslst made); rep from * for indicated number of foundation sts.

1. Chain 2.
2. Insert hook into second chain from hook.
3. Yarn over and draw up a loop (first "chain" made) (2 loops on hook).
4. Yarn over and draw through 2 loops on hook (first Fslst made).
5. Insert hook under 2 loops of "chain" just made.
6. Yarn over and draw up a loop (2 loops on hook).
7. Yarn over and draw through 2 loops on hook (Fslst made).
8. Repeat Steps 5–7 for indicated number of Foundation slip stitches.

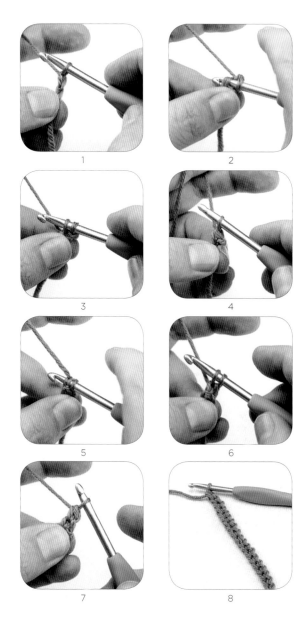

NOTE: As with all crochet stitches, the height of your foundation stitches is determined by the number of yarn overs you make before you start making your stitch. For Foundation double treble, Foundation triple treble, etc., you will simply chain higher for your first linked stitch, then yarn over the number of times you normally would for the stitch you are making.

Combination Foundation Stitches

For FAB textured fabrics such as s/dc crunch stitches (*see page 208*) you can make a matching foundation row, since all you are doing is alternating the number of yarn overs. Here is the Foundation single/double crochet stitch, but try different stitch height combinations on your own to see what kinds of interesting borders you can create for your own unique crochet fabrics.

Foundation single/double crochet (Fs/dc):

Ch 2, insert hook into second ch from hook, yo and draw up a lp, yo and draw through 1 lp (first "chain" made), yo and draw through 2 lps on hook (first Fsc made), yo, insert hook under 2 lps of the "chain" just made, yo and draw up a lp, yo and draw through 1 lp ("chain" made), [yo and draw through 2 lps on hook] 2 times (first Fdc made), *insert hook under 2 lps of the "chain" just made, yo and draw up a lp, yo and draw through 1 lp ("chain" made), yo and draw through 2 lps on hook (Fsc made), yo, insert hook under 2 lps of the "chain" just made, yo and draw up a lp, yo and draw through 1 lp ("chain" made), [yo and draw through 2 lps on hook] 2 times (Fdc made); rep from * for indicated number of foundation sts.

finished Fs/dc row

NOTE: Other foundation stitches can be made using other crochet stitches. Keep an eye open throughout this book to find adaptations of the foundation stitch technique used with other stitches.

Foundation Stitches for Extending Rows

In addition to making a beautiful and flexible starting row, foundation stitches are a great tool for extending rows—when adding sleeves to a garment or when adding asymmetrical elements to your fabrics, for example.

> **Extending Foundation single crochet (foundation sc as used for extending rows) (Ext-Fsc)**
>
> Insert hook into last st worked, yo and draw up a lp, yo and draw through 1 lp (first "chain" made), yo and draw through 2 lps on hook (first Ext-Fsc made), *insert hook under 2 lps of the "chain" just made, yo and draw up a lp, yo and draw through 1 lp ("chain" made), yo and draw through 2 lps on hook (Ext-Fsc made); rep from * for indicated number of extending foundation sts.

1. Insert hook into last stitch worked.
2. Yarn over and draw up a loop.
3. Yarn over and draw through 1 loop (first "chain" made).
4. Yarn over and draw through 2 loops on hook (first Ext-Fsc made).
5. Insert hook under 2 loops of the "chain" just made.
6. Yarn over and draw up a loop.
7. Yarn over and draw through 1 loop ("chain" made).
8. Yarn over and draw through 2 loops on hook (Ext-Fsc made).
9. Repeat Steps 5–8 for indicated number of extending Foundation single crochet stitches.

Practice Swatch

Foundation Row: Work 15 Fsc, turn.

Rows 1–10: Ch 1, sc in first st and in each st to end of row, turn.

Row 11: Ch 1, sc in first st and in each st to end of row, work 8 Ext-Fsc, turn – 23 sts.

Row 12: Ch 1, sc in first st and in each of next 14 sts, turn (leaving last 8 sts unworked) – 15 sts.

Rows 13–24: Rep Rows 1–12.

Rows 25–36: Rep Rows 1–12.

STITCH ON! Easy scarf project!
Grab your favorite yarn and keep repeating Rows 1–12 to make a longer piece of fabric.

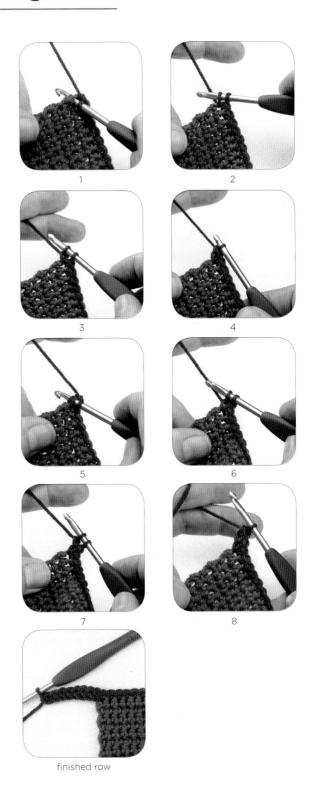

1

2

3

4

5

6

7

8

finished row

Variations on Basic Stitches

Think of the stitches in this section as the next evolution of the basic stitches you have learned so far. All of the stitches in this section make the basic stitches, but you might insert your hook into a different spot to make part of the stitch, or there might be one little extra step to completing the stitch.

Reverse Single Crochet

Reverse single crochet (sometimes called crab stitch) is worked in the opposite direction from your usual direction of work (from left to right if you stitch right-handed, right to left if you stitch left-handed). This stitch can be worked both as an edging stitch and in an overall fabric to create a FAB texture.

Reverse Single Crochet Edging

Reverse single crochet (rev-sc)

Right-handed instructions: Working from left to right, insert hook from front to back in next st to the right, yo and draw up a lp, yo and draw through 2 lps on hook. Left-handed instructions: Working from right to left, insert hook from front to back in next st to the left, yo and draw up a lp, yo and draw through 2 lps on hook.

1. Working in opposite direction of normal work (to the right if right-handed, to the left if left-handed), insert hook from front to back in next st.

2. Yarn over and draw up a loop.

3. Yarn over and draw through 2 loops on hook.

4. Continue to end of row.

Practice Swatch

This reverse single crochet edging can be worked at the end of any of your practice swatches. Simply work to the end of your last row and then, without turning your work, follow the step-out instructions below. You could even continue down the side of your swatch and work a reverse single crochet edging all around your swatch . . . Now you're on to something!

1

2

3

4

Offset Stitches

Once again, the versatility of crochet is illustrated with a stitch that is made just like a standard stitch, but the resulting fabric is dramatically altered by changing where you put your hook to make the stitches. Here, we are offsetting our stitches by inserting our hook between the posts of the stitches in the row we are working into, rather than into the heads of those stitches. The result is a beautifully textured fabric that has a woven look to it. This stitch pattern is perfect for home decor and outerwear.

Offset Half Double Crochet

Offset Half Double Crochet (offset hdc)

Yo, insert hook into the sp between the posts of the next 2 sts, yo and draw up a lp, yo and draw through all 3 lps on hook.

1. Yarn over and insert hook into the space between the posts of the next 2 stitches.
2. Yarn over and draw up a loop.
3. Yarn over and draw through all 3 loops on hook.

Practice Swatch

Foundation Row: Work 30 Fhdc (*page 105*), turn.

Rows 1–20: Ch 1, sc in first st, work offset hdc in sp between posts of next 2 sts, work offset hdc in sp between sts to last st, sc in last st, turn.

Fasten off.

1

2

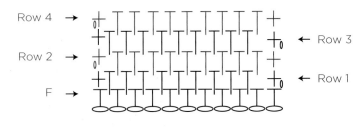

3

finished offset hdc

Row 4 →

Row 2 →

F →

← Row 3

← Row 1

Offset Double Crochet

Offset Double Crochet (offset dc)

Yo, insert hook into the sp between the posts of the next 2 sts, yo and draw up a lp, [yo and draw through 2 lps on hook] 2 times.

1. Yarn over and insert hook into the space between the posts of the next 2 stitches.
2. Yarn over and draw up a loop.
3. [Yarn over and draw through 2 loops on hook] 2 times.

1

2

3

Practice Swatch

Foundation Row: Work 30 Fdc, turn.

Rows 1–16: Ch 1, hdc in first st, work offset dc in sp between posts of next 2sts, work offset dc in sp between sts to last st, hdc in last st, turn.

Fasten off.

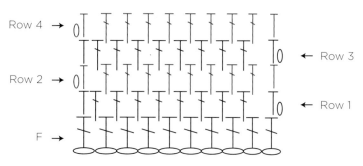

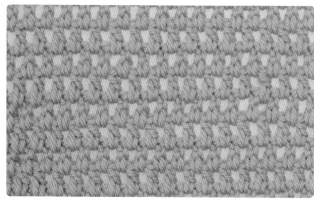

NOTE: The first and last stitches of each row of the offset hdc and offset dc practice swatches are shorter stitches than the rest of the stitches in the row—single crochet stitches on either side of offset half double crochet stitches, for example. This is because the offset stitches are shortened due to being worked below the heads of the stitches in the previous row.

Stitches Made Using One Loop Only

As we discussed in "Where to Put Your Hook" (*page 44*), inserting your hook under the front loop or back loop only of the stitch you are working into creates a whole new type of fabric, remarkably different from standard crochet stitches made by inserting your hook under both loops.

You will remember that we said making stitches by inserting your hook under the front loop of a stitch every row creates a lightweight fabric, while inserting your hook under the back loop every row creates a more dense fabric, resulting in crochet ribbing. For a review of why this happens, see "Why So Different" on page 47.

The great thing about making these new fabrics is that you already know all of the stitches you need to make them happen! All you need to do is insert your hook under either the front loop or the back loop every row and you'll have a whole new texture for your fabrics.

The most important detail to remember is that the side of the work that is facing you is always the front. Each time you turn your work, the side that is facing you is the front. The loops on the side of your work closest to you are the front loops, and the loops on the side of your work farthest away from you are the back loops.

single crochet

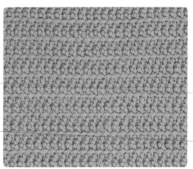

single crochet through the front loop

hook under front loop of stitch

single crochet through the back loop

hook under back loop of stitch

 # ⊥ or ✕ Single Crochet Through Front Loop Only

Single crochet through front loop only (sc-tfl)
Insert hook under front lp of indicated st, yo and draw up a lp, yo and draw through 2 lps on hook.

1. Insert hook under front loop of next stitch.
2. Yarn over and draw up a loop (2 loops on hook).
3. Yarn over and draw through 2 loops on hook.

Practice Swatch

Foundation Row: Ch 22, sc in second ch from hook and in each ch to end of row, turn – 21 sc.

Rows 1–22: Ch 1, sc in first st, sc tfl of next st and of each st to last st, sc in last st, turn.

Fasten off.

1

2

3

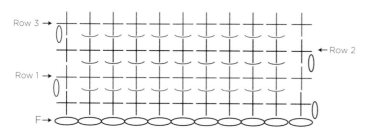

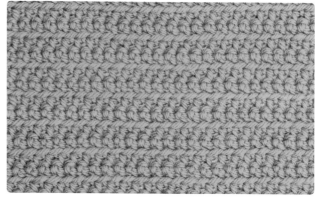

⊤ Half Double Crochet Through Front Loop Only

Half double crochet through front loop only (hdc tfl)

Yo, insert hook under front lp of indicated st, yo and draw up a lp, yo and draw through all 3 lps on hook.

1. Yarn over and insert hook under front loop of next stitch.

2. Yarn over and draw up a loop (3 loops on hook).

3. Yarn over and draw through 3 loops on hook.

Practice Swatch

Foundation Row: Ch 22, hdc in second ch from hook and in each ch to end of row, turn – 21 hdc.

Rows 1–22: Ch 1, hdc in first st, hdc tfl of next st and of each st to last st, hdc in last st, turn.

Fasten off.

1

2

3

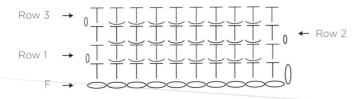

Row 3 →

← Row 2

Row 1 →

F →

⊥ or ✕ Single Crochet Through Back Loop Only

Single Crochet Through Back Loop Only (sc-tbl)

Insert hook under back lp of indicated st, yo and draw up a lp, yo and draw through 2 lps on hook.

1. Insert hook under back loop of next stitch.
2. Yarn over and draw up a loop (2 loops on hook).
3. Yarn over and draw through 2 loops on hook.

1

2

3

Practice Swatch

Foundation Row: Ch 22, sc in second ch from hook and in each ch to end of row, turn – 21 sc.

Rows 1–22: Ch 1, sc in first st, sc tbl of next st and of each st to last st, sc in last st, turn.

Fasten off.

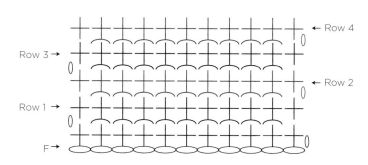

 Half Double Crochet Through Back Loop Only

Half Double Crochet Through Back Loop Only (hdc tbl)

Yo, insert hook under back lp of indicated st, yo and draw up a lp, yo and draw through all 3 lps on hook.

1. Yarn over and insert hook under back loop of next stitch.
2. Yarn over and draw up a loop (3 loops on hook).
3. Yarn over and draw through 3 loops on hook.

1

2

Practice Swatch

Foundation Row: Ch 22, hdc in second ch from hook and in each ch to end of row, turn – 21 hdc.

Rows 1–22: Ch 1, hdc in first st, hdc tbl of next st and of each st to last st, hdc in last st, turn.

Fasten off.

3

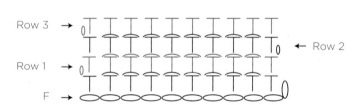

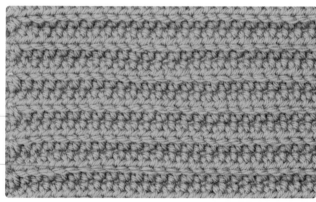

Alternating Half Double Crochet TFL/TBL

Alternating half double crochet through the front loop/through the back loop (alt hdc tfl/tbl)

Foundation Row: Work 29 Fhdc, turn.

Rows 1–22: Ch 1, hdc in first st, *hdc tfl, hdc tbl; rep from * to last 2 sts, hdc tfl, hdc in last st, turn.

Fasten off.

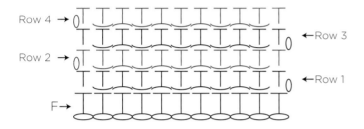

Alternating Single Crochet TFL/TBL

Alternating single crochet through the front loop/ through the back loop variation 1 (alt sc tfl/tbl var 1)

Foundation Row: Work 29 Fsc, turn.

Rows 1–22: Ch 1, sc in first st, *sc tfl, sc tbl; rep from * to last 2 sts, sc tfl, sc in last st, turn.

Fasten off.

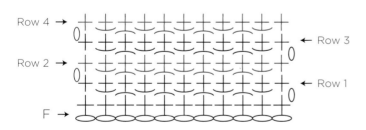

Post Stitches

Up to this point in our stitching, all of our stitches have been made by either inserting the hook into the loops of the head of the stitch or between the stitches. This next set of stitches adds a whole new dimension to crochet fabrics by working our hook around the post of the indicated stitch, rather than into the head of the stitch. This bends the head of the stitch we are working around outward and pulls the post of that same stitch up to the surface of the fabric. The result is a textured fabric that can be used for everything from home decor to garments. In addition, post stitches are the basis for a number of crochet ribbing fabrics, and are the key to making cables!

There are two types of post stitches:

1. Front Post Stitches

Front Post stitches are always worked with the hook starting in the front of the fabric and moving from front to back to front again around the post of the indicated stitch. Front Post stitches are indicated in a pattern with the abbreviation "FP" followed by the abbreviation for the height of the stitch.

For example, a Front Post double crochet stitch would be abbreviated as FPdc. A Front Post treble crochet stitch would be FPtr, and so on.

2. Back Post Stitches

Back Post stitches are always worked with the hook starting in the back of the fabric and moving from back to front to back again around the post of the indicated stitch. Back Post stitches are indicated in a pattern with the abbreviation "BP" followed by the abbreviation for the height of the stitch.

For example, a Back Post double crochet stitch would be abbreviated as BPdc. A Back Post treble crochet stitch would be BPtr, and so on.

Front Post and Back Post stitches are described exactly the same as front loop and back loop stitches. The side of the fabric that is facing you is always the front side.

Front Post Double Crochet

Front Post double crochet (FPdc)

Yo, insert hook from front to back and then to the front again around post of indicated st, yo and draw up a lp, [yo and draw through 2 lps on hook] 2 times.

1. Yarn over and insert hook from front to back of stitch post.
2. And then to front again around same stitch post.
3. Yarn over and draw up a loop.
4. [Yarn over and draw through 2 loops on hook] 2 times.

Practice Swatch

Foundation Row: Work 21 Fdc, turn.

Alternate Foundation Row: Ch 23, work Linked first-dc in first ch, dc in each ch to end of row, turn – 21 dc.

Row 1: Ch 1, sc in first st and in each st to end of row, turn.

Row 2: Ch 1, sc in first st, *FPdc around next st 2 rows below, sc in next st; rep from * to end of row, turn.

Rows 3–16: Repeat Rows 1–2.

Row 17: Repeat Row 1.

Fasten off.

Post Stitches

Unworked Heads

Note: When post stitches are made, there is always a stitch behind them that remains unworked on the next row.

1

2

3

4

Back Post Double Crochet

Back Post double crochet (BPdc)

Yo, insert hook from back to front and then to back again around post of indicated st, yo and draw up a loop, [yo and draw through 2 loops on hook] 2 times.

1. Yarn over and insert hook from back to front of stitch post.

2. And then to back again around same stitch post.

3. Yarn over and draw up a loop.

4. [Yarn over and draw through 2 loops on hook] 2 times.

Practice Swatch

Foundation Row: Work 21 Fdc, turn.

Alternate Foundation Row: Ch 23, work Linked first-dc in first ch, dc in each ch to end of row, turn – 21 dc.

Row 1: Ch 1, sc in first st and in each st to end of row, turn.

Row 2: Ch 1, sc in first st, *Fpdc around next st 2 rows below, sc in next st; rep from * to end of row, turn.

Rows 3–16: Repeat Rows 1–2.

Row 17: Repeat Row 1.

Fasten off.

1

2

3

4

Front Post/Back Post Double Crochet

The practice swatches we have done for Front Post and Back Post stitches have used each of those stitches by themselves to create a one-sided, textured fabric. Here is a commonly used stitch pattern that combines Front Post and Back Post stitches in alternating rows to create a double-sided textured fabric. This fabric is often used for ribbing around the base of hats, the hems of garments, and sleeve cuffs.

Practice Swatch

Foundation Row: Work 21 Fdc, turn.

Alternate Foundation Row: Ch 23, work Linked first-dc in first ch, sc in each ch to end of row, turn – 21 dc.

Row 1: Work first-hdc in first st, FPdc around next st, *BPdc around next st, FPdc around next st; rep from * to last st, hdc in last st, turn.

Row 2: Work first-hdc in first st, BPdc around next st, *FPdc around next st, BPdc around next st; rep from * to last st, hdc in last st, turn.

Rows 3–16: Repeat Rows 1–2.

Row 17: Ch 1, sc in first st and in each st to end of row, turn.

Fasten off.

EXPLORE ON YOUR OWN!

This combination of Front Post and Back Post stitches can be worked with stitches of any height, including treble and double treble crochet stitches. All you need to do is adjust the height of the first and last stitches of the row from half double crochet stitches to double crochet stitches to account for the height of the new post stitches.

Here are some taller post stitches for you to practice. You will see some of these later when you work on cables!

Front Post treble crochet (FPtr)

Yo 2 times, insert hook from front to back and then to front again around post of indicated st, yo and draw up a lp, [yo and draw through 2 lps on hook] 3 times.

Back Post treble crochet (BPtr)

Yo 2 times, insert hook from back to front and then to back again around post of indicated stitch, yo and draw up a lp, [yo and draw through 2 lps on hook] 3 times.

Front Post double treble crochet (FPdtr)

Yo 3 times, insert hook from front to back and then to front again around post of indicated st, yo and draw up a lp, [yo and draw through 2 lps on hook] 4 times.

Back Post double treble crochet (BPdtr)

Yo 3 times, insert hook from back to front and then to back again around post of indicated stitch, yo and draw up a lp, [yo and draw through 2 lps on hook] 4 times.

NOTE: As with all basic crochet stitches, post stitches can be made taller by making another yarn over before starting the stitch. Work your practice swatches with taller stitches by adding another yarn over before you work your hook around the post of the stitch. Just remember to adjust the height of the first and last stitches of the row to account for the height of the new post stitches.

How tall can you go?

⨍ Front Post Single Crochet

Front Post single crochet (FPsc)

Insert hook from front to back and then to the front again around post of indicated st, yo and draw up a lp, yo and draw through 2 lps on hook.

1. Insert hook from front to back of stitch post.
2. And then to front again around same stitch post.
3. Yarn over and draw up a loop.
4. Yarn over and draw through 2 loops on hook.

1   2

3   4

Practice Swatch

Foundation Row: Work 21 Fdc, turn.

Alternate Foundation Row: Ch 23, work Linked first-dc in first ch, dc in each ch to end of row, turn – 21 dc.

Row 1: Ch 1, sc in first st, FPsc around next st and each st to last st, sc in last st, turn.

Row 2: Work first-dc in first st, dc in next st and in each st to end of row, turn.

Rows 3–12: Repeat Rows 1–2.

Fasten off.

Below is an example of a lace stitch that uses FPsc to accent the waved top ridge of the lace pattern. Notice how the same stitch without the FPsc row is still a beautiful lace piece, but does not have the 3-D look of the pattern with FPsc stitches.

lace pattern stitch with addition without FPsc

lace pattern stitch with addition of FPsc

Extended Stitches

Extended stitches are a subtle variation on the basic stitches that use one additional step to create more texture and flexibility in your final fabric.

✝ Extended Single Crochet

Extended single crochet (Ext–sc)

Insert hook into indicated st or sp, yo and draw up a lp, yo and draw through 1 lp on hook, yo and draw through 2 lps on hook.

1. Insert hook into indicated stitch or space.
2. Yarn over and draw up a loop (2 loops on hook).
3. Yarn over and draw through 1 loop on hook (2 loops on hook).
4. Yarn over and draw through 2 loops on hook.
5. Repeat Steps 1–4 to make as many Extended single crochet stitches as called for in the pattern.

Practice swatch

Foundation Row: Ch 22, work Ext-sc in second ch from hook and in each ch to end of row, turn – 21 Ext-sc.

Rows 1–22: Ch 1, work Ext-sc in first st and in each st to end of row, turn.

Fasten off.

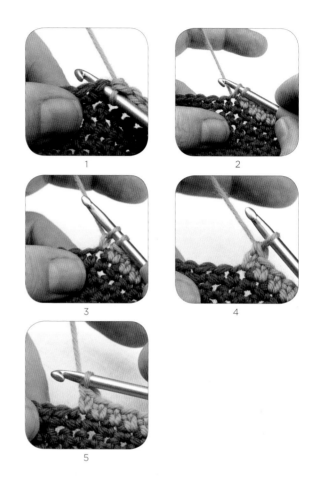

⊺ Extended Half Double Crochet

Extended half double crochet (ext-hdc)

Yo, insert hook into indicated st or sp, yo and draw up a lp (3 lps on hook), yo and draw through 1 lp on hook (3 lps on hook), yo and draw through all 3 lps on hook.

1. Yarn over and insert hook into indicated stitch or space.

2. Yarn over and draw up a loop (3 loops on hook).

3. Yarn over and draw through 1 loop on hook (3 loops on hook).

4. Yarn over and draw through all 3 loops on hook.

5. Repeat Steps 1–4 to make as many Extended half double crochet stitches as called for in the pattern.

Practice Swatch

Foundation Row: Ch 22, work Ext-hdc in second ch from hook and in each ch to end of row, turn – 21 Ext-hdc.

Rows 1–22: Ch 1, work Ext-hdc in first st and in each st to end of row, turn.

Fasten off.

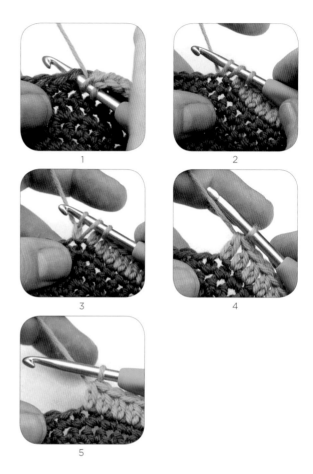

Extended Double Crochet

Extended double crochet (ext-dc)

Yo, insert hook into indicated st or sp, yo and draw up a lp (3 lps on hook), yo and draw through 1 lp on hook (3 lps on hook), [yo and draw through 2 lps on hook] 2 times.

1. Yarn over and insert hook into indicated stitch or space.

2. Yarn over and draw up a loop (3 loops on hook).

3. Yarn over and draw through 1 loop on hook (3 loops on hook).

4. Yarn over and draw through 2 loops on hook (2 loops on hook).

5. Yarn over and draw through 2 loops on hook.

6. Repeat Steps 1–5 to make as many Extended double crochet stitches as called for in the pattern.

Practice Swatch

Foundation Row: Ch 22, work Linked first Ext-dc in second ch from hook, work Ext-dc in next st and in each ch to end of row, turn – 21 Ext-dc.

Rows 1–22: Ch 1, work Ext-dc in first st and in each st to end of row, turn.

Fasten off.

1

2

3

4

5

6

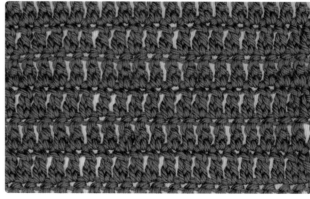

Linked Stitches

Linked stitches are another subtle variation on the basic stitches that makes a huge difference in your finished fabric. Beautifully textured fabrics are created by inserting your hook into the wraps of previous stitches in your working row to make the yarn overs of your stitches. This is a FAB stitch to have in your crochet toolkit for everything from outerwear to home decor.

⊤ Linked Half Double Crochet
   ⊥

Linked half double crochet (Lhdc)

Insert hook from top to bottom through front of horizontal wrap just below head of previous Lhdc, yo and draw up a lp (2 lps on hook), insert hook into next st, yo and draw up a lp (3 lps on hook), yo and draw through all 3 lps on hook.

1. Insert hook from top to bottom through front horizontal wrap just below the head of the previous stitch.
2. Yarn over and draw up a loop (2 loops on hook).
3. Insert hook into next st.
4. Yarn over and draw up a loop (3 loops on hook).
5. Yarn over and draw through all 3 loops on hook.

1

2

3

4

5

Practice Swatch

Foundation Row: Work 25 FLhdc, turn.

Alternate Foundation Row: Ch 26, work Linked first-hdc in second ch from hook, work Lhdc in next ch and in each ch to end of row, turn – 25 Lhdc.

Rows 1–17: Work Linked first-hdc in first st, work Lhdc in next st and in each st to end of row, turn.

Fasten off.

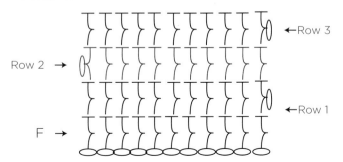

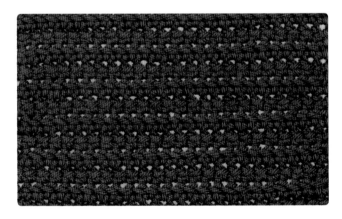

⅂ Linked Double Crochet

Linked double crochet (Ldc)

Insert hook from top to bottom through front of horizontal wrap of previous Ldc, yo and draw up a lp (2 lps on hook), insert hook into next st, yo and draw up a lp (3 lps on hook), [yo and draw through 2 lps on hook] 2 times.

1. Insert hook from top to bottom through the front of the horizontal wrap of the previous stitch.

2. Yarn over and draw up a loop (2 loops on hook).

3. Insert hook into next stitch.

4. Yarn over and draw up a loop (3 loops on hook).

5. [Yarn over and draw through 2 loops on hook] 2 times.

Practice Swatch

Foundation Row: Work 30 FLdc, turn.

Alternate Foundation Row: Ch 31, work Linked first-dc in second ch from hook, work Ldc in next st and in each ch to end of row, turn – 31 Ldc.

Rows 1–17: Work Linked first-dc in first st, work Ldc in next st and in each st to end of row, turn.

Fasten off.

1

2

3

4

5

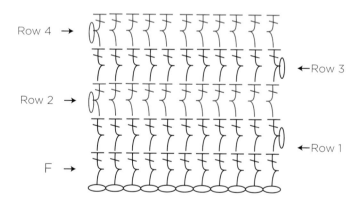

Row 4 →

Row 2 →

F →

←Row 3

←Row 1

⨎ Linked Treble Crochet

Linked treble crochet (Ltr)

Insert hook from top to bottom through front of horizontal wrap of previous Ltr, yo and draw up a lp (2 lps on hook), insert hook from top to bottom through front of next horizontal wrap, yo and draw up a lp (3 lps on hook), insert hook into next st, yo and draw up a lp (4 lps on hook), [yo and draw through 2 lps on hook] 3 times.

1. Insert hook from top to bottom through the front of the horizontal wrap of the previous stitch.

2. Yarn over and draw up a loop (2 loops on hook).

3. Insert hook from top to bottom through the front of the next horizontal wrap.

4. Yarn over and draw up a loop (3 loops on hook).

5. Insert hook into next stitch, yarn over and draw up a loop (4 loops on hook).

6. [Yarn over and draw through 2 loops on hook] 3 times.

Practice Swatch

Foundation Row: Work 30 FLtr, turn.

Alternate Foundation Row: Ch 32, work Linked first-tr in third ch from hook, work Ltr in next st and in each ch to end of row, turn – 31 Ltr.

Rows 1–17: Work Linked first-tr in first st, work Ltr in next st and in each st to end of row, turn.

Fasten off.

1

1a

2

3

4

5

5a

6

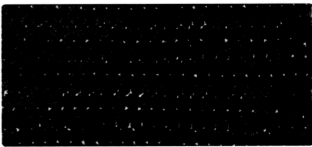

LINKED FOUNDATION STITCHES

Linked stitches are the perfect candidates to be worked as part of a foundation stitch row.

Foundation Linked Half Double Crochet

Foundation Linked half double crochet (FLhdc)

Ch 2, yo, insert hook into second ch from hook, yo and draw up a lp, yo and draw through 1 lp (first "chain" made), yo and draw through all 3 lps on hook (first Fhdc made), *insert hook from top to bottom through front of horizontal wrap just below head of previous stitch, yo and draw up a lp, insert hook under 2 lps of the "chain" just made, yo and draw up a lp ("chain" made), yo and draw through 1 lp on hook, yo and draw through all 3 lps on hook (FLhdc made); rep from * for indicated number of foundation sts.

Foundation Linked Double Crochet

Foundation Linked double crochet (FLdc)

Ch 2, insert hook into first ch from hook, yo and draw up a lp, insert hook into next ch, yo and draw up a lp (3 lps on hook), yo and draw through 1 lp (first "chain" made), [yo and draw through 2 lps on hook] 2 times (first Linked-Fdc made), *insert hook from top to bottom through front of horizontal wrap just below head of previous stitch, yo and draw up a lp, insert hook under 2 lps of the "chain" just made, yo and draw up a lp ("chain" made), yo and draw through 1 lp on hook, [yo and draw through 2 lps on hook] 2 times (FLdc made); rep from * for indicated number of foundation sts.

Herringbone Stitches

The herringbone stitch is another simple variation on the basic stitch that makes a beautifully textured fabric. The way the stitches are constructed causes the post of the stitch to lean in the direction each row is worked, giving it that signature herringbone fabric look.

The key to making herringbone stitches that lean properly is the action of making a slip stitch that secures the fabric to the first yarn over loop on your hook.

1. Yarn over and insert hook into the stitch just as you normally would.
2. Yarn over and draw up a loop through the stitch AND the first loop on hook.

This ensures that the base of the stitch is pulled toward the stitch you are working into, and causes it to lean in the direction of your work.

1   2

Herringbone Half Double Crochet

Herringbone half double crochet (herringbone hdc) (worked over any number of stitches)

Yo, insert hook into indicated st, yo and draw up a lp through st AND first lp on hook, yo and draw through both lps on hook.

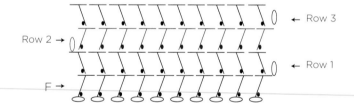

 Foundation herringbone half double crochet (Fhhdc)

Ch 2, yo, insert hook into second ch from hook, yo and draw up a lp, yo and draw through first 2 lps on hook, yo and draw through 2 lps on hook (first Fhhdc made), *yo, insert hook under 2 lps at the bottom of stitch just made, [yo and draw through 2 lps on hook] 2 times (Fhhdc made); rep from * for indicated number of foundation sts.

Practice Swatch

Foundation Row: Work 30 Fhhdc, turn.

Rows 1–16: Ch 1, herringbone hdc in first st and in each st to end of row, turn.

Fasten off.

Herringbone Double Crochet

Herringbone double crochet (worked over any number of stitches)

Yo, insert hook into indicated st, yo and draw up a lp through st AND first lp on hook, yo and draw through 1 lp on hook, yo and draw through both lps on hook.

Foundation herringbone double crochet

Ch 2, yo, insert hook into second ch from hook yo and draw up a lp, yo and draw through first 2 lps on hook, yo and draw through 1 lp on hook, yo and draw through 2 lps on hook (first Foundation herringbone dc made), *yo, insert hook under 2 lps at the bottom of stitch just made, yo and draw through 2 lps on hook, yarn over and draw through 1 lp on hook, yo and draw through 2 lps on hook (Foundation herringbone dc made); rep from * for indicated number of foundation sts.

TIP: If you like the overall fabric of herringbone stitches but need a fabric with straight edges, make the first and last stitch of your row a regular hdc or dc stitch.

Practice Swatch

Foundation Row: Work 30 Foundation herringbone dc, turn.

Rows 1-14: Ch 1, herringbone dc in first st and in each st to end of row, turn.

Fasten off.

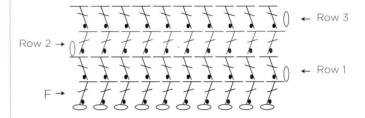

Shaping

Shaping is the term used for making changes to the width of the base section of a panel of crochet fabric. Think about looking at the front panel of a pullover: there might be shaping to decrease the hips to the waist, then shaping again to increase from the waist to the bust. Even more dramatic shaping can be seen for carving out armholes and necklines. If you were cutting out a piece of woven fabric, shaping in crochet is where you would cut into the fabric to make shapes for armholes and necklines, and to create different fit elements like waists.

Because we don't cut our crochet fabric with scissors to make different shapes, shaping is achieved by working increase and decrease stitches, either in one row or over a series of rows. Increase stitches are made by working more than one stitch into a single stitch or space; decrease stitches are made by eliminating one or more stitches.

If a designer wants to widen the sides of a panel of crochet fabric, we will add stitches to a row.

For example, an increase row might instruct you to work two dc in the first stitch and last stitch of the row. This would add one stitch at the beginning and one stitch at the end of the row, increasing the total number of stitches in that row by two.

Likewise, to narrow the sides of a panel of crochet fabric, we would take away stitches from a row.

For example, a decrease row might tell you to work a dc2tog stitch (double crochet two together—we'll get to that in a minute) at the beginning of the row, and a dc2tog stitch at the end of the row. This means that you will have decreased one stitch at the beginning and one stitch at the end of the row, decreasing the total number of stitches in that row by two.

These are simple examples of shaping by working increases and decreases at the beginning and end of a row. There are as many ways to decrease as there are stitches and stitch patterns, and every designer has their preferred way of creating shaping in their fabrics. Not only that, but different stitch patterns and the yarn they are made with might require different increases and decreases to make the shaping look smooth and elegant. Increase and decrease stitches can be worked at the beginning or end of rows (or both, as in our example), or anywhere along a row. They can even be worked all along a Transition Row, where you will be given instructions to increase or decrease a certain number of stitches over a single row, for the purpose of transitioning between two stitch patterns.

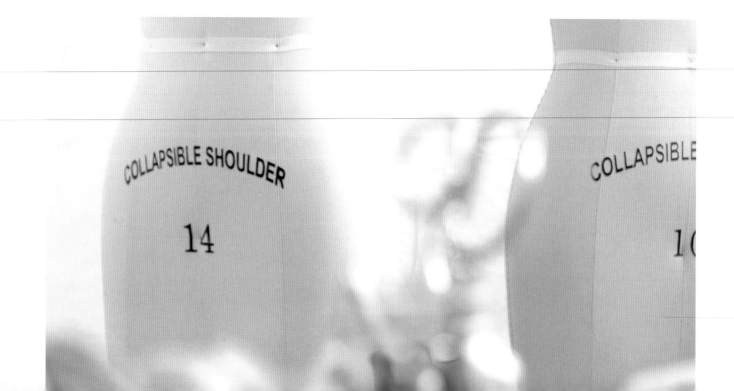

COLLAPSIBLE SHOULDER

14

COLLAPSIBLE

1(

Considerations When Working "Shaping Rows"

There are as many ways to increase and decrease as there are stitches and stitch patterns, and every designer has their preferred way of creating shaping within their fabrics. Not only that, but different stitch patterns and the yarn they are made with might require different increases and decreases to make the shaping look smooth and elegant. Some increases and decreases are highly visible on the finished crochet fabric, and designers will place them so they add a design element to the fabric. Others are nearly invisible and can be placed anywhere without disrupting the overall look of the finished crochet fabric.

If a pattern doesn't give you specific instructions for how and where to make your increase and decrease stitches, it will be up to you to experiment with your practice swatch and determine which techniques work best for your fabric for that specific project. One such example of this is when a pattern says to work in pattern stitch and increase or decrease over a certain number of rows or a certain number of times.

For example, a pattern might state:

Rows 13–24: Working in pattern stitch, increase one stitch at the beginning and end of every row.

In this case, you will need to look at the pattern stitch you are working in and determine what kind of increase you will need to use. If you have a stitch pattern that is worked at the height of single crochet stitches, you will increase by one single crochet stitch at the beginning and end of the row. For a stitch pattern worked with double crochet stitches or at the height of a double crochet stitch, you will increase by one double crochet stitch at the beginning and end of the row. You will work this increase over Rows 13 through 24: a total of 12 rows.

This could also read as "**increase** in pattern stitch" or "**decrease** in pattern stitch."

Further, if a pattern says to increase or decrease and then says to continue working "in pattern stitch as established," this means that, between your increases or decreases, you should maintain the pattern stitch as it has been worked up to this point in the pattern.

When working in this manner, there are two important factors of the pattern stitch that you need to maintain: The number of rows to repeat for pattern stitch, and the multiple of stitches to work for pattern stitch.

1. Number of rows to repeat for pattern stitch

Most patterns are worked in a pattern stitch that has a certain number of rows that will be repeated to create the pattern stitch. This will be indicated in the Pattern Stitch section as "Rep Rows X–X for pattern stitch." When working in pattern stitch as established, you must ensure that this row repeat continues.

For example:

If the instructions for a pattern stitch indicate to "Rep Rows 1–4 for pattern stitch," you will maintain that 4-row repeat as you work "in pattern stitch as established."

If the instructions for a pattern stitch end with "Rep Rows 2–4 for pattern stitch," you will maintain that 3-row repeat as you work "in pattern stitch as established."

2. Multiple of stitches to work for pattern stitch

Most patterns are worked in a pattern stitch that has a pattern repeat in multiples of a certain number of stitches. This will be indicated in the Pattern Stitch section as "(worked over a multiple of X sts)" or "(worked over a multiple of X + X sts)." When working in pattern stitch as established, you must ensure that this stitch multiple continues.

For example:

If the instructions for a pattern stitch indicate a stitch repeat as a "(multiple of 5 + 2 sts)," then once you have increased a total of 5 stitches on each side of your established pattern you will have enough increase stitches to begin working additional pattern repeats of the pattern stitch on the next row.

If the instructions for a pattern stitch indicate a stitch repeat as a "(multiple of 3 sts)," then once you have increased a total of 3 sts on each side of your established pattern you will have enough increase stitches to begin working additional pattern repeats of the pattern stitch on the next row.

In both examples, until another repeat of the pattern stitch can be established, you would work the same type of stitch (sc, dc, tr, etc.) in the increased stitches.

Similarly, if you are decreasing, to ensure that you maintain the stitch multiple, you would work your decreases, then work the same type of stitch (sc, dc, tr, etc.) until another repeat of the pattern stitch can be established.

For example:

If you are decreasing in a pattern stitch with a stitch repeat with a "(multiple of 5 + 2 sts)," and that stitch pattern is mainly double crochet stitches, you would work your decreases as indicated in the pattern, then work double crochets until another repeat of the 5-stitch pattern repeat of the pattern stitch can be worked. Likewise, at the end of a row, you would work in pattern stitch as established, then work double crochet stitches over any partial sections of the 5-stitch pattern repeat before you work your decreases.

At first glance, shaping can look daunting. But if you learn your skills, read through your patterns well, and take them one step at a time, you'll have no problem with even the most complex shaping instructions. Mark this section so you can come back to it as often as you need to when you are working the projects in this book, our other pattern books, and as you go out into the crochet universe and work on other patterns and even (maybe?) create some of your own.

Now let's take a look at how to work those increase and decrease stitches that make up shaping.

Increases

Increases are created by adding stitches to a row or over a set of rows.

One way increases are made is by working more than one stitch into a single stitch or space. Here are two examples of how increases might appear in a pattern:

If a pattern tells you to "work 2 dc in next st," you will work two full double crochet stitches into the next stitch.

1. This can also be stated as "work a 2 dc increase in next st." In both cases, you have two completely finished double crochet stitches worked into one stitch.

2. If a pattern tells you to "work 3 dc in next st," you will work three full double crochet stitches into the next stitch. This can also be stated as "work a 3 dc increase in next st." Either way, you will work three completely finished double crochet stitches into one stitch.

increase 3 dc stitches worked into one stitch

Another way increases are made is by adding stitches at the end of a row. This can be accomplished by using extending foundation stitches, as we did in the section on "Foundation Stitches for Extending Rows," on page 111, or by simply making the required number of chains at the end of the row, then working the stitches of the new length of fabric back into those chains. Usually a pattern for this sort of increase will have very specific instructions for how to make these abrupt increases, but, as with all crochet techniques and skills, feel free to experiment on a practice swatch to see which method you prefer for your fabric and your projects.

Seems simple, right? That's what we meant when we said it was important to take the pattern instructions for shaping one step at a time. If you realize that all shaping is just a combination of increase or decrease stitches, you'll have no problem with even complex patterns.

Decreases

Decreases are created by eliminating one or more stitches in a row or over a set of rows.

One way decrease stitches are made is by making a compound stitch that uses the legs of two or more stitches to create a new stitch under one head (*see "Parts of a Stitch," page 41*). Once you get the hang of how a decrease stitch is made, you will be able to create them using any height or type of stitch. The principle of how to make a basic decrease stitch is the same whether you are working a single crochet decrease or a treble crochet decrease, and the same for a double crochet stitch or a linked double crochet stitch. It is also the same for decreasing two or three stitches at a time. All you need to remember is that basic decrease stitches are created by working the number of stitches you wish to decrease stitch up to the last "yo and draw through all lps on hook" step of making a stitch. Let's take a look.

decrease dc-3 tog = decreases 3 stitches into one

Working 2 Stitches Together

⋏ Single Crochet 2 Together

Single crochet 2 together (sc2tog)
[Insert hook into next st, yo and pull up a lp] 2 times (3 lps on hook), yo and draw through all 3 lps on hook.

1.   Insert hook into next stitch, yarn over and pull up a loop (2 loops on hook).
2.   Insert hook into next stitch, yarn over and pull up a loop (3 loops on hook).
3.   Yarn over and draw through all 3 loops on hook.

1

2

3

NOTE: The sc2tog can be made by inserting your hook under both loops of the stitches you are working into or under just one loop, depending on the type of fabric you are making. **For example,** shaping in a fabric made using sc tfl stitches might look best with the sc2tog worked only under the front loops of the stitches as well. Likewise, shaping a fabric made using sc tbl stitches might look best using the back loops of the stitches to make your sc2tog. Try working a sc2tog tfl and sc2tog tbl with your sc tfl and sc tbl practice swatches.

Rolling Single Crochet 2 Together

We have found that, with fabrics made with sc tfl and sc tbl stitches, a series of sc2tog stitches can appear clunky and disrupt the flow of the overall fabric. In that case, we have found this version of a sc2tog—where we roll our hook around the front loops only or back looks only of the stitches—nearly invisible in the finished fabric.

1.   Insert hook from front to back into one loop only of the next stitch.
2.   Bring hook back to the front of the fabric and insert hook from front to back into one loop of the next stitch (3 loops on hook).
3.   Yarn over and draw a loop up through 2 loops on hook (2 loops on hook).
4.   Yarn over and draw through 2 loops on hook.

1

2

3

4

⋀ Half Double Crochet 2 Together

Half double crochet 2 together (hdc2tog)

[Yo, insert hook into next st and pull up a lp] 2 times (5 lps on hook), yo and draw through all 5 lps on hook.

1

2

3

1. Yarn over, insert hook into next stitch and pull up a loop (3 loops on hook).

2. Yarn over, insert hook into next stitch and pull up a loop (5 loops on hook).

3. Yarn over and draw through all 5 loops on hook.

Skinny Half Double Crochet 2 Together

As with the sc2tog, we found that, with some fabrics, the hdc2tog can look a little bulky and not as elegant in the finished fabric as we would like. As a remedy, we experimented and came up with a skinnier version of the hdc2tog. Having taxed our creative powers upon completion of this task, we named it the Skinny hdc2tog—because it's an hdc2tog and it's skinnier. If y'all come up with something better, feel free to let us know.

1

2

3

finished skinny hdc2tog

Skinny half double crochet 2 together

Yo, insert hook into next stitch and pull up a lp (3 lps on hook), insert hook into next stitch and pull up a lp (4 lps on hook), yo and draw through all 4 lps on hook.

1. Yarn over, insert hook into next stitch.

2. Pull up a loop (3 loops on hook).

3. Insert hook into next stitch and pull up a lp (4 loops on hook).

4. Yarn over and draw through all 5 loops on hook.

Double Crochet 2 Together

Double Crochet 2 Together (dc2tog)

[Yo, insert hook into next st, yo and draw up a lp, yo and draw through 2 lps on hook] 2 times (3 lps on hook), yo and draw through all 3 lps on hook.

1. Yarn over, insert hook into next stitch, yarn over and draw up a loop, yarn over and draw through 2 loops on hook (2 loops on hook).

2. Yarn over, insert hook into next stitch, yarn over and draw up a loop, yarn over and draw through 2 loops on hook (3 loops on hook).

3. Yarn over and draw through all 3 loops on hook.

1

2

3

A Special Note on Working Increases and Decreases

If you are working on a project and notice that your increases and decreases are causing steps or bumps in the edges of your crochet fabrics, try working the increase or decrease stitches one or two stitches from the edge. Work the first stitch of the row as written, then work your increase or decrease stitch in the next stitch. While this works very well for solid stitch fabrics, this doesn't work with all stitch patterns. After reading through your pattern, if you think you might end up with stepped edges, experiment with your practice swatch before you start your project to see if this fix works for your fabric.

TIP: Want to decrease taller stitches? Work more yarn overs at the beginning of your decrease, then work the rest of the decrease just like you've done here.

Working 3 Stitches Together

Working three stitches together follows the same principle as working two stitches together. You simply work the "Yo, insert hook into next st and pull up a lp" step one more time. Working more than three stitches together at one time can pucker or warp your fabric. Be sure to test these out in your practice swatch before starting your project.

Half Double Crochet 3 Together

Half double crochet 3 together (hdc3tog)

[Yo, insert hook into next st and pull up a lp] 3 times (7 lps on hook), yo and draw through all 7 lps on hook.

finished hdc3tog

Double Crochet 3 Together

Double crochet 3 together (dc3tog)

[Yo, insert hook into next st, yo and draw up a lp, yo and draw through 2 lps on hook] 3 times, yo and draw through all 4 lps on hook.

finished dc3tog

Treble Crochet 3 Together

Treble crochet 3 together (tr3tog)

[Yo 2 times, insert hook into next st, yo and draw up a lp, (yo and draw through 2 lps on hook) 2 times] 3 times (4 lps on hook), yo and draw through all 4 lps on hook.

finished tr3tog

Decreasing with Slip Stitches

One way of making a fast decrease at the beginning of a row is to work a slip stitch or a series of slip stitches. These slip stitches act as a way of moving across the number of stitches to be decreased without cutting your yarn and joining it again further in the row.

For example, at the beginning of a row of armhole shaping, you might read "sl st in each of first 6 sts, ch 1, sc in next st." Here you have decreased 6 sts, then picked right back up and started working again in your pattern stitch—a single crochet in our example.

The danger of working too many of these slip stitch decreases in a row is that they can become thick and show on the outside of your work, and can look bulky if sewn into a seam. To prevent this, try working your slip stitches into the back loops of the stitches you are working into. This allows the slip stitch to sit more inside and to the back of the stitch you are working into, and hides it better on the finished fabric.

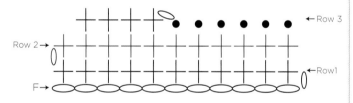

sl st in each of first 6 sts, ch 1, sc in next st chart

Skipping Stitches

Sometimes a pattern will have you work a decrease by skipping a stitch. This type of decrease is seen less often, but does occur occasionally at or near the beginning of rows.

For example, a decrease at the beginning of a row that reads "ch 1, sk first st, sc in next st," or just after the beginning of a row that reads "dc in next st, sk next st, dc in next st" will likely leave a gap where the skipped stitch is left unworked. Although it may seem like a small gap, blocking and seaming can make the gap larger and more noticeable. This is an example of where you should definitely try the suggested decrease in your practice swatch and see if you like the results. If not, it is best to use a sc2tog decrease or dc2tog decrease instead.

A more useable application of this technique is decreasing two stitches by using the steps for making a 2tog decrease (normally a decrease of 1 stitch).

For example, rather than working a dc3tog, you could work a dc2tog, but skip a stitch between the legs of your compound stitch. That would read like this:

Yo, insert hook into next st, yo and draw up a lp, yo and draw through 2 lps on hook, sk next st, yo, insert hook into next st, yo and draw up a lp, yo and draw through 2 lps on hook (3 lps on hook), yo and draw through all 3 lps on hook.

Earlier, you worked the steps for a dc2tog worked over two stitches, making a 1-stitch decrease. Now, we'll work that same decrease over three stitches resulting in a 2-stitch decrease, without the bulk off a dc3tog.

Try this in your practice swatch first to see if this decrease works best in your fabric for your project.

sl st in each of first 6 sts, ch 1, sc in next st

finished dc2tog worked over 3 sts

Variations on Increase and Decrease Stitches

These stitches are variations on the increase and decrease stitches you worked in the previous section. This means all of these stitches involve working more than one stitch into a single stitch or space, or they are made by making a compound stitch that has two or more legs under one head. This family of stitches contains some of the most iconic stitches in the crochet universe and are sure to get your crochet hooks moving and creativity flowing.

All of the stitches in this section are based on the principle of increase stitches, meaning you will work more than one stitch into a single stitch or space. We start simply with v-stitches, then work our way up to the more flamboyant shells, fans, bobbles, puffs, and popcorns!

V-stitches

V-stitches are pairs of stitches of any height, separated by any number of chain stitches worked into one stitch or space. These are narrower cousins of shells and fans and create beautiful solid stitch patterns (as in the sc-v and sc-v2), as well as lace patterns using the taller stitches. Combine two or more of them for an exciting fabric that has the characteristics of both solid and lace.

Single Crochet V-stitch

Single crochet v-stitch (sc-v)

(Sc, ch 1, sc) in indicated st or sp.

Practice Swatch

Single crochet v-stitch (sc-v) (worked over a multiple of 3 + 2 sts)

Foundation Row: Work 35 Fsc, turn.

Alternate Foundation Row: Ch 36, turn; sc in second ch from hook and in each ch to end of row, turn - 35 sts.

Row 1: Ch 1, sc in first st, sk next st, work sc-v in next st, *sk next 2 sts, work sc-v in next st; rep from * to last 2 sts, sk next st, sc in last st, turn.

Row 2: Ch 1, sc in first st, *sc-v in ch-1 sp of next sc-v; rep from * to last st, sc in last st, turn.

Rows 3–20: Rep Row 2.

Fasten off.

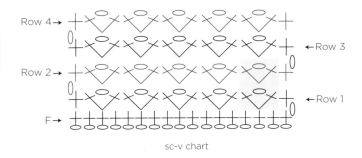

sc-v chart

Single Crochet V2-stitch

Single crochet v2-stitch (sc-v2)

(Sc, ch 2, sc) in indicated st or sp.

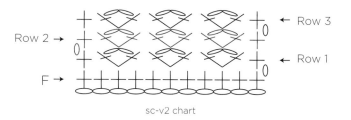

sc-v2 chart

Practice Swatch

Single crochet v2-stitch (sc-v2) (worked over a multiple of 3 + 2 sts)

Foundation Row: Work 35 Fsc, turn.

Alternate Foundation Row: Ch 36, turn; sc in second ch from hook and in each ch to end of row, turn - 35 sts.

Row 1: Ch 1, sc in first st, sk next st, work sc-v2 in next st, *sk next 2 sts, work sc-v2 in next st; rep from * to last 2 sts, sk next st, sc in last st, turn.

Row 2: Ch 1, sc in first st, *sc-v2 in ch-2 sp of next sc-v2; rep from * to last st, sc in last st, turn.

Rows 3–20: Rep Row 2.

Fasten off.

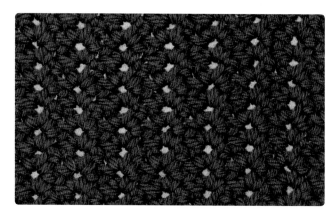

Half Double Crochet V-stitch

Half double crochet v-stitch (hdc-v)

(Hdc, ch 1, hdc) in indicated st or sp.

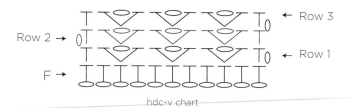

hdc-v chart

Practice Swatch

Half double crochet v-stitch (hdc-v) (worked over a multiple of 3 + 2 sts)

Foundation Row: Work 35 Fhdc, turn.

Alternate Foundation Row: Ch 36, turn; hdc in second ch from hook and in each ch to end of row, turn - 35 sts.

Row 1: Ch 1, hdc in first st, sk next st, work hdc-v in next st, *sk next 2 sts, work hdc-v in next st; rep from * to last 2 sts, sk next st, hdc in last st, turn.

Row 2: Ch 1, hdc in first st, *hdc-v in ch-1 sp of next hdc-v; rep from * to last st, hdc in last st, turn.

Rows 3–16: Rep Row 2.

Fasten off.

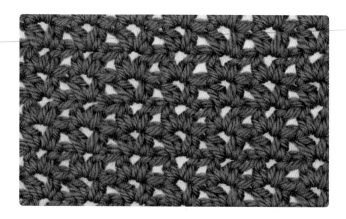

 Double Crochet V-stitch

Double crochet v-stitch (Dc-v)
(Dc, ch 1, dc) in indicated st or sp.

Practice Swatch

Double crochet v-stitch (dc-v) (worked over a multiple of 3 + 2 sts)

Foundation Row: Work 35 Fdc, turn.

Alternate Foundation Row: Ch 36, turn; dc in second ch from hook and in each ch to end of row, turn - 35 sts.

Row 1: Work first-dc in first st, sk next st, work dc-v in next st, *sk next 2 sts, work dc-v in next st; rep from * to last 2 sts, sk next st, dc in last st, turn.

Row 2: Work first-dc in first st, *dc-v in ch-1 sp of next dc-v; rep from * to last st, dc in last st, turn.

Rows 3–14: Rep Row 2.

Fasten off.

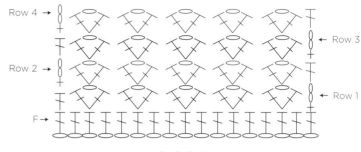

dc-v2 chart

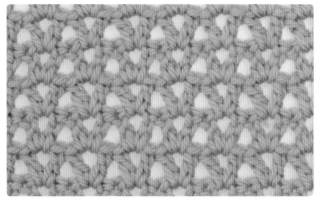

Shells and Fans

Shells and fans are interchangeable terms for the family of stitches that take increase stitches to a whole new level. These stitches involve working three or more stitches into a single stitch or space. The stitches can be separated by chains, like we did with v-stitches, or they can be full sweeps of art-deco-inspired shells and fans. While shells and fans can be worked in any height of stitch, with any number of stitches and chains, we will be working with double crochet stitches and single chains between stitches. But don't let us stop you from trying taller stitches, more stitches, and more chains! The more you experiment and play with your stitches, the more fun you'll have, and who knows what gorgeous fabrics you might come up with.

Shells

Here again we will state most adamantly that the naming of some crochet stitches is not yet a universal language and variations do exist. Here, we have chosen to call this group of stitches "shells" only for the purpose of naming and classification of a group of stitches worked in a solid stitch without any chain spaces. Also . . . we kind of think these look like a shell and the Intergalactic Council of Crochet Elders said we could.[1]

3-double crochet shell (3-dc shell)

Dc 3 times in indicated st or sp.

4-double crochet shell (4-dc shell)

Dc 4 times in indicated st or sp.

5-double crochet shell (5-dc shell)

Dc 5 times in indicated st or sp.

Fans

While the names are interchangeable, for the purposes of stitch identification and classification for teaching purposes, we will call this group of stitches that have chains worked between the double crochet stitches "fans." That is not to say that another pattern calling these same stitches "shells" is incorrect. We just happen to think the chains on the tops make these stitches look like lacy fans.

In addition to the interchangeability of the names of fans and shells, the *way* fans and shells are made is different in each pattern. For example, there are 5-dc shells where you work 5 double crochet stitches into one stitch or space. With fans, however, there is no such concise name. Sometimes a fan will be "(dc 2, ch 1, dc 2) in next st," and sometimes it will be "(dc 3, ch 1, dc 3) in next st." Both are correct. Just be sure to check the Stitch Guide or the Chart for your pattern to see what that designer's interpretation of a "dc-fan" or "dc-shell" is. If the Intergalactic Council of Crochet Elders ever comes up with a different naming convention for these, we'll let you know.[2]

Double crochet fan (dc-fan)

(Dc 2, ch 1, dc 2) in indicated st or sp.

Double crochet fan with chains (dc-fan var)

[Dc, (ch 1, dc) 3 times] in indicated st or sp.

---

1. See page 78. 2. See page 78.

Shells and Fans Practice Swatches
Solid Shells

Practice Swatch

Foundation Row: Work 37 Fsc, turn.

Row 1: (Work Linked first-dc, dc 2) in first st, sk next 2 sts, sc in next st, *sk next 2 sts, work 5-dc shell in next st, sk next 2 sts, sc in next st; rep from * to last 3 sts, sk next 2 sts, work 3 dc in last st, turn.

Row 2: Ch 1, sc in first st, *sk next 2 sts, work 5-dc shell in next sc, sk next 2 sts, sc in next st; rep from * to end of row, turn.

Rows 3–16: Rep Rows 1–2.

Fasten off.

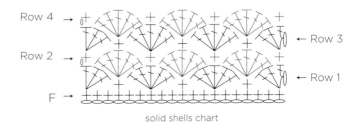

solid shells chart

Continuous Fans

Practice Swatch

Stitches you need to know to make this swatch

> **Double crochet fan (dc-fan):** (Dc 3, ch 2, dc 3) in indicated st or sp.

Foundation Row: Work 31 Fsc, turn.

Row 1: (Work Linked first-dc, dc 3) in first st, ch 1, sk next 4 sts, sc in next st, *ch 1, sk next 4 sts, dc-fan in next st, ch 1, sk next 4 sts, sc in next st; rep from * to last 5 sts, ch 1, sk next 4 sts, dc 4 times in last st, turn.

Row 2: Ch 1, sc in first st, *ch 1, dc-fan in next sc, ch 1, * sc in ch-2 sp of next dc-fan, chain 1, dc-fan in next sc; rep from * to last 5 sts, ch 1, sk next 4 sts, sc in last st, turn.

Row 3: (Work Linked first-dc, dc 3) in first st, ch 1, sc in ch-2 sp of next dc-fan, *ch 1, dc-fan in next sc, ch 1, sc in ch-2 sp of next dc fan; rep from * to last 5 stitches, chain 1, sk next 4 sts, dc 4 times in last st, turn.

Rows 4: Rep Row 2.

Rows 5–16: Rep Rows 3–4.

Fasten off.

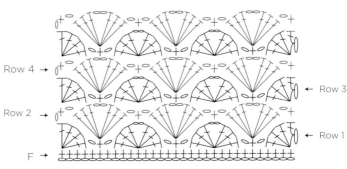

continuous fans chart

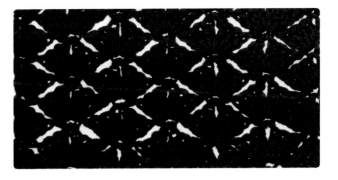

STITCH ON!

Once you have worked through how to change yarn at the end of a row for colorwork (see *Horizontal Stripes, page 194)*, come back and work these practice swatches again, changing colors every two rows for a stunning ripple effect.

Bobbles

Bobbles are one of those unmistakable texture stitches that stand out dramatically against the surface of your crochet fabrics. Worked as an accent row, in pattern with other stitches, or in a wildly bumpy 3-D fabric of their own, bobble stitches are a must-have for your crochet texture toolkit.

Bobbles are a cousin to decrease and cluster stitches, but rather than working the base of your stitches in different stitches and spaces like you would for a decrease or a cluster, you work all of the stitches for your bobble into one stitch or space.

Bobbles are unique in that they are constructed on the back side of your working row. This means that, as you are working your row of bobble stitches, the stitches will stand out against the back of the fabric. You can certainly choose to push the finished bobbles to the front side of your row, but it is the grouping of the bumps on the backs of the stitches making up the bobble that gives it that beautiful texture.

2-double crochet bobble (2-dc bobble)
Yo, insert hook into indicated st or sp and draw up a lp, yo and draw through 2 lps on hook (2 lps remain on hook), yo, insert hook into same st or sp and draw up a lp, yo and draw through 2 lps on hook, yo and draw through all 3 lps on hook.

3-double crochet bobble (3-dc bobble)
Yo, insert hook into indicated st or sp and draw up a lp, yo and draw through 2 lps on hook (2 lps on hook), [yo, insert hook into same st or sp and draw up a lp, yo and draw through 2 lps on hook] 2 times, yo and draw through all 4 lps on hook.

5 double crochet bobble (5-dc bobble)
Yo, insert hook into indicated st or sp and draw up a lp, yo and draw through 2 lps on hook (2 lps on hook), [yo, insert hook into same st or sp and draw up a lp, yo and draw through 2 lps on hook] 4 times, yo and draw through all 6 lps on hook.

Offset Bobbles

Practice Swatch
(worked over an odd number of sts)

Foundation Row: Work 29 Fsc, turn.

Row 1: Ch 1, sc in first st, *work 5-dc bobble in next st, sc in next st; rep from * to end of row, turn – 14 bobbles, 15 sc.

Row 2: Ch 1, sc in first st and in each st to end of row, turn.

Row 3: Ch 1, sc in each of first 2 sts, *work 5-dc bobble in next st, sc in next st; rep from * to last st, sc in last st, turn – 13 bobbles, 16 sc.

Row 4: Rep Row 2.

Rows 5–20: Rep Rows 1–4.

Rows 21–22: Rep Rows 1–2.

Fasten off.

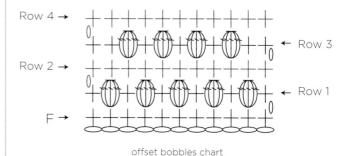

offset bobbles chart

Stacked Bobbles

Practice Swatch

(worked over an odd number of sts)

Foundation Row: Work 23 Fsc, turn.

Row 1: Ch 1, sc in first st, *work 5-dc bobble in next st, sc in next st; rep from * to end of row, turn – 14 bobbles, 15 dc.

Row 2: Ch 1, sc in first st and in each st to end of row, turn.

Rows 3–22: Rep Rows 1–2.

Fasten off.

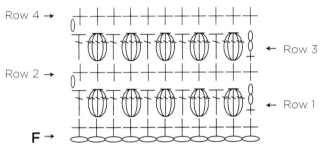

Row 4 →

← Row 3

Row 2 →

← Row 1

F →

stacked bobbles chart

STITCH ON!

We used 5-dc bobbles for the bobbles practice swatches, so that is what you see here in the photos. You could choose to make different practice swatches using 3-dc bobbles and 2-dc bobbles and compare the fabrics. Give it a try and see how dramatic the difference is in the three fabrics. We have even used the 2-dc bobble stitch in lightweight yarns for finer garments.

Puff Stitch

Puff stitches can be looked at as the evolution of the bobble stitch . . . just more . . . PUFFY! Puff stitches are made in a similar manner to bobbles, in that you start your stitches but don't finish them until you've made three or four starts, then you draw your loop through all the stitches on your hook. Puff stitches are also akin to bobbles in that they stand out on the back of the row as you are making them. Puff stitches are unique in their construction because of the pulling up of the loops to achieve the puff effect.

This is your first introduction to pulled stitches (see Pulled Stitches, page 220). With pulled stitches, you insert your hook into the indicated stitch or space, then pull the loops on the stitch up to the height of the working row. The key to making these puffy stitches puff is to keep a light tension on the working yarn as you yarn over and pull up the loops, so your stitches don't get squished down. Want more puff? Pull up more loops! The more loops you pull up and the taller those loops are, the more puff you will have!

Offset Puff Stitch

 Puff stitch (puff st)
[Yo, insert hook into indicated st, yo and draw up a lp to height of row] 3 times (7 lps on hook), yo and draw through all 7 lps on hook, ch 1 to secure top of puff.

Practice Swatch

Foundation Row: Work 23 Fsc, turn.

Row 1: Work first-dc in first st, *work puff st in next st, dc in next st; rep from * to end of row, turn – 11 puffs, 12 dc.

Row 2: Ch 1, sc in first st and in each st to end of row, turn.

Row 3: Work first-dc in first st, dc in next st, *work puff st in next st, dc in next st; rep from * to last st, dc in last st, turn – 10 puffs, 13 dc.

Row 4: Rep Row 2.

Rows 5–16: Rep Rows 1–4.

Rows 17–18: Rep Rows 1–2.

Fasten off.

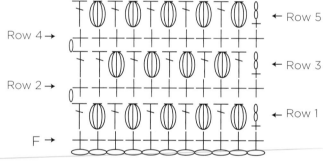

offset puff chart

Popcorn

One more branch in the family tree with bobbles and puffs contains popcorn stitches. Like bobble and puff stitches, popcorn stitches are created by working more than one stitch into a single stitch or space. From that point on, however, the family tree branches out, and popcorns claim a limb of their own. Popcorn stitches are unique because you are making several stitches into one stitch or space, then removing your hook from the last stitch, putting your hook back into the first stitch, and using a slip stitch and chain to close the top and finish the stitch. The result is a little grouping of stitches that jump out from the surface of your crochet fabric.

Stacked Popcorn Stitch

Practice Swatch

Foundation Row: Work 23 Fsc, turn.

Row 1: Work first-dc in first st, *work 5-dc popcorn st in next st, dc in next st; rep from * to end of row, turn – 11 popcorns, 12 dc.

Row 2: Ch 1, sc in first st and in each st to end of row, turn.

Rows 3–16: Rep Rows 1–2.

Fasten off.

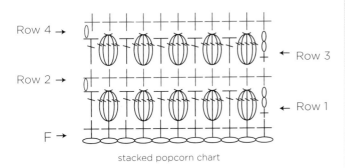

stacked popcorn chart

STITCH ON!

What would happen if you worked this same practice swatch using a 7-dc popcorn or an 8-dc or 9-dc popcorn? That's crazy talk, right? Find out for yourself. Use different weights of yarn and more stitches to make up your own popcorns and see what kind of fabric you can create!

Offset Popcorn Stitch

5-double crochet popcorn (5-dc popcorn)
Work 5 dc in next st, remove hook from last lp on hook, insert hook from front to back into top of first dc made, insert hook back into lp and draw through st, ch 1 to create top of st.

Practice Swatch

Foundation Row: Work 23 Fsc, turn.

Row 1: Work first-dc in first st, *work 5-dc popcorn st in next st, dc in next st; rep from * to end of row, turn – 11 popcorn, 12 dc.

Row 2: Ch 1, sc in first st and in each st to end of row, turn.

Row 3: Work first-dc in first st, dc in next st, *work 5-dc popcorn st in next st, dc in next st; rep from * to last st, dc in last st, turn – 10 puffs, 13 dc.

Row 4: Rep Row 2.

Rows 5–16: Rep Rows 1–4.

Rows 17–18: Rep Rows 1–2.

Fasten off.

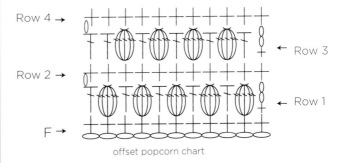

offset popcorn chart

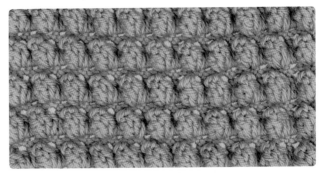

Variations on Decrease Stitches

The stitches in this section are based on the principle of decrease stitches. For each of these you will make more than one base and post and finish them off under a single head. We start here with the basic cluster stitches which you will build on in the future for more elaborate pattern stitches such as star stitches and Catherine wheels.

Clusters

Cluster stitches are the next step to texture stitches after you have learned decrease stitches (*see Decreases, page 139*). Cluster stitches, like decrease stitches, are a type of compound stitch in that the legs of two or more stitches are worked together to create a new stitch under one head. Unlike decrease stitches, however, cluster stitches are made as part of a pattern stitch, rather than as a way of actually making a decrease in the row. In the practice swatches for this section, you will be working your cluster stitches across three stitches and/or spaces every row to create a beautifully textured fabric suitable for everything from home decor to garments. More extravagant applications of the cluster stitch technique can be seen in the Catherine Wheel stitch pattern in the Pattern Stitches section (*page 232*).

2-Double Crochet Cluster

This cousin to the dc2tog stitch is called the 2-dc cluster or the inverted dc-v stitch because it does mirror the dc-v stitch nicely. The difference here is that this stitch is worked into a pattern and does not actually decrease the number of stitches in a row.

2 double crochet cluster (2-dc cluster)

Yo, insert hook into last st you just worked, yo and draw up a lp, yo and draw through 2 loops on hook (2 lps on hook), sk next st, yo, insert hook into next st, yo and draw up a lp, yo and draw through 2 lps on hook, (3 lps on hook), yo and draw through all 3 lps on hook.

1. Yarn over and insert hook into the last stitch you just worked.

2. Yarn over and draw up a loop (3 loops on hook).

3. Yarn over and draw through 2 loops on hook (2 loops on hook).

4. Skip the next stitch, yo and insert hook into next stitch.

5. Yarn over and draw up a loop (3 loops on hook).

6. Yarn over and draw through all 3 loops on hook.

Practice Swatch

Foundation Row: Work 31 Fsc, turn.

Row 1: Work first-dc in first st, ch 1, yo, insert hook into next st, yo and draw up a lp, yo and draw through 2 lps on hook, sk next st, yo, insert hook into next st, yo and draw up a lp, yo and draw through 2 lps on hook, yo and draw through all 3 lps on hook, ch 1, *work 2-dc cluster by inserting hook into last worked st, sk next st, then into next st, ch 1; rep from * to last st, dc in last st, turn – 14 clusters, 15 chs, 2 dc.

Rows 2-10: Work first-dc in first st, ch 1, work 2-dc cluster using next 2 ch-1 sps, ch 1, *work 2-dc cluster by using ch-1 sp just worked, and next ch-1 sp, ch 1; rep from * to last st, dc in last st, turn.

Fasten off.

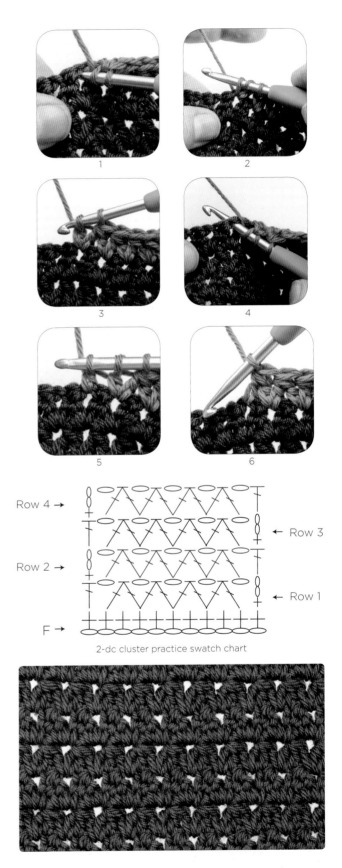

2-dc cluster practice swatch chart

3-Double Crochet Cluster

3-double crochet cluster (3-dc cluster)

Yo, insert hook into indicated st, yo and draw up a lp, yo and draw through 2 lps on hook (2 lps on hook), [yo, insert hook into next indicated st, yo and draw up a lp, yo and draw through 2 lps on hook] 2 times (4 lps on hook), yo and draw through all 4 lps on hook.

1. Yarn over and insert hook into the last stitch you just worked.

2. Yarn over and draw up a loop, yarn over and draw through 2 loops on hook (2 loops on hook).

3. Yarn over and insert hook into the next stitch, yarn over and draw up a loop, yarn over and draw through 2 loops on hook (3 loops on hook).

4. Repeat Step 3 (4 loops on hook).

5. Yarn over and draw through all 4 loops on hook.

Practice Swatch

Foundation Row: Work 31 Fsc, turn.

Row 1: Work first-dc in first st, ch 1, work 3-dc cluster over next 3 sts, ch 1, *work 3-dc cluster by inserting hook into last worked st, then into each of next 2 sts, ch 1; rep from * to last st, dc in last st, turn – 14 clusters, 15 chs, 2 dc.

Rows 2-10: Work first-dc in first st, ch 1, work 3-dc cluster by inserting hook into next ch-1 sp, head of cluster, and next ch-1 sp of previous row, ch 1, *work 3-dc cluster by inserting hook into ch-1 sp just worked, head of cluster, and next ch-1 sp of previous row, ch 1; rep from * to last st, dc in last st, turn.

Fasten off.

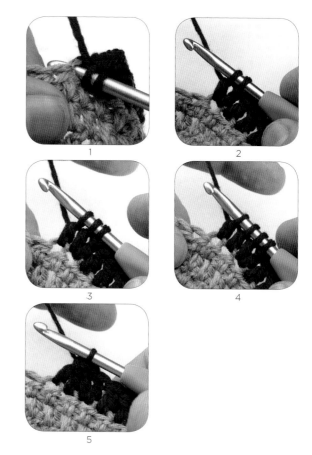

Row 4 →   ← Row 3

Row 2 →   ← Row 1

F →

3-dc cluster chart

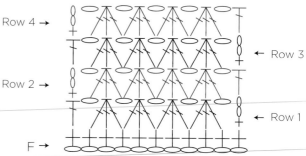

The Star Stitch is a stunning stitch pattern based on the cluster stitch technique. Be sure to check out this special stitch in the "Pattern Stitches" section on page 230.

Joining New Yarn

The technique for changing yarn is the same whether you have run out of the yarn you are working with and need to add another ball or you want to change colors. Working to the end of the row or round and changing yarn, or changing yarn or colors mid-row, you will always use the same technique:

Joining New Yarn:

Work the last stitch of the current yarn or color up to the last "yo and draw through all lps on hook," yarn over with the new yarn and draw through the remaining loops on your hook. Hold both previous and new yarn tails snug to adjust tension of the last stitch. Continue with new yarn.

Changing Yarn at the **End** of a Row

In this example, we are using two different colors of yarn so you can more easily see the changeover from one yarn to the other.

1. Work a double crochet stitch made up to the last "yo and draw through all lps on hook."

2. Yarn over with the new yarn.

3. And draw through remaining loops on hook.

4. Hold both previous and new yarn tails snug to adjust tension of the last stitch made.

5. Continue with new yarn.

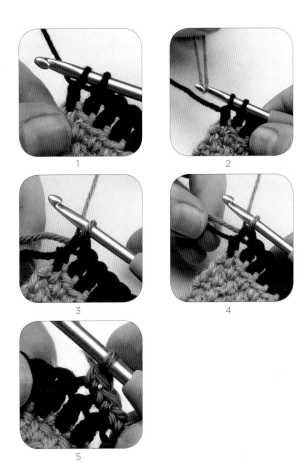

Changing Yarn in the **Middle** of a Row

As we said, this same technique works if you are adding yarn or changing color in the middle of a row. Again, we are using two colors of yarn so you can see the change more easily.

1. Work a double crochet stitch made up to the last "yo and draw through all lps on hook."
2. Yarn over with the new yarn.
3. And draw through remaining loops on hook.
4. Hold both previous and new yarn tails snug to adjust tension of the last stitch made.
5. Continue with new yarn.

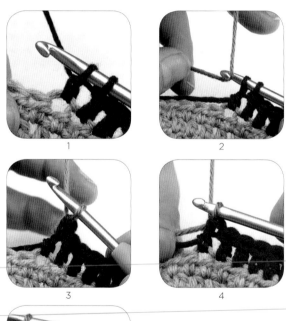

1

2

3

4

5

Standing Stitches

Standing stitches are appropriately named because they can stand on their own, without being attached to a chain-up at the beginning of a row or to a previous stitch in the middle of a row of stitches. Because of the unique way they are constructed, standing stitches are invaluable when used as first stitches when you are starting a new ball of yarn, a new color, or when you are starting a new section of a garment that is not attached to the section next to it. Anywhere you need to start a new stitch that isn't attached to your current work, use a standing stitch.

The key to making a successful standing stitch is the way you wrap the yarn around your hook to make the head of the stitch.

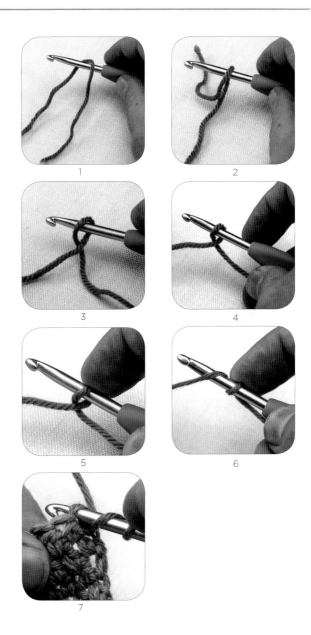

Starting a Standing Stitch

1. Bring the tail of the new yarn over the hook from back to front.
2. Cross the tail along the side of your working yarn that is closest to the hook end of your crochet hook.
3. Cross the tail to the back of the working yarn toward the hand that holds your crochet hook.
4. Hold the tail firmly with the same hand that is holding your crochet hook.
5. Lock the loop on your hook down by holding firmly with your finger.
6. Yarn over the number of times needed for the height of your stitch (here we are doing one yarn over for a double crochet) and insert your hook into the first stitch of the row or of the new section.
7. Finish your stitch as you normally would.

TIP: The standing stitches technique works equally well at the beginning of a row or in the middle of a row, and with any height of stitch. Practice making standing stitches with different heights of stitches so you can use this technique effortlessly in the future.

Motifs

The dictionary gives us a few definitions for the word "motif." The first definition—"a decorative design or pattern"—certainly applies here to crochet. Another definition applies to music: "a short succession of notes producing a single impression; a brief melodic or rhythmic formula out of which longer passages are developed." That particular definition resonates loudly with our artistic side and could be adapted to apply to crochet motifs as: "a short succession of stitches producing a single impression; a brief decorative pattern of stitches out of which larger decorative designs or patterns are developed."

The bottom line is that crochet motifs are these amazing little chunks of crochet creativity that combine individual stitches into one beautiful package. Use them alone as decorations or ornaments, or join them together to make everything from home decor to fashionable garments and accessories (*see Seams & Joins, page 256*). Motifs are the perfect tool for exploring your creativity and come in every shape and size imaginable. Start with the practice motifs in this section using worsted-weight, lace-weight, and even thread- and jumbo-weight yarns, to see what kind of creativity you spark in yourself.

There are as many motif patterns out there in the yarny universe as there are possible combinations of stitches. The five practice motifs in this section are meant to teach you the basics of starting and increasing your motif properly. After you have worked them in different weights of yarn, and maybe even made an afghan or market bag for yourself, go forth into the world and explore different motifs and the wonderful things they can make.

At left is an example of just how far you can go with motifs. This is the Motif Maxi Skirt from our book *Designer Crochet*, which uses Join-As-You-Go techniques to combine motifs with lace to create an overall fabric that is visually stunning. Yes, after you work through this book and work on a few of our projects, you will be ready to move on to more advanced show stoppers like this skirt!

Working from the Center Out

Back in the first part of this book, where we talked about direction of work, we discussed working in the round, in turned rounds, and working in a spiral. When creating motifs, any one of those techniques could be applied since motifs are generally worked from the center out. In order to work from the center out, you have to have a strong center to work from. Here are three ways to get started with your center-out motifs. Each of these has its own purpose and its own strengths and weaknesses. Experiment with each to see which you like, using different yarn weights and motifs.

ℰ Adjustable Ring

The adjustable ring is most useful when the center of your motif must be closed tightly. The ring is adjustable in size, so you can work any number of stitches into the ring, in any yarn weight. Once your first row is worked, you simply tighten the ring to close the center of your motif.

The reason most folks like this method is that you are working your stitches over the loops of the wraps, meaning the tail is already worked in and is less likely to come loose. That said, always test the center of your motif by pulling on it to see if it will come open again after tightening. If your yarn is slick, you might need to wrap the yarn once more over your finger for the initial ring, or use a yarn needle to weave the tail more securely within the bases of the first round of stitches.

1. Wrap yarn tail twice from front to back around your index finger, ensuring the yarn tail ends behind your finger.
2. Grip the ring and tail firmly between your middle finger and index finger. Insert hook through center of ring.
3. Yarn over and draw up a loop.
4. Chain 1 to secure the loop.
5. Work stitches of first round into ring (here we are making 10 double crochet stitches).
6. After first round has been worked, pull gently but firmly on yarn tail to close ring.

If needed to secure the center, you can use a yarn needle to weave the tail more securely within the of bases of the first round of stitches.

Adjustable Ring

Wrap yarn twice in ring around index finger, ensuring the yarn tail falls behind the working yarn. Grip ring and tail firmly between middle finger and thumb. Insert hook through center of ring, yo (with working yarn) and draw up a lp, ch 1 to secure the lp. Work sts of first rnd in ring created by the wraps. After the first rnd of sts has been worked, pull gently but firmly on yarn tail to tighten ring.

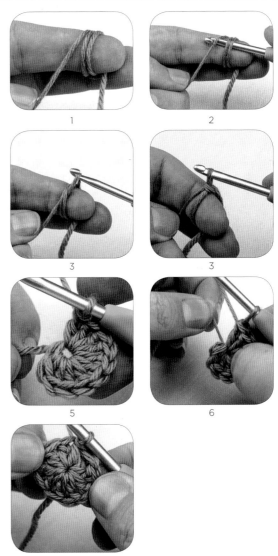

1

2

3

3

5

6

TA-DA!

⬡ Chain Ring

The chain ring is most useful when you want to keep the center of your motif open. Making fewer or more chains before you join the chain ring will determine the size of the hole in the center of your motif. Most patterns will give you a certain number of chains to make, but don't be afraid to add or subtract a chain to achieve the desired effect.

Chain Ring

Make indicated number of chain sts, join with sl st to first ch st made.

| 1 | 2 |

1. Make the indicated number of chain stitches (here we are making 5).
2. Join with slip stitch to first chain stitch made.

◯ Slip Ring

The slip ring method of starting a center-out motif is the same as making a slip knot on your hook before you start stitching (*see page 79*). With the slip ring, you will keep the opening of the slip knot wider so you can work your first round of stitches into the ring. After the first round is made, tighten the center of your ring.

With this method, it is important that you leave enough of a tail to weave in securely. If you trim this tail too closely the knot will come undone and the center of your motif will fall apart.

Another thing to watch out for with this method is the knot in the center of your motif. Even when weaving in the tail, this knot can often still be seen, keeping your motifs from looking their absolute best.

Before you start your practice motifs, review some of the stitches and special techniques you will need. As with any other pattern (*see Pattern Reading, page 52*), read through the practice motif patterns and see if there are any stitches or techniques you need to brush up on or learn before starting.

Motif Stitch Guide

First double crochet (First-dc)

Choose which one is your favorite from the First Stitches of a Row section on page 96.

Foundation double crochet (Fdc)

You will use this for your rectangle motif, and can find the tutorial on page 106.

Special Techniques

Bridge Double Crochet

Bridge double crochet (bridge-dc):

Dc in top lps of first st of rnd. **Note:** Use this stitch as a substitute for the last ch-3 sp in a motif round.

Joining Chain

Joining chain (joining-ch):

Insert hook from front to back through corresponding ch sp or st of neighboring motif, yo and draw up a lp through corresponding ch sp or st of neighboring motif and lp on hook.

Joining Double Crochet

Joining double crochet (joining-dc):

Remove lp from hook, insert hook from front to back through indicated st of corresponding neighboring motif, return lp to hook, yo, insert hook in indicated st of current motif, yo and draw up a lp, yo and draw through 2 lps on hook, yo and draw through 2 lps on hook and through corresponding st of neighboring motif.

Join with Duplicate Stitch

See "Join with Duplicate Stitch" section on page 251.

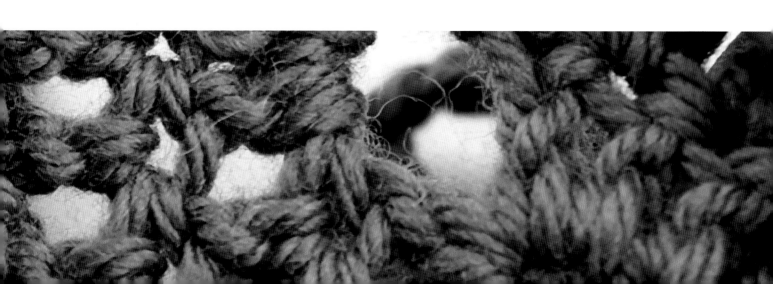

Granny Square

"All granny squares are motifs, but not all motifs are granny squares."

A common misconception is that every square motif is a granny square. In fact, a traditional granny square is made in the style of "filet crochet," by working multiple double crochet stitches into a chain space, creating an overall lace effect of stacked blocks and open spaces.

Round 1: First-dc in Adjustable Loop, dc 2 times in Adjustable Loop, ch 3, [dc 3 times in Adjustable Loop, ch 3] 2 times, dc 3 times in Adjustable Loop, join rnd with bridge-dc in first-dc – 1 first-dc, 1 bridge-dc, 3 ch-3 sps, 11 dc.

Round 2: Sl st in bridge-dc sp, ch 1, (first-dc, dc 2 times, ch 3, dc 3 times) in bridge-dc sp, [ch 1, sk next 3 sts, (dc 3 times, ch 3, dc 3 times) in next ch-3 sp] 3 times, ch 1, join rnd with sl st to first-dc – 1 first-dc, 4 ch-1 sps, 4 ch-3 sps, 23 dc.

Round 3: Sl st in each of next 2 sts and in next ch-3 sp, ch 1, (first-dc, dc 2 times, ch 3, dc 3 times) in ch-3 sp, [ch 1, sk next 3 sts, dc 3 times in next ch-1 sp, ch 1, sk next 3 sts, (dc 3 times, ch 3, dc 3 times) in next ch-3 sp] 3 times, ch 1, sk next 3 sts, dc 3 times in next ch-1 sp, ch 1, join rnd with sl st to first-dc – 1 first-dc, 4 ch-3 sps, 8 ch-1 sps, 35 dc.

Round 4: Sl st in each of next 2 sts and in next ch-3 sp, ch 1, (first-dc, dc 2 times, ch 3, dc 3 times) in ch-3 sp, [(ch 1, sk next 3 sts, dc 3 times in next ch-1 sp) 2 times, ch 1, (dc 3 times, ch 3, dc 3 times) in next ch-3 sp] 3 times, [ch 1, sk next 3 sts, dc 3 times in next ch-1 sp] 2 times, ch 1 – 1 first-dc, 4 ch-3 sps, 12 ch-1 sps, 47 dc.

Cut yarn, leaving approximately 8″ tail for weaving in. Join rnd with Duplicate Stitch.

STITCH ON! ✏

Make a classic granny square afghan by using the Join-As-You-Go technique from page 262. Use your favorite color to make it a monochromatic masterpiece, or mix and match colors to create a visual party. The choice is up to you, and your only limit is your own imagination!

Circle Motif

Round 1: (First-dc, dc 9 times) in Adjustable Loop, join rnd with sl st to first-dc – 1 first-dc, 9 dc.

Round 2: (First-dc, dc) in first st, [dc 2 times in next st] 9 times, join rnd with sl st to first-dc – 1 first-dc, 19 dc.

Round 3: First-dc, dc 2 times in next st, *dc in next st, dc 2 times in next st; rep from * around, join rnd with sl st in first-dc – 1 first-dc, 29 dc.

Round 4: First-dc, dc in next st, dc 2 times in next st, *dc in each of next 2 sts, dc 2 times in next st; rep from * around, join rnd with sl st in first-dc – 1 first-dc, 39 dc.

Round 5: First-dc, dc in each of next 2 sts, dc 2 times in next st, *dc in each of next 3 sts, dc 2 times in next st; rep from * around – 1 first-dc, 49 dc.

Cut yarn, leaving approximately 8″ tail for weaving in. Join rnd with Duplicate Stitch.

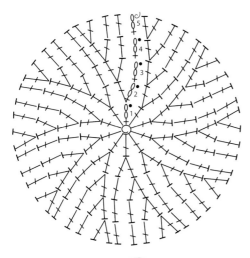

Increasing to Make a Flat Circle

Working a circular increase that results in a flat circle is a simple matter of continuing to make stacked increases. Stacked increases are necessary to ensure that your circle will lie flat once blocked, without waves or ripples around the edge. Stacked increases are made by working the increase into one of the previous increase stitches. See an increase? Make another increase!

There are two ways to keep track of these stacked increases:

Look: When you make an increase, you will have two stitches made into one stitch, so they are easy to spot. Every time you come to an increase stitch, make another increase in that stitch.

Count: In your practice swatch, you worked Round 2 by increasing in every stitch. After that, your increases will happen at regular intervals, adding one stitch between the increases each round.

For example:

Round 3: Work 1 regular stitch, make increase.

Round 4: Work 2 regular stitches, make increase.

Round 5: Work 3 regular stitches, make increase.

Round 6: Work 4 regular stitches, make increase.

Round 7: Work 5 regular stitches, make increase.

Round 8: Work 6 regular stitches, make increase.

STITCH ON!

A circular motif very easily turns into a hat, and any of the motifs can be made into a FAB market bag. Just keep working stacked increases until your flat motif is large enough, then continue working in the round without doing any more increases and your flat motif will become a tube of stitches. Make a short tube and you have a hat; make a longer tube, add a handle, and you have a bag!

Square Motif

Round 1: First-dc in Adjustable Loop, dc 2 times in Loop/Ring, ch 3, [dc 3 times in Adjustable Loop, ch 3] 2 times, dc 3 times in Adjustable Loop, join rnd with bridge-dc in first-dc – 1 first-dc, 1 bridge-dc, 3 ch-3 sps, 11 dc.

Round 2: Sl st in bridge-dc sp, ch 1, (first-dc, ch 3, dc) in bridge-dc sp, dc in each of next 3 sts, *(dc, ch-3, dc) in next ch-3 sp, dc in each of next 3 sts; rep from * around, join rnd with sl st to first-dc – 1 first-dc, 4 ch-3 sps, 19 dc.

Round 3: Sl st in next ch-3 sp, ch 1, (first-dc, dc, ch 3, dc 2 times) in ch-3 sp, dc in each of next 5 sts, *(dc 2 times, ch 3, dc 2 times) in next ch-3 sp, dc in each of next 5 sts; rep from * around, join rnd with sl st to first-dc – 1 first-dc, 4 ch-3 sps, 35 dc.

Round 4: Sl st in next st and in next ch-3 sp, ch 1, (first-dc, dc, ch 3, dc 2 times) in ch-3 sp, dc in each of next 9 sts, *(dc 2 times, ch 3, dc 2 times) in next ch-3 sp, dc in each of next 9 sts; rep from * around, join rnd with sl st to first-dc – 1 first-dc, 4 ch-3 sps, 51 dc.

Round 5: Sl st in next st and in next ch-3 sp, ch 1, (first-dc, ch 3, dc 2 times) in ch-3 sp, dc in each of next 13 sts, *(dc 2 times, ch 3, dc 2 times) in next ch-3 sp, dc in each of next 13 sts; rep from * around – 1 first-dc, 4 ch-3 sps, 67 dc.

Cut yarn, leaving approximately 8″ tail for weaving in. Join rnd with Duplicate Stitch.

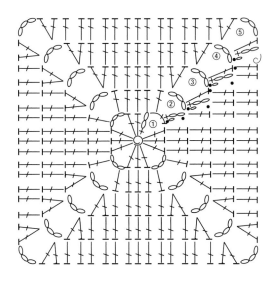

Note: These practice motifs become extraordinary when they are worked in bulky or jumbo yarns. Just keep working stacked increases until you have a FAB throw rug, a trendy bulky afghan to snuggle up under, or even a wall hanging!

Triangle Motif

Round 1: First-dc in Adjustable Loop, dc 2 times in Adjustable Loop, [ch 3, dc 3 times in Adjustable Loop], 2 times, join rnd with bridge-dc in first-dc – 1 first-dc, 1 bridge-dc, 8 dc.

Round 2: Sl st in bridge-dc sp, ch 1, (first-dc, dc, ch 3, dc 2 times) in bridge-dc sp, [dc in each of next 3 sts, (dc 2 times, ch 3, dc 2 times) in next ch-3 sp] 2 times, dc in each of next 3 sts, join rnd with sl st to first-dc – 1 first-dc, 3 ch-3 sps, 20 dc.

Round 3: Sl st in next st and in next ch-3 sp, ch 1, (first-dc, dc 2 times, ch 3, dc 3 times) in ch-3 sp, dc in each of next 7 sts, [(dc 3 times, ch 3, dc 3 times) in next ch-3 sp, dc in each of next 7 sts] 2 times, join rnd with sl st to first-dc – 1 first-dc, 3 ch-3 sps, 38 dc.

Round 4: Sl st in each of next 2 sts and in next ch-3 sp, ch-1 (first dc, dc 2 times, ch 3, dc 3 times) in ch-3 sp, dc in each of next 13 sts, [(dc 3 times, ch 3, dc 3 times) in next ch-3 sp, dc in each of next 13 sts] 2 times, join rnd with sl st to first-dc – 1 first-dc, 3 ch-3 sps, 56 dc.

Round 5: Sl st in each of next 2 sts and in next ch-3 sp, (first dc, dc 2 times, ch 3, dc 3 times) in ch-3 sp, dc in each of next 19 sts, [(dc 3 times, ch 3, dc 3 times) in next ch-3 sp, dc in each of next 19 sts] 2 times – 1 first-dc, 3 ch-3 sps, 74 dc.

Cut yarn, leaving approximately 8″ tail for weaving in. Join rnd with Duplicate Stitch.

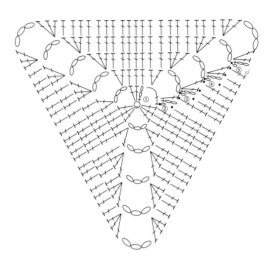

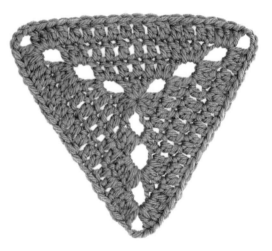

> **Note:** Experiment with piecing together different motifs to make larger shapes! What happens if you combine squares and triangles to make different geometric shapes? Give it a try and maybe you'll surprise yourself with a FAB new fabric!

Rectangle Motif

Round 1: Work 8 Fdc, ch 3, rotating work to the right dc 3 times in bottom of last Fdc made, ch 3, continue to rotate work to the right and dc in bottom of last Fdc made, dc in bottom of each of next 7 Fhdc, ch 3, dc 3 in bottom of first Fdc made, join rnd with bridge-dc – 1 bridge-dc, 3 ch-3 sps, 8 Fdc, 14 dc.

Round 2: Sl st in bridge-dc sp, ch 1, (first-dc, dc, ch 3, dc 2 times) in bridge-dc sp, dc in each of next 8 sts, (dc 2 times, ch 3, dc 2 times) in next ch-3 sp, dc in each of next 3 sts, (dc 2 times, ch 3, dc 2 times) in next ch-3 sp, dc in each of next 8 sts, (dc 2 times, ch 3, dc 2 times) in next ch-3 sp, dc in each of next 3 sts, join rnd with sl st to first-dc – 1 first-dc, 4 ch-3 sps, 37 dc.

Round 3: Sl st in next st and in next ch-3 sp, ch 1, (first-dc, dc, ch 3, dc 2 times) in ch-3 sp, dc in each of next 12 sts, (dc 2 times, ch 3, dc 2 times) in next ch-3 sp, dc in each of next 7 sts, (dc 2 times, ch 3, dc 2 times) in next ch-3 sp, dc in each of next 12 sts, (dc 2 times, ch 3, dc 2 times) in next ch-3 sp, dc in each of next 7 sts, join rnd with sl st to first-dc – 1 first-dc, 4 ch-3 sps, 53 dc.

Round 4: Sl st in next st and in next ch-3 sp, ch 1, (first-dc, dc, ch 3, dc 2 times) in ch-3 sp, dc in each of next 16 sts, (dc 2 times, ch 3, dc 2 times) in next ch-3 sp, dc in each of next 11 sts, (dc 2 times, ch 3, dc 2 times) in next ch-3 sp, dc in each of next 16 sts, (dc 2 times, ch 3, dc 2 times) in next ch-3 sp, dc in each of next 11 sts – 1 first-dc, 4 ch-3 sps, 69 dc.

Cut yarn, leaving approximately 8″ tail for weaving in. Join rnd with Duplicate Stitch.

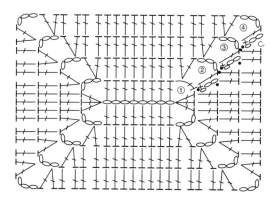

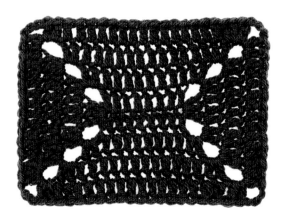

NOTE: Unlike other motifs, the rectangle motif does not start with a ring in the center. It is still worked from the center out, but the base is a row of foundation chains or, as in the case of this practice pattern, a row of foundation double crochet stitches. That makes this particular motif unique in that you can easily customize your starting length to create rugs, afghans, and the bottoms for bags.

Spiral

A spiral is a unique motif in that, for any stitches taller than a single crochet, the beginning of your first round must start with shorter stitches, then increase up to the tallest stitch you will use in the spiral. Without this gradual increasing in the first round, you will not be able to continue in a spiral when you come to the first stitch of the second round.

Remember our discussion about "Working in a Spiral in the Direction of Work" section, (*page 69*)? You should definitely place a stitch marker in the first stitch of your spiral round, to keep track of where one round ends and the next round begins.

Round 1: (Sc, hdc 2 times, dc 7 times) in Adjustable Loop – 10 sts.

Round 2: (First-dc, dc) in first st, [dc 2 times in next st] 9 times – 20 sts.

Round 3: (First-dc, dc) in first st, dc in next st, *dc 2 times in next st, dc in next st; rep from * around – 30 sts.

Round 4: (First-dc, dc) in first st, dc in each of next 2 sts, *dc 2 times in next st, dc in each of next 2 sts; rep from * around – 40 sts.

Round 5: (First-dc, dc) in first st, dc in each of next 3 sts, *dc 2 times in next st, dc in each of next 3 sts; rep from * around – 50 sts.

Round 6: (First-dc, dc) in first st, dc in each of next 4 sts, *dc 2 times in next st, dc in each of next 4 sts; rep from * around, hdc in each of next 2 sts, sc in next st, sl st tbl of next st – 60 dc, 2 hdc, 1 sc, 1 sl st.

Cut yarn, leaving approximately 8" tail for weaving in. Join rnd with Duplicate Stitch.

NOTE: Experiment with piecing together different motifs to make larger shapes! What happens if you combine squares and triangles to make different geometric shapes? Give it a try and maybe you'll surprise yourself with a FAB new fabric!

STITCH ON!

As with the circle motif, you can keep increasing to make a flat spiral until your spiral is as large as you want, then work the end of your last round like you did here in Round 6 to taper off the end. We have made many rag rugs, pet beds, and washcloths this way. Give it a try!

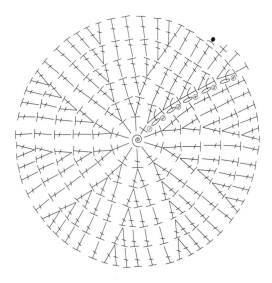

Cables

Now that you have worked on a variety of basic stitches and their variations, you are ready to combine two different stitch techniques into one glorious skill to create crochet cables!

Crochet cables use different combinations of crossed post stitches and crossed standard stitches to create intricate stitch patterns that weave in and out of one another and cross back and forth across your crochet fabric. The resulting fabric is visually dramatic, and is ideal for everything from home decor to garments, depending on the weight of yarn you use.

A cable is a stitch pattern that is created by using crossed stitches, or stitches that are worked out of order. If we labeled the stitches in a row as ABCD in the order of normal work, you would work those in the order of CDAB to create crossed stitches, making a cable:

1. Stitches are ABCD in normal working order.

2. Skip stitches A and B, insert hook into stitch C, and make a stitch.

3. Insert hook into stitch D and make a stitch.

4. Working in front of the two stitches just made, go back and insert hook into stitch A and make a stitch.

5. Insert hook into stitch B and make a stitch.

6. ABCD becomes CDAB.

All crossing stitches and cables are made in this manner, by working the stitches out of their normal working order.

Three Types of Cables

1. Standard Crochet Stitch Cables - Crossed Stitches

This type of cable uses standard stitches that cross. This means the crossed stitches are worked into the heads of the stitches from the previous row, just as a normal crochet stitch is made. This type of cable looks the same from the front and the back of the fabric, and the stitches are not as raised on the face of the finished fabric as the post stitch style of cables.

1. crossed stitches

2. Combination: Standard and Post Stitch Cables

These cable stitches are created using both standard stitches worked into the heads of the stitches of the previous row and post stitches. Cables using this combination of stitches are usually part of a larger stitch pattern, where the standard stitch is not seen on the front of the fabric at all—instead, the post stitch appears to travel off on its own.

2. standard and post stitch cables

3. Front Post/Back Post Stitch Cables

This type of cable uses a combination of Front Post and Back Post stitches that cross every row. Cable fabric made using both Front Post and Back Post stitches will have noticeable spaces between the stitches.

3. front/back post stitch cables

3a. Front Post Only Stitch Cables

Front Post Only cable fabric is created by working alternating rows of post stitch cable stitches with rows of sc or hdc stitches. This creates a much more stable fabric, since there is a row of solid sc or hdc stitches running between the crossed post stitches. This type of fabric has the raised post stitches on one side while the other side is flat, making this fabric ideal for garments or for any project for which you want a lighter-weight fabric.

3a. front only post stitch cables

Naming of a Stitch

Crochet cables are indicated in a pattern with an abbreviation that includes the number of the crossing stitches, the type and the height of the crossed stitches used, and the direction the crossed stitches on the front of the fabric lean in relation to where the base of the stitch is made.

For example, a cable that uses two sets of 2 crossing double crochet stitches, where the stitches on the front of the fabric lean to the left, would be called a 2-over-2 double crochet left cross, and would be abbreviated as 2x2 dc left cross or 2/2 dc LC. The same cable with the stitches on the front of the fabric leaning to the right would be abbreviated as 2x2 dc right cross or 2/2 dc RC.

Additionally, if the cable uses only Front Post or Back Post stitches, the abbreviation would include that information: 2x2 FPdc LC, 2/2 FPdc LC, or 2/2 FPdc RC, for example.

There are cables that use a combination of crossed and uncrossed stitches, with the uncrossed stitches occurring between the crossed stitches. The uncrossed stitches act to stabilize and widen the cable, either for greater visual impact or as a setup to start a wandering cable pattern. In these cases, the abbreviation includes the same information as a regular cable cross with the addition of the uncrossed stitch.

For example, a 2-1-2 FPdc LC or 2/1/2 FPdc RC would have 4 double crochet post stitches that cross over 1 uncrossed stitch (usually a single crochet or a half double crochet, depending on the fabric desired).

Crochet cables are as varied as the imagination of the designer can stretch, with different numbers of stitches crossing, wide cables, and traveling cables. We will explore many of these and their variations throughout this section.

2-over-2 double crochet left cross

2-over-2 double crochet right cross

Standard Crochet Stitch Cables - Crossed Stitches

Crossed stitches utilize standard crochet stitches. Once you learn these basic cross combinations and get the hang of how to cross those stitches correctly, you will be ready to combine your knowledge of crossed stitches and post stitches to create increasingly more complex crochet cables!

How a stitch is named is the key to your success when making crochet cables. Remember, if a stitch is named as a left cross (LC), then the stitch on the front of the fabric will lean to the left in relation to where you inserted your hook to make the base of the stitch. Likewise, if a stitch is named a right cross (RC), then the stitch on the front of the fabric will lean to the right in relation to where you inserted your hook to make the base of the stitch.

We'll start off with crossed stitches that involve standard crochet stitches worked out of order. In this example, we will use double crochet stitches, but the same fabrics could be worked using treble crochet, double treble crochet, or taller stitches.

1x1 Double Crochet Left Cross

1x1 double crochet left cross (1x1 dc LC) (worked over 2 sts)

Sk next st, dc in next st, working in front of dc just made, dc in skipped st.

1. Skip next stitch.
2. Work a dc in next stitch.
3. Working in front of dc just made.
4. Work a dc in skipped stitch.

1x1 double crochet left cross

1x1 Double Crochet Right Cross

1x1 double crochet right cross (1x1 dc RC) (worked over 2 sts)

Sk next st, dc in next st, working behind dc just made, dc in skipped st.

1. Skip next stitch.
2. Work a dc in next stitch.
3. Working behind dc just made.
4. Work a dc in skipped stitch.

1x1 double crochet right cross

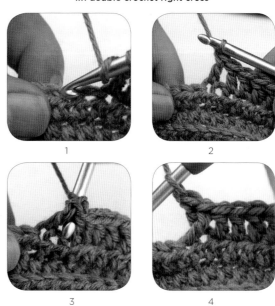

2x2 Treble Crochet Left Cross

**2x2 treble crochet left cross
(2x2 tr LC) (worked over 4 sts)**

Sk next 2 sts, tr in each of next 2 sts; working in front of 2 tr just made, tr in first skipped st, tr in second skipped st.

1. Skip next 2 stitches.
2. Work a tr in each of next 2 stitches.
3. Working in front of 2 tr just made.
4. Work a tr in first skipped stitch.
5. Work a tr in second skipped stitch.

2x2 treble crochet left cross

2x2 Treble Crochet Right Cross

**2x2 treble crochet right cross
(2x2 tr RC) (worked over 4 sts)**

Sk next 2 sts, tr in each of next 2 sts; working behind 2 tr just made, tr in first skipped st, tr in second skipped st.

1. Skip next 2 stitches.
2. Work a tr in each of next 2 stitches.
3. Working behind 2 tr just made.
4. Work a tr in first skipped stitch.
5. Work a tr in second skipped stitch.

2x2 treble crochet right cross

3x3 Treble Crochet Left Cross

**3x3 treble crochet left cross
(3x3 tr LC) (worked over 6 sts)**

Sk next 3 sts, tr in each of next 3 sts; working in front of 3 tr just made, tr in first skipped st, tr in second skipped st, tr in third skipped st.

1. Skip next 3 stitches.
2. Work a tr in each of next 3 stitches.
3. Working in front of 3 tr just made.
4. Work a tr in first skipped stitch.
5. Work a tr in second skipped stitch.
6. Work a tr in third skipped stitch.

3x3 treble crochet left cross

3x3 Treble Crochet Right Cross

**3x3 treble crochet right cross
(3x3 tr RC) (worked over 6 sts)**

Sk next 3 sts, tr in each of next 3 sts; working behind 3 tr just made, tr in first skipped st, tr in second skipped st, tr in third skipped st.

1. Skip next 3 stitches.
2. Work a tr in each of next 3 stitches.
3. Working behind 3 tr just made.
4. Work a tr in first skipped stitch.
5. Work a tr in second skipped stitch.
6. Work a tr in third skipped stitch

3x3 treble crochet right cross

Combination: Standard and Post Stitch Cables

These crossed stitches use basic crochet stitches and post stitches in combination to create a surface texture similar to cables. These types of stitch combinations are used in larger crochet cable patterns to create traveling cables, and are flatter in texture since the post stitch crosses a non-post stitch.

The naming convention for these stitch combinations is the same as for other crossed stitches and includes the number of crossing stitches, the height of the stitches used, and the direction the stitch on the front of the fabric leans in relation to where the base of the stitch is made.

NOTE: Cables made using post stitches add another level of dimension to your crochet fabrics, since all of the stitches are raised above the front of your finished fabric. There are an infinite number of cable combinations using different heights of stitches and the number of stitches crossed both right and left. Once you work through these cables and the practice swatches, you should be ready to tackle any crochet cable project, like the cable version of the Signature Vests in the "Projects" section on page 287.

1x1 Half Double Crochet/Front Post Treble Crochet Right Cross

> **1x1 half double crochet/Front Post treble crochet right cross (1x1 hdc/FPtr RC) (worked over 2 sts)**
> Sk next st, FPtr around st 2 rows below next st; working behind FPtr just made, hdc in skipped st.

1. Skip next stitch.
2. Work a FPtr around stitch 2 rows below next stitch.
3. Working behind FPtr just made.
4. Work a hdc in skipped stitch.

1

2

3

4

5

Practice Swatch

Diagonal post stitch (worked over any even number of sts)

Foundation Row: Work 22 Fhdc, turn.

Alternate Foundation Row: Ch 23, work first-hdc in second ch from hook, hdc in next st and in each st to end of row, turn – 22 hdc.

Row 1: Ch-1, hdc in first st, hdc in next st and in each st to end of row, turn.

Row 2: Work first-hdc in first st, *work 1x1 hdc/FPtr LC; rep from * to last st, hdc in last st, turn.

Row 3: Rep Row 1.

Row 4: Ch-1, hdc in first st, hdc in next st, *work 1x1 hdc/FPtr LC; rep from * to last 2 sts, hdc in each of last 2 sts, turn.

Rows 5–8: Rep Rows 1–4.

Row 9: Rep Row 1.

Row 10: Ch-1, hdc in first st, *work 1x1 hdc/FPtr RC; rep from * to last st, hdc in last st, turn.

Row 11: Rep Row 1.

Row 12: Ch-1, hdc in first st, hdc in next st, *work 1x1 hdc/FPtr RC; rep from * to last 2 sts, hdc in each of last 2 sts, turn.

Rows 13–16: Rep Rows 9–12.

Row 17: Rep Row 1.

Fasten off.

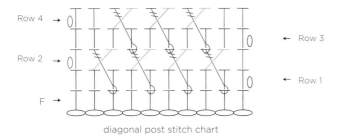

diagonal post stitch chart

diagonal post stitch practice swatch

1x1 Half Double Crochet/Front Post Treble Crochet Left Cross

> **1x1 half double crochet/Front Post treble crochet left cross (1x1 hdc/FPtr LC) (worked over 2 sts)**
>
> Sk next st, hdc in next st; working in front of hdc just made, FPtr around post of st 2 rows below skipped st.

1. Skip next stitch.
2. Work a hdc in next stitch.
3. Working in front of hdc just made.
4. Work a FPtr around post of stitch 2 rows below skipped stitch.

finished cable

1-over-1 Front Post Double Crochet Left Cross

1-over-1 Front Post double crochet left cross (1/1 FPdc LC) (worked over 2 sts)

Sk next st, FPdc around post of next st; working in front of FPdc just made, FPdc around post of skipped st.

1. Skip next stitch.
2. Work a FPdc around post of next stitch.
3. Working in front of FPdc just made, work a FPdc around post of skipped stitch.

1-over-1 Front Post Double Crochet Right Cross

1-over-1 Front Post double crochet right cross (1/1 FPdc RC) (worked over 2 sts)

Sk next st, FPdc around post of next st; working behind FPdc just made, FPdc around post of skipped st.

1. Skip next stitch, work a FPdc around post of next stitch.
2. Working behind FPdc just made (this means you will insert your hook between the FPdc you just made and the fabric in order to work your hook around the skipped stitch).
3. Work a FPdc around post of skipped stitch (use hook to pull the post of the stitch you are working around up to the top of your work so you don't get your yarn overs tangled up with the stitch).

3

finished cable

1-over-1 Back Post Double Crochet Left Cross

**1-over-1 Back Post double crochet left cross
(1/1 BPdc LC) (worked over 2 sts)**

Sk next st, BPdc around post of next st; working in front of BPdc just made, BPdc around post of skipped st.

NOTE: Stitch is worked on the back side of the fabric, but will cross to the left on the right side of the finished fabric.

1. Skip next stitch, work a BPdc around post of next stitch.
2. Working in front of the BPdc just made (this means you will insert your hook between the BPdc just made and the fabric in order to work your hook around the skipped stitch).
3. Work a BPdc around post of skipped stitch.
4. When you turn your work over, you will see the left cross.

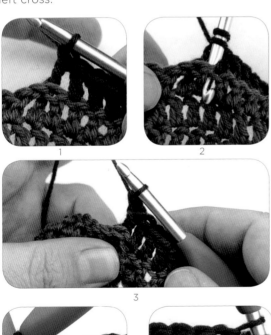

front of work   back of work

1-over-1 Back Post Double Crochet Right Cross

**1-over-1 Back Post double crochet right cross
(1/1 BPdc RC) (worked over 2 sts)**

Sk next st, BPdc around post of next st; working behind BPdc just made, BPdc around post of skipped st.

1. Skip next stitch, work a BPdc around post of next stitch.
2. Working behind BPdc just made.
3. Work a BPdc around post of skipped stitch .
4. Turn your work over and you will see the right cross.

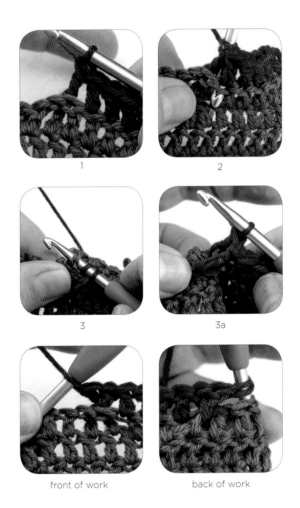

1   2

3   3a

front of work   back of work

2-over-2 Front Post Double Crochet Left Cross

2-over-2 Front Post double crochet left cross (2/2 FPdc LC) (worked over 4 sts)

Sk next 2 sts, [FPdc around post of next st] 2 times; working in front of 2 FPdc just made, FPdc around post of first skipped st, FPdc around post of next skipped st

1. Skip next 2 stitches, work a FPdc around post of next stitch.
2. Work a FPdc around post of next stitch.
3. Working in front of the 2 FPdc just made, work a FPdc around post of first skipped stitch.
4. Work a FPdc around post of next skipped stitch.

1

2

3

4

front of work

2-over-2 Front Post Double Crochet Right Cross

**2-over-2 Front Post double crochet right cross
(2/2 FPdc RC) (worked over 4 sts)**

Sk next 2 sts, [FPdc around post of next st] 2 times;
working behind 2 FPdc just made, FPdc around post of
first skipped st, FPdc around post of next skipped st.

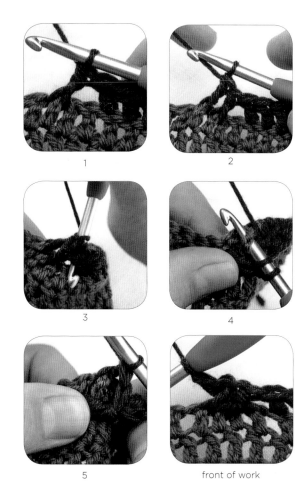

1. Skip the next 2 stitches, work a FPdc around post of next stitch.

2. Work a FPdc around post of next stitch.

3. Working behind the 2 FPdc you just made (this means you will insert your hook between the FPdc you just made and the fabric in order to work your hook around the skipped stitches).

4. Work a FPdc around post of first skipped stitch (use hook to pull the post of the stitch you are working around up to the top of your work so you don't get your yarn overs tangled up with the stitch).

5. Work a FPdc around post of next skipped stitch (again, use hook to pull the post of the stitch you are working around up to the top of your work so you don't get your yarn overs tangled up with the stitch).

2-over-2 Back Post Double Crochet Left Cross

2-over-2 Back Post double crochet left cross (2/2 BPdc LC) (worked over 4 sts)

Sk next 2 sts, [BPdc around post of next st] 2 times; working in front of 2 BPdc just made, BPdc around post of first skipped st, BPdc around post of next skipped st.

1. Skip next 2 stitches, work a BPdc around post of next stitch.

2. Work a BPdc around post of next stitch.

3. Working in front of the 2 BPdc just made (this means you will insert your hook between the BPdc you just made and the fabric in order to work your hook around the skipped stitches).

4. Work a BPdc around post of first skipped stitch.

5. Work a BPdc around post of next skipped stitch.

6. Turn your work over to see the left cross.

1

2

3

4

5

front of work

back of work

2-over-2 Front Post Treble Crochet Left Cross

2-over-2 Front Post treble crochet left cross (2/2 FPtr LC) (worked over 4 sts)

Sk next 2 sts, FPtr around each of next 2 sts 2 rows below; working in front of FPtr just made, FPtr around each of 2 skipped sts 2 rows below.

2-over-2 Front Post Treble Crochet Right Cross

2-over-2 Front Post treble crochet right cross (2/2 FPtr RC) (worked over 4 sts)

Sk next 2 sts, FPtr around each of next 2 sts 2 rows below; working behind FPtr just made, FPtr around each of 2 skipped sts 2 rows below.

3-over-3 Front Post Treble Crochet Left Cross

3-over-3 Front Post treble crochet left cross (3/3 FPtr LC) (worked over 6 sts)

Sk next 3 sts, FPtr around each of next 3 sts; working in front of 3 FPtr just made, FPtr around each of 3 skipped sts.

3-over-3 Front Post Treble Crochet Right Cross

3-over-3 Front Post treble crochet right cross (3/3 FPtr RC) (worked over 6 sts)

Sk next 3 sts, FPtr around each of next 3 sts; working behind 3 FPtr just made, FPtr around each of 3 skipped sts.

3-over-3 Front Post Double Treble Crochet Left Cross

3-over-3 Front Post double treble crochet left cross (3/3 FPdtr LC) (worked over 6 sts)

Sk next 3 sts, FPdtr around each of next 3 sts 2 rows below; working in front of FPdtr just made, FPdtr around each of 3 skipped sts 2 rows below.

3-over-3 Front Post Double Treble Crochet Right Cross

3-over-3 Front Post double treble crochet right cross (3/3 FPdtr RC) (worked over 6 sts)

Sk next 3 sts, FPdtr around each of next 3 sts 2 rows below; working behind FPdtr just made, FPdtr around each of 3 skipped sts 2 rows below.

4-over-4 Front Post Double Treble Crochet Left Cross

4-over-4 Front Post double treble crochet left cross (4/4 FPdtr LC) (worked over 8 sts)

Sk next 4 sts, FPdtr around each of next 4 sts; working in front of 4 FPdtr just made, FPdtr around each of 4 skipped sts.

4-over-4 Front Post Double Treble Crochet Left Cross

4-over-4 Front Post double treble crochet left cross (4/4 FPdtr LC) (worked over 8 sts)

Sk next 4 sts, FPdtr around each of next 4 sts; working in front of 4 FPdtr just made, FPdtr around each of 4 skipped sts.

Anchored Cables

Anchored cables are a more complex version of the combination standard and post stitch cables we worked on earlier in this section. Anchored cables are wider and have an uncrossed stitch worked in the middle of the crossed cables. This uncrossed stitch allows for a wider cable, but also gives the cable fabric greater stability by eliminating the gap associated with wide cables.

2-1-2 Front Post Treble Crochet Left Cross

2-1-2 Front Post treble crochet left cross (2/1/2 FPtr LC) (worked over 5 sts)

Sk next 3 sts, FPtr around each of next 2 sts; working behind 2 FPtr just made, hdc in third skipped st; working in front of hdc AND 2 FPtr just made, FPtr around each of first 2 skipped sts.

1. Skip next 3 stitches, work a FPtr around post of each of the next 2 stitches.

2. Working behind the 2 FPtr you just made, work a regular hdc in the third skipped stitch.

3. Working in front of hdc AND 2 FPtr just made, work a FPtr around each of first 2 skipped stitches.

1

2

3

finished cable

2-1-2 Front Post Treble Crochet Right Cross

2-1-2 Front Post treble crochet right cross (2/1/2 FPtr RC) (worked over 5 sts)

Sk next 3 sts, FPtr around each of next 2 sts; working behind 2 FPtr just made, hdc in third skipped st; working in front of hdc just made AND behind 2 FPtr just made, FPtr around each of first 2 skipped sts.

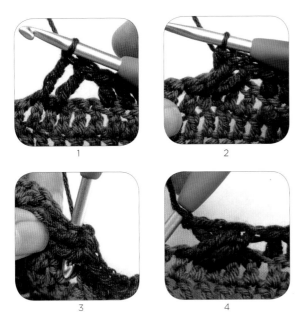

1

2

3

4

1. Skip next 3 stitches, work a FPtr around post of each of the next 2 stitches.

2. Working behind the 2 FPtr you just made, work a regular hdc in the third skipped stitch.

3. Working in front of the hdc just made AND behind the 2 FPtr just made (this means you will insert your hook between the 2 FPtr stitches you just made and the fabric [including the hdc] in order to work your hook around the skipped stitches) (Remember to use hook here to pull the stitches up to the top or your work to avoid tangles).

4. Work a FPtr around each of first 2 skipped stitches.

3-1-3 Front Post Treble Crochet Left Cross

3-1-3 Front Post treble crochet left cross (3/1/3 FPtr LC) (worked over 7 sts)

Sk next 4 sts, FPtr around each of next 3 sts; working behind 3 FPtr just made, hdc in fourth skipped st; working in front of hdc AND 3 FPtr just made, FPtr around each of first 3 skipped sts.

3-1-3 Front Post Treble Crochet Right Cross

3-1-3 Front Post treble crochet right cross (3/1/3 FPtr RC) (worked over 7 sts)

Sk next 4 sts, FPtr around each of next 3 sts; working behind 3 FPtr just made, hdc in fourth skipped st; working in front of hdc just made AND behind 3 FPtr just made, FPtr around each of first 3 skipped sts.

4-1-4 Front Post Treble Crochet Left Cross

4-1-4 Front Post treble crochet left cross (4/1/4 FPtr LC) (worked over 9 sts)

Sk next 5 sts, FPtr around each of next 4 sts; working behind 4 FPtr just made, hdc in fifth skipped st; working in front hdc AND 4 FPtr just made, FPtr around each of first 4 skipped sts.

4-1-4 Front Post Treble Crochet Right Cross

4-1-4 Front Post treble crochet right cross (4/1/4 FPtr RC) (worked over 9 sts)

Sk next 5 sts, FPtr around each of next 4 sts; working behind 4 FPtr just made, hdc in fifth skipped st; working in front of hdc just made AND behind 4 FPtr just made, FPtr around each of first 4 skipped sts.

Post Stitch Cables

Continuous Cables

Stitches you need to know to make this swatch:

> **4-over-4 Front Post double treble/triple treble crochet left cross (4/4 FPdtr/trtr LC) (worked over 8 sts)**
>
> Sk next 4 sts, FPdtr around each of next 4 sts; working in front of FPdtr just made, FPtrtr around each of 4 skipped sts.

Practice Swatch

Foundation Row: Work 32 Fdc, turn.

Row 1: First-dc, FPdc around next st, BPdc around each of next 8 sts, *FPdc around each of next 2 sts, BPdc around each of next 8 sts; rep from * to last 2 sts, FPdc around next st, dc in last st, turn.

Row 2 (RS): First-dc, BPdc around next st, work 4/4 FPdtr/trtr LC, *BPdc around each of next 2 sts, work 4/4 FPdtr/trtr LC; rep from * last 2 sts, BPdc around next st, dc in last st, turn.

Rows 3–9: Rep Rows 1–2.

Fasten off.

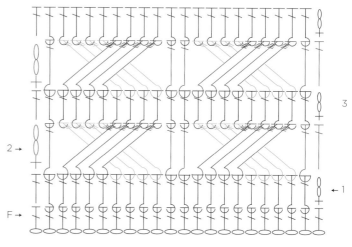

4/4 FPdtr/trtr LC chart

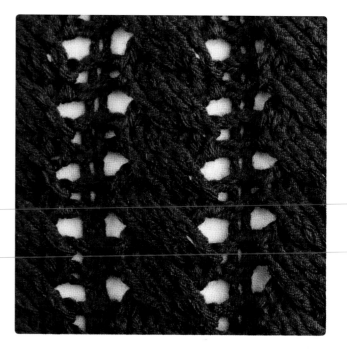

1x1 and 2x2 Cables

Practice Swatch

Foundation Row: Work 14 Fdc, turn.

Row 1: Ch 1, sc in first st and in each st to end of row, turn.

Row 2: Ch 1, sc in first st, sc in next st, work 1x1 left cross, sc in next st, FPdc around each of next 4 sts 2 rows below, sc in next st, work 1x1 right cross, sc in each of next 2 sts, turn.

Row 3: Rep Row 1.

Row 4: Ch 1, sc in first st, sc in next st, work 1x1 left cross, sc in next st, work 2x2 left cross, sc in next st, work 1x1 right cross, sc in each of next 2 sts, turn.

Rows 5–8: Rep Rows 1–4.

Row 9: Rep Row 1.

Row 10: Rep Row 2.

Row 11: Rep Row 1.

Row 12: Ch 1, sc in first st, sc in next st, work 1x1 left cross, sc in next st, work 2x2 right cross, sc in next st, work 1x1 right cross, sc in each of next 2 sts, turn.

Rows 13–16: Rep Rows 9–12.

Row 17: Rep Row 1.

Row 18: Rep Row 2.

Fasten off.

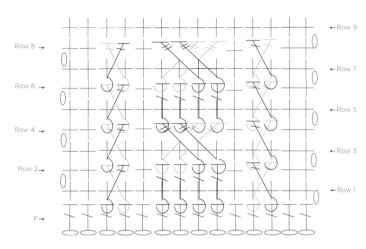

1/1 and 2/2 Cables Practice Swatch chart

2-1-2 Cables

Practice Swatch

Foundation Row: Work 23 Fhdc, turn.

Row 1: Ch 1, sc in first st and in each st to end of row, turn.

Row 2: Ch 1, hdc in first st and in each st to end of row, turn.

Row 3: Rep Row 1.

Row 4: Ch 1, hdc in first st, [work 2-1-2 left cross, hdc in each of next 3 sts] 2 times, work 2-1-2 left cross, hdc in last st, turn.

Row 5: Rep Row 1.

Row 6: Ch 1, hdc in first st, [FPdc around each of next 2 sts 2 rows below, hdc in next st, FPdc around each of next 2 sts 2 rows below, hdc in each of next 3 sts] 2 times, FPdc around each of next 2 sts 2 rows below, hdc in last st, turn.

Rows 7–14: Rep Rows 3–6.

Row 15: Rep Row 1.

Row 16: Ch 1, hdc in first st, [work 2-1-2 right cross, hdc in each of next 3 sts] 2 times, work 2-1-2 right cross, hdc in last st, turn.

Row 17: Rep Row 1.

Row 18: Rep Row 6.

Rows 19–22: Rep Rows 15–18.

Rows 23–24: Rep Rows 15–16.

Fasten off.

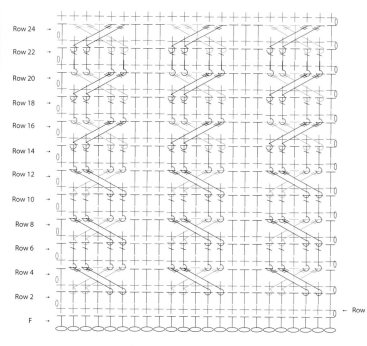

2-1-2 cables chart

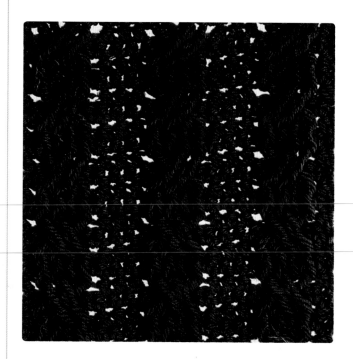

Wandering Paths Cable Pattern

Stitches you need to know to work this swatch:

2-1-2 Front Post tr/dtr left cross (2-1-2 FPLC) (worked over 5 sts)

Sk next 3 sts, FPtr around each of next 2 sts 2 rows below; working behind FPtr just made, sc in third skipped st; work in front of FPtr just made, FPdtr around each of first 2 skipped sts 2 rows below.

2-1-2 Front Post dtr/tr right cross (2-1-2 FPRC) (worked over 5 sts)

Sk next 3 sts, FPdtr around each of next 2 sts 2 rows below; working behind FPdtr just made, sc in third skipped st; working behind FPdtr but in front of sc just made, FPtr around each of first 2 skipped sts 2 rows below.

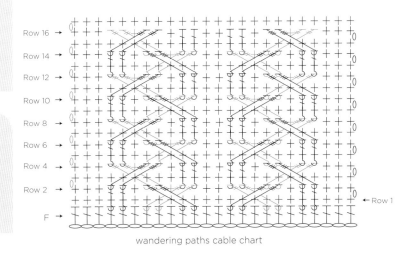

wandering paths cable chart

Practice Swatch

Foundation Row: Work 24 Fdc, turn.

Row 1 (WS): Ch 1, sc in first st, sc in each st to end of row, turn.

Row 2 (RS): Ch 1, sc in first st, [sc in next st] 2 times, [FPdc around next st 2 rows below] 2 times, sc in next st, work 2-1-2 FPRC, [sc in next st] 2 times, work 2-1-2 FPLC, sc in next st, [FPdc around next st 2 rows below] 2 times, [sc in next st] 3 times, turn.

Row 3: Rep Row 1.

Row 4: Ch 1, sc in first st, [sc in next st] 2 times, work 2-1-2 FPLC, sc in next st, [FPdc around next st 2 rows below] 2 times, [sc in next st] 2 times, [FPdc around next st 2 rows below] 2 times, sc in next st, work 2-1-2 FPRC, [sc in next st] 3 times, turn.

Rows 5–12: Rep Rows 1–4.

Rows 13–15: Rep Rows 1–3.

Fasten off.

Colorwork

From stripes to colorblocking to making intricate mosaic designs, crochet colorwork creates stunning fabrics and is as easy as making your basic stitches and changing yarns. We'll start off with easy striping techniques, then move on to more advanced colorwork techniques. After you have worked through these techniques, watch for places throughout the Stitch Patterns section of this book where we will suggest other stitches for you to experiment with using color changes.

Horizontal Stripes

We will start off our colorwork section by using the simplest of the colorwork techniques: horizontal stripes of color created by changing yarns at the end of a row. The good news is that you already know how to do this! We covered how to change yarn at the end of a row with a step-by-step photo tutorial in the "Joining New Yarn" lesson (*see page 159*), so be sure to look at that if you haven't already.

The key here is to make sure that you are changing yarns to the next color at the end of the row, *AND* carrying the unworked color up the side of your work with proper tension while weaving it into the end stitches of your rows. With a little practice, you will be able to finesse your carried yarn so it is barely visible.

Color Change at the End of a Row

Carry yarn up side of work. Work to last stitch of row, work last stitch of row up to last "yo and draw through," pass carried yarn from front to back over working yarn and hold to back of work, yarn over and draw through remaining loops as usual; turn, pass carried yarn from front to back over working yarn, chain 1, and continue with row.

Repeat for each row, being careful of the tension in the carried yarn.

If this yarn is pulled too snug, your fabric will not block properly. Similarly, if tension in the carried yarn is too loose, your fabric may have holes along the side or loose strands of yarn.

Of note in colorwork patterns is some terminology we haven't seen before, when working in different colors, rather than referring to them by color name, patterns will refer to the different colors as Color A, Color B, Color C, etc. They might also say MC (main color), then Color A, B, and so on. Here we are using two colors: Color A and Color B.

1. With Color A, work to the last stitch of the row.
2. Insert hook into last stitch of the row and pass Color B (the carried yarn) from back to front over the hook and hold to the front of your work.
3. Yarn over with Color A.
4. Draw up a loop (trapping Color B).
5. Pick up Color B with your yarn hand (Color B is now the working yarn) and pass Color A from back to front over the working yarn.
6. Yarn over and draw up a loop with Color B (the working yarn).
7. Turn your work.
8. Pass Color A from front to back between the hook and the working yarn.
9. Chain 1, trapping Color A (the new carried yarn).
10. Continue with your new row in Color B.

For taller stitches, there is one extra step because you need to carry the yarn up the inside of the stitch so it is at the level of the new row. We'll demonstrate here with a double crochet stitch.

1. With Color A, work to the last stitch of the row.
2. Insert the hook into the last stitch of the row and pass Color B (the carried yarn) from back to front over the hook and hold to the front of your work.
3. Yarn over and draw up a loop with Color A (trapping Color B).
4. Yarn over and draw through 2 loops on hook.
5. Pick up Color B with your yarn hand (Color B is now the working yarn) and hold Color A to the back of your work with your hook hand.
6. Yarn over with Color B and draw through the remaining 2 loops on the hook.

7. Turn your work.
8. Pass Color A from front to back between the hook and the working yarn.
9. Chain 1 (trapping Color A—the new carried yarn).
10. Work your favorite first-dc stitch. Here we are working the Linked first-dc (see First Stitches of a Row, page 96).
11. Continue with your new row in Color B.

For taller stitches, on the row where you will change yarn colors, you will change to the next color on Step 6, just as you would when changing to a new yarn or a new color as described in the "Joining New Yarn" tutorial (page 159).

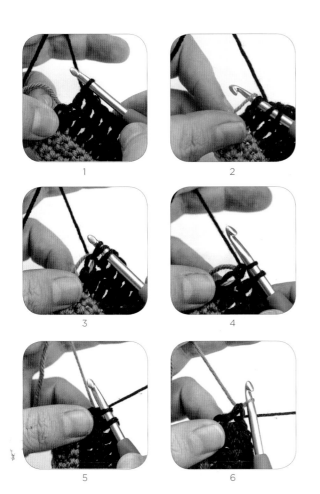

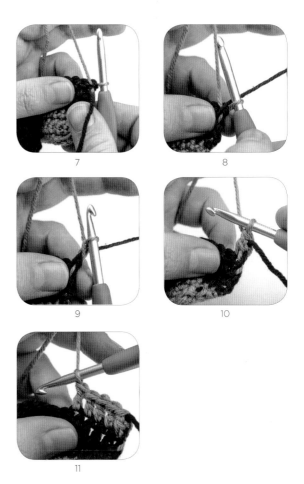

So now let's practice carrying yarn up the side of our work and changing colors in our swatch. We will be using the single crochet linen stitch, with color changes every other row. Single crochet linen stitch is a favorite of ours for fashion fabrics, and you will see it again in the Signature Vests pattern in the "Projects" section (*see page 287*).

The effect of changing colors every other row in this stitch pattern is dramatic and will make your fabrics look amazing.

The first time through this swatch, work your color changes every other row: work with Color A for Rows 1–2, then change over to Color B at the end of Row 2 and continue with Color B for Rows 3–4. Also at the end of Row 2, you will begin carrying Color A up the side of your work so you are ready to switch over to it at the end of Row 4. Alternate colors every other row like this until you are comfortable with the technique and have smoothed out your transitions on the ends of the rows.

Single Crochet Linen Stitch (sc linen st) (worked over a multiple of 2 + 1 sts)

Practice Swatch

Foundation Row: Work 41 Fsc, turn.

Row 1: Ch 1, sc in first st, *ch 1, sk next st, sc in next st; rep from * to end of row, turn.

Row 2: Ch 1, sc in first st, sc in next ch-1 sp, *ch 1, sk next st, sc in next ch-1 sp; rep from * to last st, sc in last st, turn.

Row 3: Ch 1, sc in first st, *ch 1, sk next st, sc in next ch-1 sp; rep from * to last 2 sts, ch 1, sk next st, sc in last st, turn.

Rows 4–32: Rep Rows 2–3.

Fasten off.

STITCH ON!
Feel like you have this technique down pat? Once you are confident with carrying yarn up the sides of your work, try making this swatch again, changing yarn every row! This is more of a challenge because you will be working with two balls of each color, for a total of four balls of yarn. Give it a try and see just how stunning the effect is. Here's this technique used in the bottom hem of our Cross Front Vest pattern from our book *Designer Crochet*.

BONUS TECHNIQUE APPLICATIONS!

"Pooling" is a special term crocheters use for the dreaded occasion when your beautiful variegated, hand-dyed, or kettle-dyed yarn creates blobs of color all over your project. While these yarns look gorgeous on their own, when they are worked into rows the colors can pool together to create unfortunate blobs of color that can draw the eye in unwanted ways. Imagine a gorgeous pullover with a few not-so-well-placed pools of color. YIKES!

To prevent this color horror from occurring, change yarn at the end of every other row. This mixes up the color sections of your yarn and allows the randomness of the color to shine through—without any pools or blobs.

Changing yarn every other row also works well when you need to use two different dye lots of the same color of yarn. When yarn is dyed, it is often dyed in batches that are assigned "dye lot numbers" that can be found on the ball band of your yarn (*see Ball Bands, page 36*). These dye lot numbers are assigned because each time a batch of yarn is dyed, the resulting color can be slightly different. Because of this, it is important, when buying yarn, to buy enough in the same dye lot, or you could end up with part of your garment in one shade and the rest in another, rather than with a uniform color throughout.

If you absolutely must work with two different dye lots of the same color, divide the balls of yarn into halves and alternate between the two dye lots every other row. This will blend the color together over the entirety of your garment and should be completely unnoticeable.

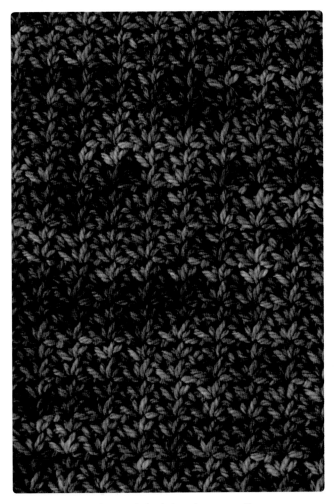

hand-dyed yarn stitched changing every other row

Fair Isle, Jacquard, and Intarsia Colorwork: A Primer

In the hand stitching fiber arts world, there are three types of colorwork: Fair Isle, jacquard, and intarsia.

Fair isle colorwork is done by carrying your yarn along the back of your work as you switch from color to color, giving it the nickname "stranded colorwork." Color changes are frequent, and each color is only worked a few stitches at a time. Generally, the stranded side of the work is meant to be the back of the fabric. No more than two colors are usually carried along a row at a time (three if you are really wild!). The more strands to carry, the more hectic the back of the work can become, making it necessary to line the back of the finished fabric unless your strands are very well tended.

Intarsia colorwork is worked with large blocks of colors and uses a different ball of yarn for each color section. No yarn is carried along the back of the work since the color blocks are too long and the strands of carried yarn would become unruly. Instead, each color of yarn is often divided into smaller balls that are more manageable.

Both sides of a colorwork design worked using intarsia can show the pattern as long as your stitches are neat and tidy.

Jacquard, often referred to as tapestry crochet, is a style of colorwork in which the strands of yarn in the color not being used are carried along the top of the row you are working into, and are covered by the stitches you are making. This creates a denser fabric, since you have an additional layer of yarn running under your stitches. These are made larger because you are working them over the head of the stitch you are working into *and* the strand of unworked yarn. In addition, if your yarn colors are very different, you will likely be able to see the carried color under the stitches of the working color. Because of the thickening of your fabric, the contrast in the colors you are using, or if you are carrying more than one color along your rows and you don't need a two-sided fabric, you might want to consider Fair Isle to keep the fabric less dense and to keep your stitches from becoming distorted.

Colorwork Patterns

Reading colorwork patterns is very different from reading other crochet patterns because the patterns are not usually written out. Instead, the patterns are presented in a colorwork grid in which the individual boxes each represent a stitch and the color of each box indicates a color. For our practice swatches in this section and for our Colorblock Throw in the "Projects" section (*see page 279*), we will use single crochet stitches.

Here is an example of a colorwork chart for a simple checkerboard pattern. Because we are changing colors every three stitches, we can choose to use either Fair Isle/stranded or jacquard/tapestry crochet to make this practice swatch. But, for the sake of practice, let's do both!

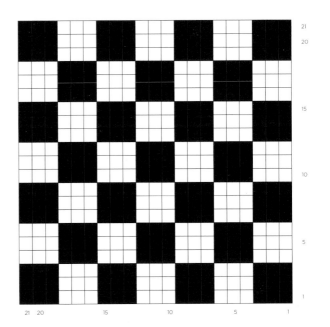

Fair Isle

fair isle stripes colorwork

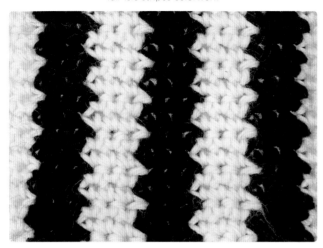

With Strands on Back of Work

1. With Color A, sc up to last "yarn over and draw through all loops on hook."
2. Passing Color B under Color A, pick up Color A with your hook hand and pick up Color B with your yarn hand.
3. Yarn over with Color B and draw through both loops on the hook to finish the sc.
4. Drop Color A and continue with Color B.
5. Repeat Steps 1–4, alternating colors as needed.

Fair Isle with strands on back of work

1   2

3   4

With Strands on Front of Work

1. With Color A, sc up to last "yarn over and draw through all loops on hook."
2. Passing Color B under Color A, pick up Color B with your yarn hand (Color B becomes the working yarn) and pass Color A from back to front between the hook and the working yarn, allowing Color A to fall to the front of the work.
3. Yarn over with Color B and draw through both loops on the hook to finish the sc.
4. Continue with Color B.
5. Repeat Steps 1–4, alternating colors as needed.

Fair Isle with strands on front of work

1   2

3   4

5

Jacquard

Looking at the fronts of the two swatches below and opposite, you might not be able to tell which colorwork technique was used to make which swatch. The back of the fabric tells the real tale. It is easy to see the strands of yarn carried across the back of the work in the Fair Isle swatch, while the back of the jacquard swatch is a mirror image of the front.

As we have said many times before, you need to make choices about which techniques you use to create the fabrics you need for your projects. If you were making a garment that was going to be put on and taken off many times, you might not want strands of yarn running along the inside of the fabric, for fear of snagging them and ruining your project. That said, you might not mind the short strands of yarn as much as you do the added thickness of the fabric when worked in the tapestry style of colorwork. Ultimately, the choice is up to you to pick the right technique to create the right fabric for your project.

jacquard stripes colorwork

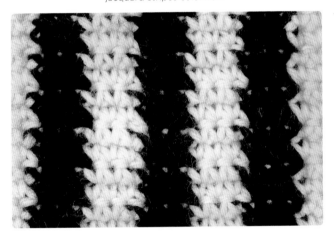

1. With Color A, sc up to last "yarn over and draw through all loops on hook."

2. Holding Color A out of the way, pick up Color B with your yarn hand.

3. Yarn over with Color B and draw through both loops on the hook to finish the sc.

4. Hold Color A so the yarn lies across the tops of the next stitches.

5. Continue with Color B, working into the stitches and over the unworked strand of Color A to the next color change.

6. Repeat Steps 1–5, alternating colors as needed.

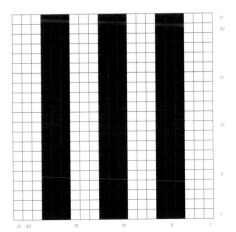

vertical stripe pattern for fair isle and jacquard colorwork

Let's try another practice swatch.

This time we will use the intarsia method of colorwork because our pattern calls for large blocks of color.

This is the colorwork chart for one block from the Colorblock Throw in the "Projects" section of this book. For this block, you will need to use three different balls of yarn to make the color changes. Your first few rows start out with one color, then you switch to using two colors, then three. While you can certainly use three colors that make you happy, we used purple, white, and red as indicated in the colorwork chart.

Intarsia

1. Sc with Color A up to the last "yarn over and draw through all loops on hook."
2. Pick up Color B with your yarn hand.
3. Bring Color A from back to front between the hook and Color B.
4. Continue to work with Color B up to the next color change.
5. Repeat Steps 1–4, alternating colors.

As you can see, each of these colorwork techniques has its own strengths and weaknesses. Practice them all, and keep them in your crochet bag of skills so you can decide which one works best for your fabric for your project.

Key

■ Color A
□ Color B
■ Color C

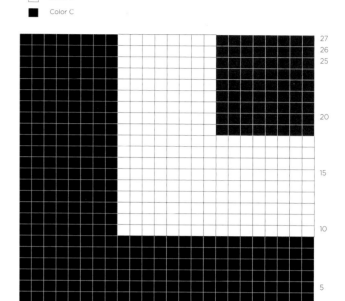

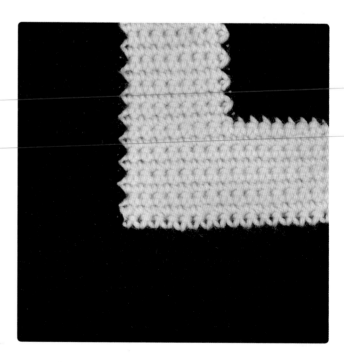

STITCH ON! ◣━━━
Now that you've made a practice swatch, you can jump right to the Colorblock Throw (*see page 279*) and start on your very first project while you work on the rest of your techniques and stitches!

Pattern Stitches

This section is designed to take your hooking skills to the next level. Each one of the pattern stitches in this section uses a combination of the stitches and techniques in this book to make new fabrics and to give you an application for your new knowledge and skills. Not only will you create exciting fabrics, but you will cement your learning even further so you can proceed to make thrilling projects of your own.

To help you work on these FAB stitches, we have provided you with practice swatch patterns for each one.

If you find a stitch pattern you really love and want to use it to make a larger piece of fabric for a project of your own (longer swatches make great scarves, and wider swatches make beautiful wraps!), or to substitute one of these pattern stitches into an existing pattern, you need to consider two pieces of information: the Stitch Multiple and the Row Repeat. We covered both of these in-depth in "Number of rows to repeat for pattern stitch" and "Multiple of stitches to work for pattern stitch" in the Shaping section on page 137. Go back and use that section for reference, but here is a quick review.

Stitch Multiple

The stitch multiple is the number of stitches needed to work one repeat of a pattern stitch. When working with pattern stitches, you will often see the phrase "worked over a multiple of," followed by numbers with a plus sign between them such as 3 + 2, 5 + 2, etc. This information is telling you exactly how many stitches you need in order to work this pattern stitch evenly across a row.

Row Repeat

The row repeat, like the stitch multiple, is the number of rows needed to work one repeat of a pattern stitch. When you look at the practice swatch patterns for each pattern stitch here, you will see a set of written-out rows, and then you will see a set of rows grouped together, where the pattern instructions say to "Repeat Rows XX–XX."

If you see a pattern stitch you really love and want to work up into a larger piece of fabric, with the stitch multiple and row repeat information in hand, you can take the stitch multiple, work out the number of stitches you need, then just keep working your row repeats and you're on your way to making your own fabric! The row repeats are a simple matter of working the rows given as repeats in the pattern; stitch multiples involve some actual math and calculating. To help you out with the stitch multiples, we've included a Stitch Multiples Worksheet in the "Resources" section of this book on page 316.

Have fun learning these different pattern stitches, and be sure to look for little notes from us throughout this section. We will give you tips on how to use some of these pattern stitches for easy projects you can make up on your own, like scarves, wraps, and afghans, and, of course, some are used in the "Projects" section (*see page 271*).

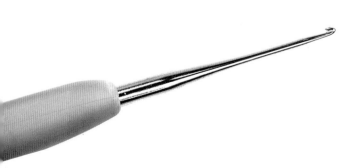

Single Crochet Linen Stitch

Single Crochet Linen Stitch (sc linen st)
(worked over a multiple of 2 + 1 sts)

Foundation Row: Work 41 Fsc, turn.

Row 1: Ch 1, sc in first st, *ch 1, sk next st, sc in next st; rep from * to end of row, turn.

Row 2: Ch 1, sc in first st, sc in next ch-1 sp, *ch 1, sk next st, sc in next ch-1 sp; rep from * to last st, sc in last st, turn.

Row 3: Ch 1, sc in first st, *ch 1, sk next st, sc in next ch-1 sp; rep from * to last 2 sts, ch 1, sk next st, sc in last st, turn.

Rows 4–32: Rep Rows 2–3.

Fasten off.

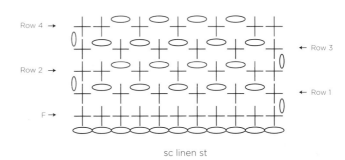

sc linen st

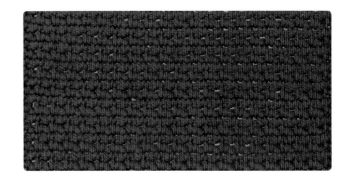

Single Crochet Grid

Single crochet grid (sc grid)
(worked over a multiple of 2 + 1 sts)

Foundation Row: Work 29 Fsc, turn.

Row 1: Ch 1, sc in first st, ch 1, sk next st, *sc in next st, ch 1, sk next st, rep from * to last st, sc in last st, turn.

Row 2: Ch 1, sc in first st, ch 1, sk next ch-1 sp, *sc in next st, ch 1, sk next ch-1 sp; rep from * to last st, sc in last st, turn.

Rows 3–22: Rep Row 2.

Fasten off.

sc grid

STITCH ON! ◄━━━

If you haven't already given this a go in the Colorwork section on *page 194*, try working this same swatch changing colors every other row, then every row. This makes a stunning color variation that will really show off your stitching skills!

Single Crochet Grid through the Front Loop

Single crochet grid through the front loop (worked over a multiple of 2 + 1 sts)

Foundation Row: Work 29 Fsc, turn.

Row 1: Ch 1, sc in first st, ch 1, sk next st, *sc-tfl in next st, ch 1, sk next st; rep from * to last st, sc in last st, turn.

Row 2: Ch 1, sc in first st, ch 1, sk next ch-1 sp, *sc-tfl in next st, ch 1, sk next ch-1 sp; rep from * to last st, sc in last st, turn.

Rows 3-22: Rep Row 2.

Fasten off.

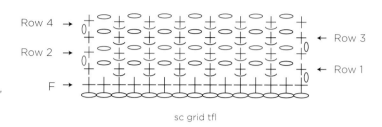

sc grid tfl

Single/Double Crochet Crunch Stitch

Single/double crochet crunch st (sc/dc crunch st) (worked over any even number of stitches)

Foundation Row: Work 32 Fsc, turn.

Row 1: Ch 1, sc in first st, dc in next st, *sc in next st, dc in next st; rep from * to end of row, turn.

Rows 2-21: Rep Row 1.

Fasten off.

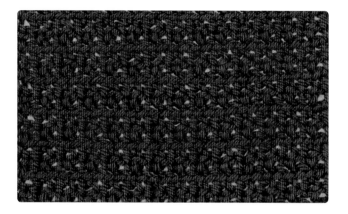

sc/dc crunch st

Explore different textures by substituting treble and double treble crochet stitches for the double crochet stitches in this sc/dc crunch stitch swatch. The higher the crunched stitch, the more textured and interesting the fabrics become!

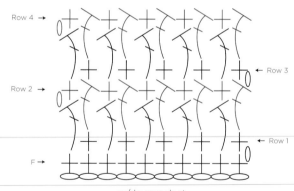

Evolving V-stitch

Evolving v-stitch (worked over a multiple of 3 + 2 sts)

Foundation Row: Work 35 Fsc, turn.

Alternate Foundation Row: Ch 36, turn; sc in second ch from hook and in each ch to end of row, turn - 35 sts.

Row 1: Work first-dc in first st, sk next st, work dc-v in next st, *sk next 2 sts, work dc-v in next st; rep from * to last 2 sts, sk next st, dc in last st, turn – 11 dc-v, 1 first-dc, 1 dc.

Rows 2–3: Work first-hdc in first st, work hdc-v in next ch-1 sp and in each ch-1 sp to last 2 sts, sk next st, hdc in last st, turn – 11 hdc-v, 1 first-hdc, 1 hdc.

Rows 4–6: Ch 1, sc in first st, work sc-v2 in next ch-1 sp and in each ch-1 sp to last 2 sts, sk next st, hdc in last st, turn – 11 sc-v2, 2 sc.

Rows 7–24: Rep Rows 1–6.

Fasten off.

STITCH ON!

Grab your favorite yarn and keep working repeats of the evolving v-st rows until you have a FAB lace scarf! First, work the row repeats until your fabric is about half the length of the scarf you want to make, then go back to the foundation row and work in the opposite direction by working Row 1 in the bottom of the foundation single crochet stitches. Work the same number of rows in the opposite direction and VOILA! You have a FAB accessory to go show off!

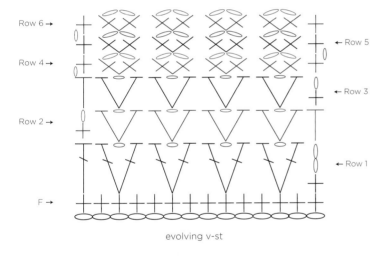

evolving v-st

Papyrus Stitch

This is a fun variation on the Solid Shells practice swatch from earlier (*see Shells and Fans, page 150*), that makes the stitch pattern a little more open and even incorporates some pulled stitches. This one has a little bit of everything!

Stitches you need to know to make this swatch

Papyrus Stitch (worked over a multiple of 6 + 1 sts)

Pulled single crochet (pulled-sc): Working over sc, insert hook into dc 2 rows below, yo and draw up a lp to the height of the first sc in row, yo and draw through 2 lps on hook.

Papyrus Stitch

Practice Swatch

Foundation Row: Work 37 Fsc, turn.

Row 1: (Work Linked first-dc, dc 2) in first st, sk next 2 sts, sc in next st, *sk next 2 sts, work 5-dc shell in next st, sk next 2 sts, sc in next st; rep from * to last 3 sts, sk next 2 sts, work 3 dc in last st, turn.

Row 2: Ch 1, sc in first st, *ch 2, sk next 2 sts, dc in next st, ch 2, sk next 2 sts, sc in next st; rep from * to end of row, turn.

Row 3: Ch 1, sc in first st, sk next ch-2 sp, work 5-dc shell in next st, sk next ch-2 sp, *work pulled-sc, sk next ch-2 sp, work 5-dc shell in next st, sk next ch-2 sp; rep from * to last st, sc in last st, turn.

Row 4: Work Linked first-dc in first st, ch 2, sk next 2 sts, sc in next st, *ch 2, sk next 2 sts, dc in next st, ch 2, sk next 2 sts, sc in next st; rep from * to last 3 sts, ch2, sk next 2 sts, dc in last st, turn.

Row 5: (Work Linked first-dc, dc 2) in first st, sk next ch-2 sp, *work pulled-sc, sk next ch-2 sp, work 5-dc shell in next st, sk next ch-2 sp; rep from * to last st, work 3 dc in last st, turn.

Rows 6–19: Rep Rows 2–5.

Fasten off.

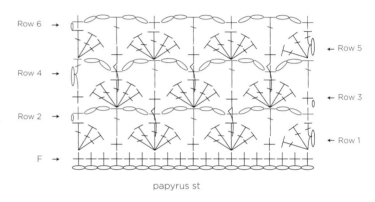

papyrus st

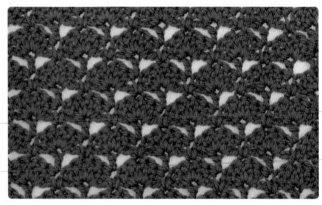

Corner to Corner Pattern Stitch

The Corner to Corner pattern stitch is a technique that crocheters have used for years to make everything from scarves, afghans, rugs, baby blankets, to garments. The versatility of the pattern allows you to "eyeball" just how large your piece of fabric is going to be while working the increase side of the pattern stitch. Then finish up your masterpiece by simply working the decrease side of the pattern stitch. The stitch takes a little practice, but making multiple Corner to Corner squares can be rewarding—just sew them together to make a unique creation of your own!

Stitches you need to know to make this swatch

Increase row: Work First Square, *sk next 3 sts, sl st in next ch-3 sp, ch 3, dc 3 times in same ch-3 sp; rep from * to last ch-3 sp, sk next 3 sts, sl st in next ch-3 sp, turn.

Decrease row: Sl st in each of first 3 sts, *sl st in next ch-3 sp, ch 3, dc 3 times in same ch-3 sp, sk next 3 sts; rep from * to last ch-3 sp, sl st in last ch-3 sp, turn.

Corner to Corner Square

Practice Swatch

First Square: Ch 6, dc in fourth ch from hook, dc in each of next 2 chs – 3 dc, 1 ch-3 sp.

Increase side

Row 1: Work First Square, turn.

Row 2: Work First Square, sk next 3 sts, sl st in next ch-3 sp, ch 3, dc 3 times in same ch-3 sp, turn – 2 squares.

Row 3: Work First Square, [sk next 3 sts, sl st in next ch-3 sp, ch 3, dc 3 times in same ch-3 sp] 2 times, turn – 3 squares.

Row 4: Work First Square, [sk next 3 sts, sl st in next ch-3 sp, ch 3, dc 3 times in same ch-3 sp] 3 times, turn – 4 squares.

Row 5: Work First Square, [sk next 3 sts, sl st in next ch-3 sp, ch 3, dc 3 times in same ch-3 sp] 4 times, turn – 5 squares.

Decrease side

Row 6: Sl st in each of first 3 sts, [sl st in next ch-3 sp, ch 3, dc 3 times in same ch-3 sp, sk next 3 sts] 4 times, sl st in next ch-3 sp – 4 squares.

Row 7: Sl st in each of first 3 sts, [sl st in next ch-3 sp, ch 3, dc 3 times in same ch-3 sp, sk next 3 sts] 3 times, sl st in next ch-3 sp – 3 squares.

Row 8: Sl st in each of first 3 sts, [sl st in next ch-3 sp, ch 3, dc 3 times in same ch-3 sp, sk next 3 sts] 2 times, sl st in next ch-3 sp – 2 squares.

Row 9: Sl st in each of first 3 sts, sl st in next ch-3 sp, ch 3, dc 3 times in same ch-3 sp, sk next 3 sts, sl st in last ch-3 sp – 1 square.

Fasten off.

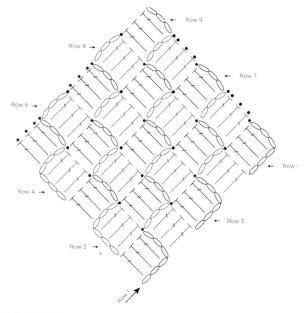

Corner to Corner Rectangle

Practice Swatch

First Square: Ch 6, dc in fourth ch from hook, dc in each of next 2 chs – 3 dc, 1 ch-3 sp.

Row 1: Work First Square, turn.

Row 2: Work First Square, sk next 3 sts, sl st in next ch-3 sp, ch 3, dc 3 times in same ch-3 sp, turn – 2 squares.

Row 3: Work First Square, [sk next 3 sts, sl st in next ch-3 sp, ch 3, dc 3 times in same ch-3 sp] 2 times, turn – 3 squares.

Rows 4–6: Work First Square, *sk next 3 sts, sl st in next ch-3 sp, ch 3, dc 3 times in same ch-3 sp; rep from * to end of row, turn – 6 squares at end of Row 6.

Row 7: Work First Square, *sk next 3 sts, sl st in next ch-3 sp, ch 3, dc 3 times in same ch-3 sp; rep from * to last ch-3 sp, sl st in last ch-3 sp, turn – 6 squares.

Row 8: Sl st in each of first 3 sts, *sl st in next ch-3 sp, ch 3, dc 3 times in same ch-3 sp, sk next 3 sts; rep from * to last ch-3 sp, sl st in last ch-3 sp, ch 3, dc 3 times in same ch-3 sp, turn.

Row 9: Rep Row 7.

Rows 10–13: Sl st in each of first 3 sts, *sl st in next ch-3 sp, ch 3, dc 3 times in same ch-3 sp, sk next 3 sts; rep from * to last ch-3 sp, sl st in last ch-3 sp, turn – 2 squares at end of Row 13.

Row 14: Sl st in each of first 3 sts, sl st in next ch-3 sp, ch 3, dc 3 times in same ch-3 sp, sk next 3 sts, sl st in last ch-3 sp – 1 square.

Fasten off.

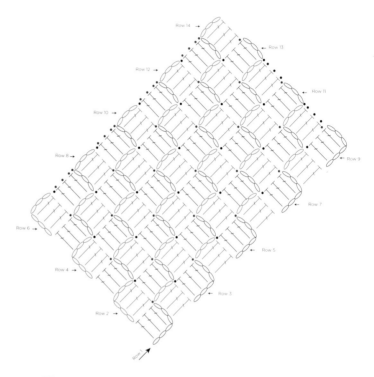

STITCH ON! ━━━━

You can make your own Corner to Corner afghan by repeating Row 4 of the Corner to Corner Rectangle pattern stitch. Just keep working your repeats until the short side of your afghan is as wide as you'd like, then start working Row 10 until you're down to 2 squares, then work Row 14 and fasten off. This is a non-pattern that people have been using for many years to create family heirloom afghans and throws. Try changing yarn colors every few rows to create a diagonal strip sequence! This is a FAB way to use up scrap yarns and to create unique pieces that suit your home decor.

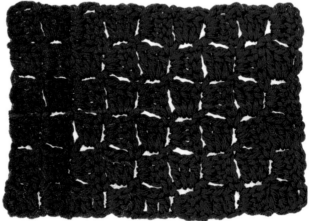

Chevron Stitch Patterns

Chevrons are a classic crochet stitch pattern that has adorned couches and beds with vibrant-colored throws and afghans, as well as the runways of the world, seen frequently in the designs of fashion icons like Missoni. A chevron stitch pattern is characterized by the sharp angles—made with quick increases and decreases worked into one stitch or space—that create the points of the pattern. Each of these points are separated by any number of regular stitches that create the straight edges of the pattern.

The popularity of chevrons could be attributed to how easy they are to just sit down and start making, without worrying much about paying attention to a pattern. Once you get the hang of the 3-stitch increase and the 3-stitch decrease rhythm of these examples, try different variations on stitch height and color. With all the possible combinations, you'll never run out of FAB crochet fabrics to create!

Single Crochet Chevron

Single Crochet Chevron (sc chevron)
(worked over a multiple of 18 + 1 sts)

Foundation Row: Ch 56, turn.

Row 1: Ch 1 sc 2 times in second ch from hook, sc in each of next 7 sts, sc3tog, sc in each of next 7 sts, *sc 3 times in next st, sc in each of next 7 sts, sc3tog, sc in each of next 7 sts; rep from * to last st, sc 2 times in last st, turn – 55 sts.

Row 2: Ch 1, sc 2 times in first st, sc in each of next 7 sts, sc3tog, sc in each of next 7 sts, *sc 3 times in next st, sc in each of next 7 sts, sc3tog, sc in each of next 7 sts; rep from * to last st, sc 2 times in last st, turn.

Rows 3–10: Rep Row 2.

Fasten off.

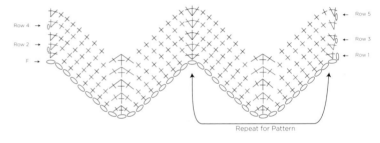

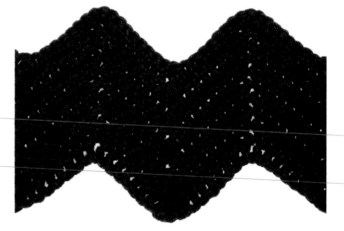

STITCH ON!

Now that you have this pattern down in regular single crochet, give it a try using single crochet through the back loop (sc tbl). This ribbed chevron stitch is a favorite of ours, and we have used it in our own afghans here at home.

Half Double Crochet Chevron

Half Double Crochet Chevron (hdc chevron)
(worked over a multiple of 18 + 1 sts)

Foundation Row: Ch 56, turn.

Row 1: (Work first-hdc, hdc) in second ch from hook, hdc in each of next 7 sts, hdc3tog, dc in each of next 7 sts, *hdc 3 times in next st, hdc in each of next 7 sts, hdc3tog, hdc in each of next 7 sts; rep from * to last st, hdc 2 times in last st, turn - 55 sts.

Row 2: Ch 1, hdc 2 times in first st, hdc in each of next 7 sts, hdc3tog, hdc in each of next 7 sts, *hdc 3 times in next st, hdc in each of next 7 sts, hdc3tog, hdc in each of next 7 sts; rep from * to last st, hdc 2 times in last st, turn.

Rows 3–10: Rep Row 2.

Fasten off.

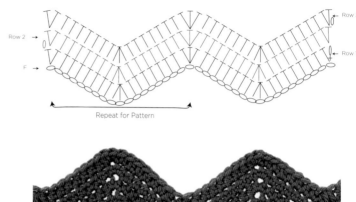

Double Crochet Chevron

Double Crochet Chevron (dc chevron)
(worked over a multiple of 18 + 1 sts)

Foundation Row: Ch 56, turn.

Row 1: (Work first-dc, dc) in second ch from hook, dc in each of next 7 sts, dc3tog, dc in each of next 7 sts, *dc 3 times in next st, dc in each of next 7 sts, dc3tog, dc in each of next 7 sts; rep from * to last st, dc 2 times in last st, turn - 55 sts.

Row 2: Ch 1, dc 2 times in first st, dc in each of next 7 sts, dc3tog, dc in each of next 7 sts, *dc 3 times in next st, dc in each of next 7 sts, dc3tog, dc in each of next 7 sts; rep from * to last st, dc 2 times in last st, turn.

Rows 3–10: Rep Row 2.

Fasten off.

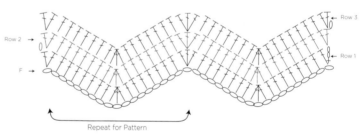

STITCH ON! ⟵

Ready to create your own classic? Here's the un-pattern for our chevron stitch afghan (pictured below). We did this using sale yarn and just playing with stitches, so don't be afraid to play with your own variations.

Foundation Row: Ch 235, turn.

Row 1: Ch 1, sc 2 times in second ch from hook, sc in each of next 7 sts, sc3tog, sc in each of next 7 sts, *sc 3 times in next st, sc in each of next 7 sts, sc3tog, sc in each of next 7 sts; rep from * to last st, sc 2 times in last st, turn – 234 sts.

Rows 2–6: Ch 1, sc 2 times in first st, sc tbl in each of next 7 sts, sc3tog, sc tbl in each of next 7 sts, *sc 3 times in next st, sc tbl in each of next 7 sts, sc3tog, sc tbl in each of next 7 sts; rep from * to last st, sc 2 times in last st, turn.

Row 7: Ch 1, dc 2 times in first st, dc in each of next 7 sts, dc3tog, dc in each of next 7 sts, *dc 3 times in next st, dc in each of next 7 sts, dc3tog, dc in each of next 7 sts; rep from * to last st, dc 2 times in last st, turn.

Row 8: Ch 1, sc in first st, FPsc around next st and each st to last st, sc in last st, turn.

Row 9: Rep Row 7.

Row 10: Ch 1, sc in each st to end of row, turn.

Row 11: Ch 1, sc 2 times in first st, sc tbl in each of next 7 sts, sc3tog, sc tbl in each of next 7 sts, *sc 3 times in next st, sc tbl in each of next 7 sts, sc3tog, sc tbl in each of next 7 sts; rep from * to last st, sc 2 times in last st, turn.

Just repeat Rows 2–11 until you have the length you want! We changed colors after every set of sc stitches, but you can work this un-pattern up in solid colors, variegated colors, stripes . . . whatever YOU want. It's your masterpiece!

Ripple Stitch Patterns

Ripple stitch patterns are the more laid-back cousins of chevrons. Ripple stitch patterns are characterized by slow and easy curves that undulate evenly across the fabric, using slower increases and decreases worked over more than one stitch. The rise and fall of each section is created by dramatic increases and slow decreases. The ubiquitous ripple has influenced designers of home decor and fashion since crocheters began putting hook to yarn, and there are as many variations on the theme as there are stitches and stitch combinations in the crochet universe. Here are two of our favorites to get you started.

Feather and Fan

Feather and Fan (worked over a multiple of 19 + 2 sts)

Foundation Row: Work 59 Fsc, turn.

Row 1: Work first-tr in first st, *work 5 tr in next st, tr in next st, [sk next st, tr in next st] 8 times, work 5 tr in next st; rep from * to last st, tr in last st, turn.

Rows 2–8: Rep Row 1.

Fasten off.

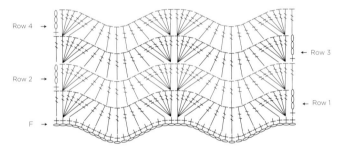

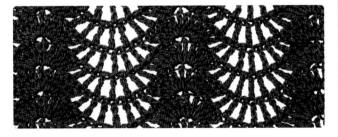

Feather and Fan with FPsc

**Feather and Fan with FPsc
(worked over a multiple of 19 + 2 sts)**

Foundation Row: Work 59 Fsc, turn.

Row 1: Work first-tr in first st, *work 5 tr in next st, tr in next st, [sk next st, tr in next st] 8 times, work 5 tr in next st; rep from * to last st, tr in last st, turn.

Row 2: Ch 1, sc in first st, FPsc around next st and each st to last st, sc in last st, turn.

Rows 3–16: Rep Rows 1–2.

Fasten off.

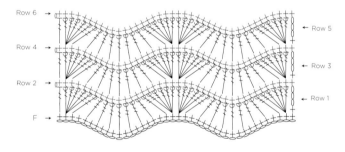

STITCH ON!

Wouldn't this make a FAB scarf or wrap? For a stylish scarf, just keep working repeats of Rows 1 and 2. Need it wider? The pattern is worked over a multiple of 19 + 2 stitches, so add an extra 19 stitches to your swatch pattern, or use the Stitch Multiples Worksheet on page 316 in the "Resources" section of this book for larger pieces of fabric like wraps and ruanas.

Wave Stitch Patterns

Single Wave

Single Wave (worked over a multiple of 14 + 1 sts)

Foundation Row: Work 43 Fsc, turn.

Row 1: Ch 1, sc in first st, *sc in next st, hdc in each of next 2 sts, dc in each of next 2 sts, tr in each of next 3 sts, dc in each of next 2 sts, hdc in each of next 2 sts, sc in each of next 2 sts; rep from * to end of row, turn.

Row 2: Ch 1, sc in first st and in each st to end of row, turn.

Row 3: Ch 1, work first-tr in first st, *tr in next st, dc in each of next 2 sts, hdc in each of next 2 sts, sc in each of next 3 sts, hdc in each of next 2 sts, dc in each of next 2 sts, tr in each of next 2 sts; rep from * to end of row, turn.

Row 4: Rep Row 2.

Rows 3–22: Rep Rows 1–4.

Fasten off.

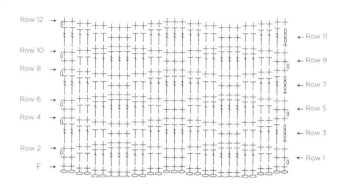

Double Wave

Double Wave (worked over a multiple of 14 + 1 sts)

Foundation Row: Work 43 Fsc, turn.

Rows 1–2: Ch 1, sc in first st, *sc in next st, hdc in each of next 2 sts, dc in each of next 2 sts, tr in each of next 3 sts, dc in each of next 2 sts, hdc in each of next 2 sts, sc in each of next 2 sts; rep from * to end of row, turn.

Row 3: Ch 1, sc in first st and in each st to end of row, turn.

Rows 4–5: Work first-tr in first st, *tr in next st, dc in each of next 2 sts, hdc in each of next 2 sts, sc in each of next 3 sts, hdc in each of next 2 sts, dc in each of next 2 sts, tr in each of next 2 sts; rep from * to end of row, turn.

Row 6: Rep Row 3.

Rows 7–18: Rep Rows 1–6.

Fasten off.

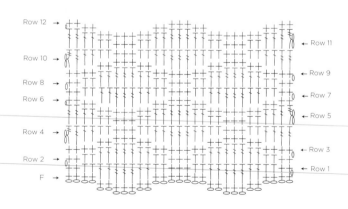

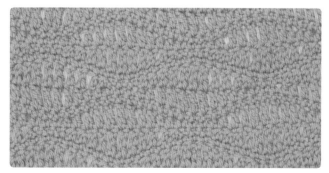

STITCH ON!
Now that you have the hang of it, show off your stitching prowess by using this pattern stitch to make the Rectangle Wrap Vest on page 283.

Half Double Crochet/ Slip Stitch Wave

**Half double crochet slip stitch wave
(worked over a multiple of 10 + 5 sts)**

Foundation Row: Ch 36, turn.

Row 1: Sl st in bottom bump of second ch from hook, sl st in bottom bump of each of next 4 sts, *hdc in bottom bump of each of next 5 sts, sl st in bottom bump of each of next 5 sts; rep from * to end of row, turn.

Row 2: Ch 1, sl st tbl in each of first 5 sts, *hdc tbl in each of next 5 sts, sl st tbl in each of next 5 sts; rep from * to end of row, turn—35sts.

Rows 3–4: Work first-hdc tbl in first st, hdc tbl in each of next 4 sts, *sl st tbl in each of next 5 sts, hdc tbl in each of next 5 sts; rep from * to end of row, turn.

Rows 5–6: Ch 1, sl st tbl in each of first 5 sts, *hdc tbl in each of next 5 sts, sl st tbl in each of next 5 sts; rep from * to end of row, turn.

Rows 7–26: Rep Rows 3–6.

Fasten off.

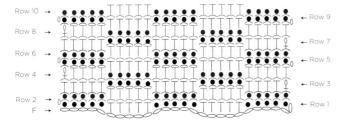

Pulled Stitches

This category of stitches is sometimes referred to as stretched, long, or spike stitches. Regardless of the name, the technique for creating these unique stitches is the same, as discussed in the "Where to Put Your Hook" section of this book (*page 44*). Pulled stitches are worked by inserting your hook two or more rows below the working row and pulling up a loop to the height of the stitches in the working row. The key to making successful pulled stitches is to keep a light tension on the working yarn, to keep the fabric from being scrunched up and squished.

Double Linen Stitch

Here are two versions of the single crochet linen stitch that uses pulled stitches to really accentuate the woven look of the single crochet linen stitch. Both use pulled single crochet stitches, but one version works into a chain space 2 rows below, and the other works into a single crochet stitch 2 rows below. Try them both and think of what kinds of projects you would like to use them for.

Stitches you need to know to make this swatch

Pulled single crochet (pulled sc)

Working over ch-1 sp, insert hook into indicated st or sp 2 rows below, yo and pull up a lp to the height of current row (2 lps on hook), yo and draw through both lps on hook.

Double Linen Stitch 1

Double Linen Stitch 1 (worked over a multiple of 2 + 1 sts)

Foundation Row: Work 25 Fsc, turn.

Alternate Foundation Row: Ch 26, sc in second ch from hook and in each ch to end of row, turn – 25 sc.

Row 1: Ch 1, sc in first st, *ch 1, sk next st, sc in next st; rep from * to end of row, turn.

Row 2: Ch 1, sc in first st, work pulled sc in st 2 rows below, *ch 1, sk next st, work pulled sc in st 2 rows below; rep from * to last st, sc in last st, turn.

Row 3: Ch 1, sc in first st, *ch 1, sk next st, work pulled sc in st 2 rows below; rep from * to last 2 sts, ch 1, sk next st, sc in last st, turn.

Rep Rows 2-3 for pattern stitch.

Fasten off.

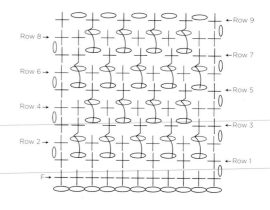

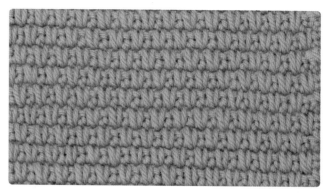

Double Linen Stitch 2

Double Linen Stitch 2 (worked over multiple of 2 + 1 sts)

Foundation Row: Work 25 Fsc, turn.

Alternate Foundation Row: Ch 26, sc in second ch from hook and in each ch to end of row, turn – 25 sc.

Row 1: Ch 1, sc in first st, *ch 1, sk next st, sc in next st; rep from * to end of row, turn.

Row 2: Ch 1, sc in first st, *ch 1, sk next ch sp, sc in next st; rep from * to end of row, turn.

Row 3: Ch 1, sc in first st, work pulled sc in ch-1 sp 2 rows below, *ch 1, sk next st, work pulled sc in ch-1 sp 2 rows below; rep from * to last st, sc in last st, turn.

Row 4: Ch 1, sc in first st, sc in next st, *ch 1, sk next ch sp, sc in next st; rep from * to last st, sc in last st, turn.

Row 5: Ch 1, sc in first st, *ch 1, sk next st, work pulled sc in ch-1 sp 2 rows below; rep from * to last 2 sts, ch 1, sk next st, sc in last st, turn.

Rep Rows 2–5 for pattern stitch.

Fasten off.

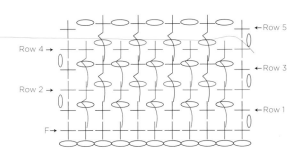

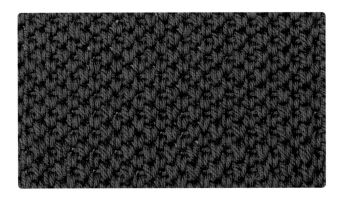

Spike Wedge Stitch

This stitch pattern is a showstopper! Worked in a solid color or with alternating rows of colors, this pattern takes pulled stitches to another level, creating an overall graphic design on your crochet fabric that you'll want to use for home decor, accessories, and garments. The swatch below is written with the color changes included. If you want to make it in one color, just skip the instructions that say to fasten off and join another color. Try this pattern stitch in different color combinations and in different weights of yarn to see what types of FAB fabrics you can come up with!

Stitches you need to know to make this swatch

Spike Wedge (worked over 5 sts)

Spike in next st 6 rows below, Spike in next st 5 rows below, Spike in next st 4 rows below, Spike in next st 3 rows below, Spike in next st 2 rows below.

Spike Wedge Stitch (worked over a multiple of 10 + 5 sts)

Foundation Row: Work 45 fsc, turn.

With Color A

Rows 1–5: Ch 1, sc in each st across, turn.

Row 6: Ch 1, sc in each st across, turn.

Fasten off A, join B.

With Color B

Row 7: Ch 1, sc in first 5 sts, *Work Spike Wedge over next 5 sts, sc in next 5 sts; rep from * across, turn.

Rows 8–11: Ch 1, sc in each st to end of row, turn.

Row 12: Ch 1, sc in each st to end of row, turn.

Fasten off B, join A.

With Color A

Row 13: Ch 1, Work Spike Wedge over first 5 sts, *sc in next 5 sts, Work Spike Wedge over next 5 sts; rep from * across, turn.

Rows 14–17: Ch 1, sc in each st to end of row, turn.

Row 18: Ch 1, sc in each st to end of row, turn. Fasten off A, join B.

Rows 19–30: Rep Rows 7–18.

Fasten off.

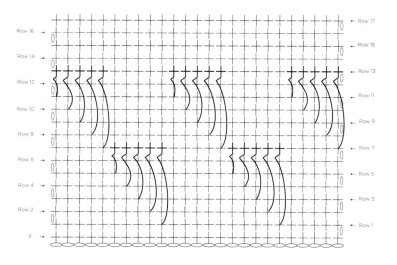

Feathered Columns

The feather stitch combines the technique for pulled stitches with cluster stitches like we've seen earlier in this book. The way the pulled stitches work together and seem to layer one on top of the other makes this a stunning texture stitch for all types of projects.

Feathered Columns (worked over a multiple of 2 + 1 sts)

Foundation Row: Work 41 Fhdc, turn.

Row 1: Ch 1, hdc in first st, *ch 1, sk next st, hdc in next st; rep from * to end of row, turn.

Row 2: Ch 1, hdc in first st, ch 1, work Beginning Feather, ch 1, *work Feather, ch 1; rep from * to last st, hdc in last st, turn.

Rows 3–21: Rep Row 2.

Fasten off.

Stitches you need to know to make this swatch

Beginning Feather

Yo, insert hook into last ch-1 spof previous row, yo and draw up a lp even with lps on hook (3 lps on hook), yo, insert hook into ch-1 sp one row below same sp just worked, yo and draw up a lp even with lps on hook (5 lps on hook), yo, insert hook into next ch-1 sp, yo and draw up a lp even with lps on hook, yo and draw through all 7 lps on hook.

Feather

Yo, insert hook into same ch-1 sp as last Feather, yo and draw up a lp even with lps on hook (3 lps on hook), yo, insert hook into skipped st or ch-1 sp one row below same sp, yo and draw up a lp even with lps on hook (5 lps on hook), yo, insert hook into next ch-1 sp, yo and draw up a lp even with lps on hook, yo and draw through all 7 lps on hook.

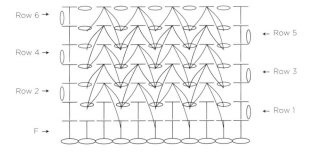

Wrapped Stitches

Wrapped Double Crochet

This pattern stitch combines the concept of a cable (working stitches out of order) with pulled stitches. Previously we worked pulled stitches by inserting our hook into rows that had already been worked. This visually interesting pattern stitch uses a pulled stitch worked by inserting your hook into a skipped stitch, then pulled over two or three double crochet stitches, making a pulled stitch that wraps over the standing stitches.

Stitches you need to know to work these swatches

Wrapped double crochet stitch (wrapped-dc)

Yo, holding working yarn to back of work, insert hook into indicated st or sp, yo and draw up a lp to the height of the working row, ensuring that stitch wraps around previously made stitches evenly, [yo and draw through 2 lps on hook] 2 times.

Wrapped double crochet (wrapped dc)
(worked over a multiple of 3 + 2 stitches)

Foundation Row: Work 35 Fsc sts, turn.

Row 1: Work first-dc in first st, sk next st, *dc in each of next 2 sts, work wrapped-dc in skipped st; rep from * to last st of row, dc in last st, turn.

Row 2: Ch 1, sc in first st and in each st to end of row, turn.

Rows 3–22: Rep Rows 1–2.

Fasten off.

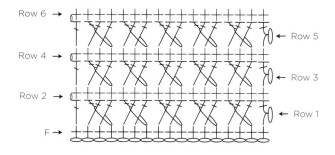

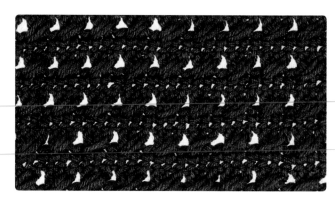

Crossed Dc and Bobble

Here's a fun variation on wrapped stitches that still uses a wrapped-dc, but that works the crossed stitches into chain spaces on either side of a bobble.

Crossed Dc and Bobble
(worked over a multiple of 3 + 2 sts)

Foundation Row: Work 35 Fsc, turn.

Alternate Foundation Row: Ch 36, work sc in second ch from hook and in each ch to end of row, turn – 35 sc.

Row 1: Work Linked first-dc in first st, *sk next 2 sts, dc in next st, ch 1, working in front of dc just made, dc in first skipped st; rep from * to last st, dc in last st, turn.

Row 2: Work Linked first-dc in first st, *ch 1, work 3-dc bobble in next ch-1 sp, ch 1; rep from * to last st, dc in last st, turn.

Row 3: Work Linked first-dc in first st, *sk next ch-1 sp and next 3-dc bobble, dc in next ch-1 sp, working in front of dc just made dc in skipped ch-1 sp; rep from * to last st, dc in last st, turn.

Rows 4–13: Rep Rows 2–3.

Fasten off.

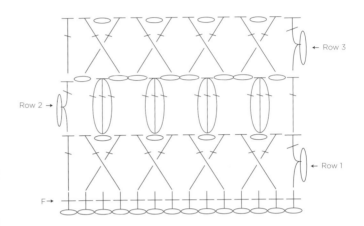

Ribbing 6 Ways

Offered here for your reference and future use are six versions of crochet ribbing. These techniques for working ribbing are useful for everything from hats and sleeve cuffs to the hems and necklines of garments.

Single Crochet Reversible Ribbing

Single Crochet Reversible Ribbing (sc tbl ribbing)
(worked over any multiple of stitches)

If you're experiencing deja vu, it's because you HAVE seen this stitch before. This is the same stitch you worked on way back in the "Variations on Basic Stitches" section (*see page 113*). Working continuous rows of sc tbl does, indeed, make a beautiful, lightweight, springy crochet ribbing. Just turn your swatch so the ends of the rows are at the top and bottom, and you can see the welts and troughs that make ribbing. Get ready to see this FAB little stitch again in Signature Vests pattern on page 287 in the "Projects" section of this book.

So now that you have this one mastered, move on to the other five versions of crochet ribbing here.

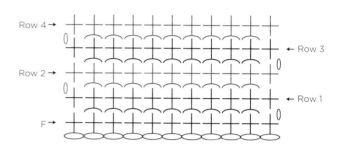

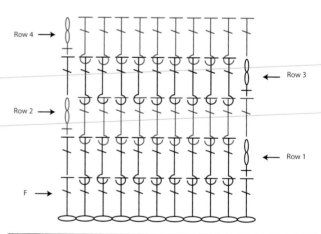

Alternating Front Post and Back Post Reversible Ribbing

Alternating Front Post and Back Post Reversible Ribbing (FP/BP reversible ribbing)
(worked over a multiple of 2 + 1 sts)

Foundation Row: Work 25 Fdc, turn.

Row 1: Work first-dc in first st, work BPdc around next st, *work FPdc around next st, work BPdc around next st; rep from * to last st, dc in last st, turn.

Row 2: Work first-dc in first st, work FPdc around next st, *work BPdc around next st, work FPdc around next st; rep from * to last st, dc in last st, turn.

Rows 3–14: Rep Rows 1–2.

Fasten off.

Horizontal Half Double Crochet Reversible Post Stitch Ribbing

Horizontal half double crochet reversible post stitch ribbing (FPhdc ribbing) (worked over any multiple of sts)

Foundation Row: Work 25 Fhdc, turn.

Row 1: Ch 1, work FPhdc around first st and each st to end of row, turn.

Rows 2–22: Rep Row 1.

Fasten off.

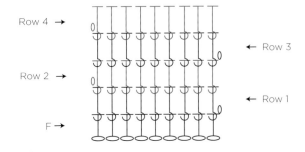

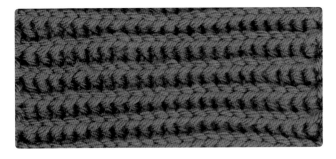

Horizontal Double Crochet Reversible Post Stitch Ribbing

Horizontal double crochet reversible post stitch ribbing (FPdc ribbing) (worked over any multiple of sts)

Foundation Row: Work 25 Fdc, turn.

Row 1: Work first dc in first st, work FPdc around first st and each st to end of row, turn.

Rows 2–18: Rep Row 1.

Fasten off.

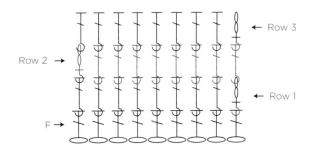

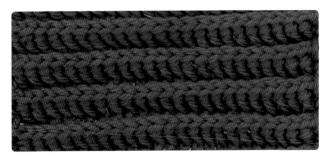

Horizontal One-Sided Post Stitch Ribbing

Horizontal one-sided post stitch ribbing (worked over any multiple of sts)

Foundation Row: Work 25 Fdc, turn.

Row 1: Ch 1, work FPdc around first st and around each st to end of row, turn.

Row 2: Ch 1, work BPdc around first st and around each st to end of row, turn.

Rows 3–14: Rep Rows 1–2.

Fasten off.

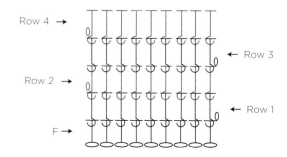

Vertical One-Sided Post Stitch Ribbing

Vertical one-sided post stitch ribbing (worked over a multiple of 2 + 1 sts)

Foundation Row: Work 25 Fdc, turn.

Row 1: Ch 1, sc in first st and in each st to end of row, turn.

Row 2 (RS): Ch 1, sc in first st, *FPdc around next st 2 rows below, sc in next st; rep from * to end of row, turn.

Rows 3–14: Rep Rows 1–2.

Fasten off.

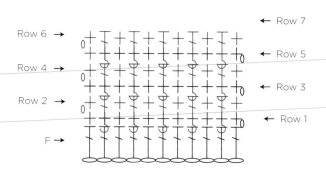

Post Stitch Basketweave

This basketweave pattern stitch is highly textural, and depending on the weight of yarn you use, can be used to create fabrics for everything from cozy home decor items to FAB textured garments. Try this one using worsted-weight yarn, then try a fingering-weight or sock-weight yarn to see how dramatic the difference is in the fabrics.

Post Stitch Basketweave

**Post Stitch Basketweave
(worked over a multiple of 8 + 6 sts)**

Foundation Row: Work 38 Fdc, turn.

Row 1: Work first-hdc in first st, work FPdc around each of next 4 sts, *work BPdc around each of next 4 sts, work FPdc around each of next 4 sts; rep from * to last st, hdc in last st, turn.

Row 2: Work first-hdc in first st, work BPdc around each of next 4 sts, *work FPdc around each of next 4 sts, work BPdc around each of next 4 sts; rep from * to last st, hdc in last st, turn.

Fasten off.

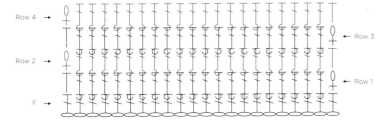

Star Stitch

A Star Stitch is a special kind of cluster stitch (*see Variations on Increase and Decrease Stitches, page 146*) that works into different parts of neighboring stitches to create a complex-looking textured stitch with multiple legs that radiate from a center point.

Star Stitch

Practice Swatch

(worked over a multiple of 3 + 1 sts)

Foundation Row: Work 28 Fsc, turn.

Row 1: Work First Star, work Star st across to end of row, turn.

Row 2: Ch 1, sc in eye of First Star, *sc tfl of next st (arm of Star), sc in eye of next Star; rep from * to last st, sc in last st, turn.

Rows 3–14: Rep Rows 1–2.

Fasten off.

Stitches you need to know to make this swatch

First Star Stitch (First-Star)

Ch 2, insert hook into first ch from hook, yo and draw up a lp, insert hook into next ch, yo and draw up a lp (3 lps hook), insert hook into first st of row, yo and draw up a lp to height of other lps on hook (4 lps on hook), insert hook into next st, yo and draw up a lp to height of other lps on hook (5 lps on hook), yo and draw through all 5 lps on hook, ch 1 to close "Star" and form "eye" of Star.

Star Stitch (Star st)

Insert hook into ch-1 of last Star st made, yo and draw up a lp, insert hook into back of fifth lp of last Star made, yo and draw up a lp to height of first lp (3 lps on hook), [insert hook into next st, yo and draw up a lp to height of previous lps] 2 times, (5 lps on hook), yo and draw through all 5 lps on hook, ch 1 to close Star and form "eye" of Star.

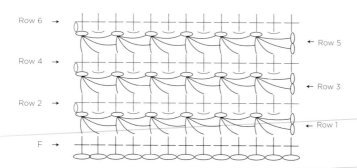

"IT IS TOTALLY OKAY FOR YOU TO EXPERIMENT AND TINKER AROUND WITH STITCHES AND STITCH PATTERNS."

There! We said it.

Experimenting and playing is how new techniques are born, and how fun and innovative stitch patterns and designs are created. And we do it here in our studio all the time . . . ALL THE TIME!

One such tinkering session occurred when we were looking at the swatch for the Catherine Wheels (see *pages 232–233*). We just weren't happy with that teeny little gap where the wheel didn't come all the way around. So the playing and experimenting began, and we came up with a variation on the Catherine Wheel that we liked better.

Moral of the story: **Don't be afraid to experiment!**

Catherine Wheels

Catherine Wheels are a combination of rows of cluster stitches alternating with rows of fans/shells. These have always been a favorite of crocheters and can be found in projects from hats to home decor, scarves, wraps, and garments.

Catherine Wheel

Catherine Wheel (worked over a multiple of 8 + 1 sts)

Foundation Row: Work 33 Fsc, turn.

Row 1: Ch 1, sc in first st, *sc in next st, sk next 2 sts, work 7-dc fan, sk next 2 sts, sc in each of next 2 sts; rep from * to end of row, turn.

Row 2: Work first 4-dc cluster, ch 3, sc in same st as last leg of first 4-dc cluster, *sc in each of next 2 sts, ch 3, work 7-dc cluster, ch 3, sc in same st as last leg of first 4-dc cluster; rep from * to last 6 sts, sc in each of next 2 sts, ch 3, work 4-dc cluster, turn.

Row 3: (Work first-dc, dc 3 times) in top of 4-dc cluster, sk next ch-3 sp, sc in each of next 3 sts, *work 7-dc fan in top of next cluster st, sk next ch-3 sp, sc in each of next 3 sts; rep from * to last cluster st, dc 4 times in top of last cluster st, turn.

Row 4: Ch 1, sc in each of first 2 sts, ch 3, work 7-dc cluster, ch 3, sc in same st as last leg of 7-dc cluster, *sc in each of next 2 sts, ch 3, work 7-dc cluster, sc in same st as last leg of 7-dc cluster; rep from * to last st, sc in last st, turn.

Row 5: Ch 1, sc in first st, *sc in next st, sk next ch-3 sp, work 7-dc fan, sk next ch-3 sp, sc in each of next 2 sts; rep from * to end of row, turn.

Rows 6–14: Rep Rows 2–5, ending last rep on Row 2.

Fasten off.

Stitches you need to know to make this swatch

7-dc fan: Work 7 dc in indicated st.

7-dc cluster: [Yo, insert hook into next st, yo and draw up a lp, yo and draw through 2 lps on hook] 7 times (8 lps on hook), yo and draw through all 8 lps on hook, ch 1 to create top of 7-dc cluster.

4-dc cluster: [Yo, insert hook into next st, yo and draw up a lp, yo and draw through 2 lps on hook] 4 times (5 lps on hook), yo and draw through all 5 lps on hook, ch 1 to create top of 4-dc cluster.

First 4-dc cluster: Without making a chain-up, sc in first st, ch 1 (counts as first leg of cluster), [yo, insert hook into next st, yo and draw up a lp, yo and draw through 2 lps on hook] 3 times (4 lps on hook), yo and draw through all 4 lps on hook, ch 1 to create top of first 4-dc cluster.

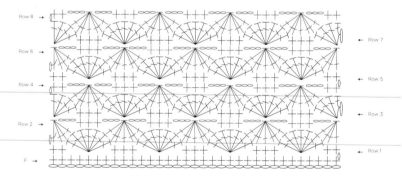

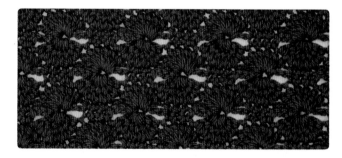

Catherine Wheel Variations

Catherine Wheel Variation 1 (Catherine Wheel var 1)
(worked over a multiple of 8 + 1 sts)

Foundation Row: Work 33 Fsc, turn.

Row 1: Ch 1, sc in first st, *sc in next st, sk next 2 sts, work 7-dc fan, sk next 2 sts, sc in each of next 2 sts; rep from * to end of row, turn.

Row 2: Work first 5-dc cluster, ch 3, sc in same st as last leg of first 5-dc cluster, *sc in each of next 2 sts, ch 3, work 9-dc cluster, ch 3, sc in same st as last leg of first 5-dc cluster; rep from * to last 6 sts, sc in each of next 2 sts, ch 3, work 5-dc cluster, turn.

Row 3: (Work first-dc, dc 3 times) in top of 5-dc cluster, sk next ch-3 sp, sc in each of next 3 sts, *work 7-dc fan in top of next cluster st, sk next ch-3 sp, sc in each of next 3 sts; rep from * to last cluster st, dc 4 times in top of last cluster st, turn.

Row 4: Ch 1, sc in each of first 2 sts, ch 3, work 9-dc cluster, ch 3, sc in same st as last leg of 9-dc cluster, *sc in each of next 2 sts, ch 3, work 9-dc cluster, sc in same st as last leg of 9-dc cluster; rep from * to last st, sc in last st, turn.

Row 5: Ch 1, sc in first st, *sc in next st, sk next ch-3 sp, work 7-dc fan, sk next ch-3 sp, sc in each of next 2 sts; rep from * to end of row, turn.

Rows 6–14: Rep Rows 2–5, ending last rep on Row 2.

Fasten off.

Stitches you need to know to make this swatch

7-dc fan: Work 7 dc in indicated st.

9-dc cluster: Yo, insert hook into same st as last sc made, yo and draw up a lp, yo and draw through 2 lps on hook, [yo, insert hook into next st, yo and draw up a lp, yo and draw through 2 lps on hook] 8 times (10 lps on hook), yo and draw through all 10 lps on hook, ch 1 to create top of 9-dc cluster.

5-dc cluster: Yo, insert hook into same st as last sc made, yo and draw up a lp, yo and draw through 2 lps on hook, [yo, insert hook into next st, yo and draw up a lp, yo and draw through 2 lps on hook] 4 times (6 lps on hook), yo and draw through all 6 lps on hook, ch 1 to create top of 5-dc cluster.

First 5-dc cluster: Without making a chain-up, sc in first st, ch 1 (counts as first leg of cluster), [yo, insert hook into next st, yo and draw up a lp, yo and draw through 2 lps on hook] 4 times (5 lps on hook), yo and draw through all 5 lps on hook, ch 1 to create top of first 5-dc cluster.

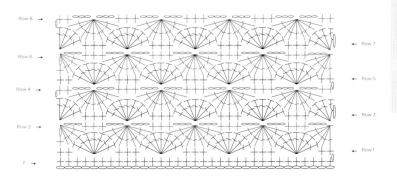

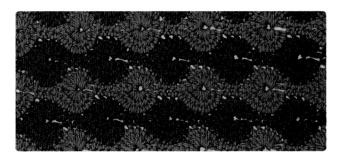

Mesh Stitches

This family of stitches creates mesh fabrics that can be used as stand-alone fabrics for garments, accessories, and home decor. They are also the base fabric used to create the grids for making filet crochet fabrics.

Half Double Crochet Squared Mesh

Half double crochet squared mesh (worked over a multiple of 2 + 1 sts)

Foundation Row: Work 29 Fsc, turn.

Row 1: Work first-hdc in first st, *ch 1, sk next st, hdc in next st; rep from * to end of row, turn.

Rows 2–14: Rep Row 1.

Fasten off.

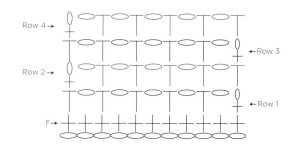

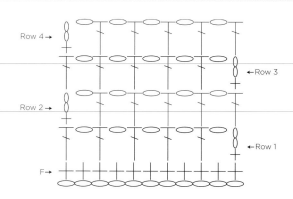

Double Crochet Squared Mesh

Double crochet squared mesh (worked over a multiple of 2 + 1 sts)

Foundation Row: Work 29 Fsc, turn.

Row 1: Work first-dc in first st, *ch 1, sk next st, dc in next st; rep from * to end of row, turn.

Rows 2–14: Rep Row 1.

Fasten off.

Offset Half Double Crochet Mesh

**Offset half double crochet mesh
(offset hdc mesh) (worked over a multiple of 2 + 1 sts)**

Foundation Row: Work 29 Fsc, turn.

Row 1: Work first-hdc in first st, *ch 1, sk next st, hdc in next st; rep from * to end of row, turn.

Row 2: Work first-hdc in first st, hdc in next ch-1 sp, *ch 1, sk next st, hdc in next ch-1 sp; rep from * to last st, hdc in last st, turn.

Row 3: Work first-hdc in first st, *ch 1, sk next st, hdc in next ch-1 sp; rep from * to end of row, turn.

Rows 4–16: Rep Rows 2–3.

Fasten off.

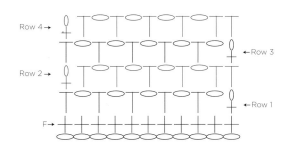

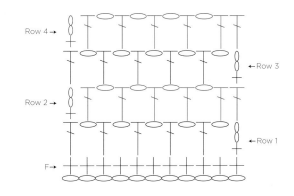

Offset Double Crochet Mesh

**Offset double crochet mesh
(offset dc mesh) (worked over a multiple of 2 + 1 sts)**

Foundation Row: Work 29 Fsc, turn.

Row 1: Work first-dc in first st, *ch 1, sk next st, dc in next st; rep from * to end of row, turn.

Row 2: Work first-dc in first st, dc in next ch-1 sp, *ch 1, sk next st, dc in next ch-1 sp; rep from * to last st, dc in last st, turn.

Row 3: Work first-dc in first st, *ch 1, sk next st, dc in next ch-1 sp; rep from * to end of row, turn.

Rows 4–16: Rep Rows 2–3.

Fasten off.

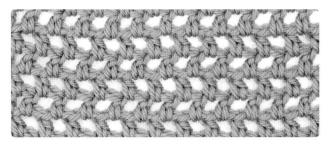

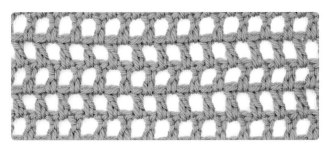

Blocks and Squares

This stitch pattern is a classic example of filet crochet using blocks and spaces to create a graphic pattern that looks stunning when worked up into larger pieces of fabric. Try this one with your practice yarn first, then work your way down to progressively finer yarn until you are able to work in crochet thread. Shout out to the future "Threadies" out there!

Blocks and Squares (worked over a multiple of 3 + 1 sts)

Foundation row: Work 40 Fsc, turn.

Row 1: Work first-dc in first st, dc in each of next 3 sts, *[ch 2, sk next 2 sts, dc in next st] 3 times, dc in each of next 3 sts; rep from * to end of row, turn.

Row 2: Work first-dc in first st, ch-2, sk next 2 sts, dc in next st, *[ch 2, sk next ch-2 sp, dc in next st] 2 times, dc 2 times in next ch-2 sp, dc in next st, ch 2, sk next 2 sts, dc in next st; rep from * to end of row, turn.

Row 3: Work first-dc in first st, ch 2, sk next ch-2 sp, dc in next st, *ch 2, sk next 2 sts, dc in next st, dc 2 times in next ch-2 sp, dc in next st, [ch 2, sk next ch-2 sp, dc in next st] 2 times; rep from * to end of row, turn.

Row 4: Work first-dc in first st, ch 2, sk next ch-2 sp, dc in next st, *dc 2 times in next ch-2 sp, dc in next st, ch 2, sk next 2 sts, dc in next st, [ch 2, sk next ch-2 sp, dc in next st] 2 times; rep from * to end of row, turn.

Row 5: Work first-dc in first st, *[ch 2, sk next ch-2 sp, dc in next st] 2 times, dc 2 times in next ch-2 sp, dc in next st, ch 2, sk next 2 sts, dc in next st; rep from * to last ch-2 sp, ch 2, sk last ch-2 sp, dc in last st, turn.

Row 6: Work first-dc in first st, *[ch 2, sk next ch-2 sp, dc in next st] 2 times, ch 2, sk next 2 sts, dc in next st, dc 2 times in next ch-2 sp, dc in next st; rep from * to last ch-2 sp, ch 2, sk last ch-2 sp, dc in last st, turn.

Row 7: Work first-dc in first st, dc 2 times in next ch-2 sp, dc in next st, *ch 2, sk next 2 sts, dc in next st, [ch 2, sk next ch-2 sp, dc in next st] 2 times, dc 2 times in next ch-2 sp, dc in next st; rep from * to end of row, turn.

Rows 8–19: Rep Rows 2–7.

Fasten off.

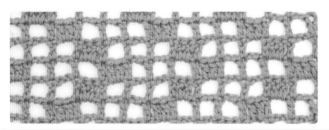

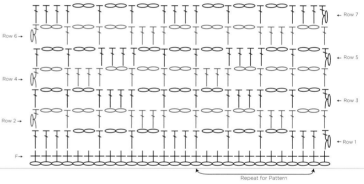

Double/Single Crochet Combination Grid

Double/single crochet combination grid (dc/sc combo grid) (worked over a multiple of 3 + 1 sts)

Foundation Row: Work 34 Fsc, turn.

Row 1: Work first-dc in first st, *ch 2, sk next 2 sts, dc in next st; rep from * to end of row, turn.

Rows 2–3: Ch 1, sc in first st, *ch 2, sk next ch-2 sp, sc in next st; rep from * to end of row, turn.

Row 4: Work first-dc in first st, *ch 2, sk next ch-2 sp, dc in next st; rep from * to end of row, turn.

Rows 5–16: Rep Rows 2–4.

Fasten off.

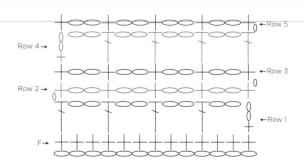

Trellis Stitch

Trellis Stitch (worked over a multiple of 4 + 1 sts)

Foundation Row: Work 29 Fsc, turn.

Row 1: Ch 1, sc in first st, *ch 5, sk next 3 sts, sc in next st; rep from * to end of row, turn.

Row 2: Work first-dc in first st, ch 3, *sc in next ch-5 sp, ch 5; rep from * to last ch-5 sp, sc in last ch-5 sp, ch 3, dc in last st, turn.

Row 3: Ch 1, sc in first st, ch 5, *sc in next ch-5 sp, ch 5; rep from * to last st, sc in last st, turn.

Rows 4–19: Rep Rows 2–3.

Fasten off.

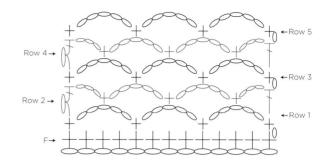

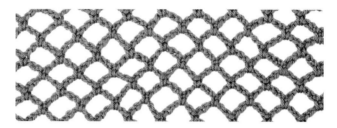

Picot Trellis Stitch

Picot Trellis Stitch (worked over a multiple of 4 + 1 sts)

Foundation Row: Work 29 Fsc, turn.

Row 1: Ch 1, sc in first st, *ch 5, sk next 3 sts, sc in next st; rep from * to end of row, turn.

Row 2: Work first-dc in first st, ch 3, *work picot in next ch-5 sp, ch 5; rep from * to last ch-5 sp, work picot in last ch-5 sp, ch 3, dc in last st, turn.

Row 3: Ch 1, sc in first st, ch 5, *work picot in next ch-5 sp, ch 5; rep from * to last st, sc in last st, turn.

Rows 4–19: Rep Rows 2–3.

Fasten off.

Stitches you need to know to make this swatch

Picot: (Sc, ch 3, sl st in back bump of third ch from hook, sc) in indicated st or sp.

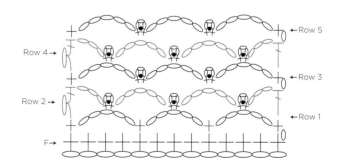

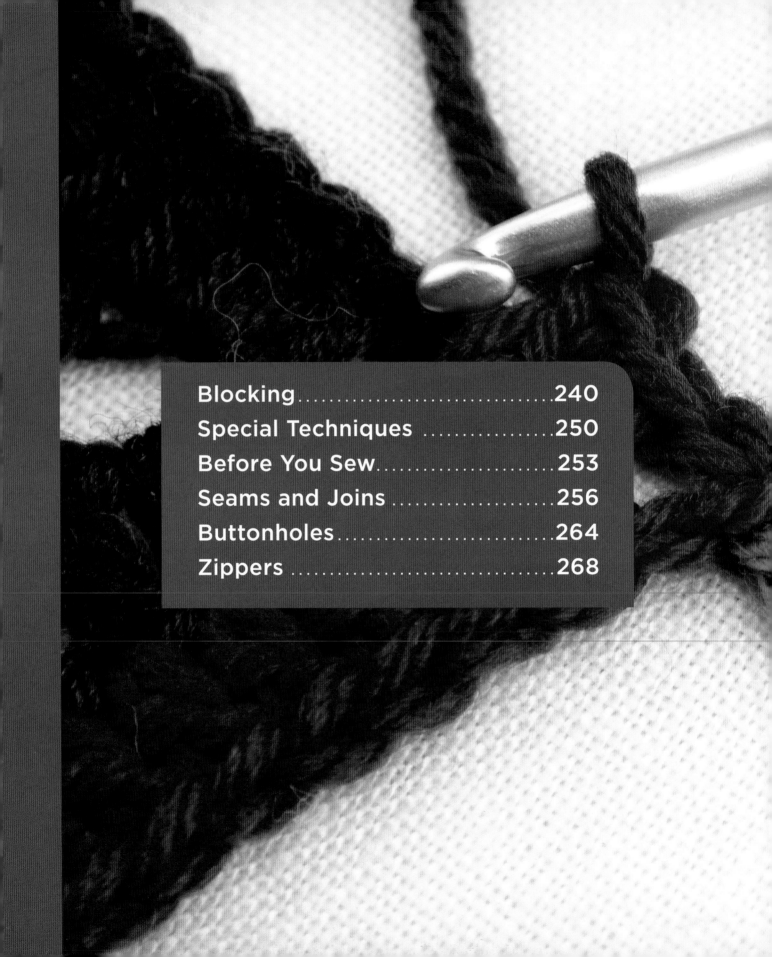

"The biggest compliment a crocheter can receive about their finishing is no compliment at all."

FINISHING

Blocking

Now that you have made the fabric for your project, it is time to put the polish on and give it a professional look with great finishing. In one sense, finishing is the process of creating a "Finished Fabric," which means that the fabric has been blocked and the ends have been woven in. However, finishing also includes the process of sewing seams, adding closures like buttons or zippers, and steaming out any final wrinkles or bumps.

It is easy to understand how your finishing work is just as important to the success of your project as the ability to make good stitches. You can make beautiful stitches with gorgeous yarn, but all that work will be overshadowed if your ends aren't woven in well or your seams are sloppy. Finishing is the work that fades into the background and becomes invisible, allowing the real artistry of your work to come into full view and shine. In the end, great finishing, done correctly, won't even be noticed.

Blocking is the first step in finishing your fabrics. Blocking introduces moisture into your crochet fabric and is an essential part of your work, both during the swatching process, when you are testing your fabric, and during the finishing process, before weaving in ends and seaming. Blocking serves several valuable purposes:

Restoring Your Fibers

Blocking allows the fibers in your yarn to expand and return to their natural state. During the processing of most fibers, there are chemicals used to treat those fibers, and the fibers are put through machines that can flatten them out a bit when the twist is put into the yarn. Introducing moisture into your fabric allows those fibers to relax and open up, and even to expand in some cases. Wools in particular will relax and the fibers will open up, creating a more pliable and supple fabric. The same is true of plant-based fibers and even acrylics, if the process is done correctly. Think of a dry sponge that swells up when placed in water. The result is not nearly as dramatic, but the effect is the same. The water is absorbed into the fiber and relaxes it beautifully.

Cleaning

As far as those processing chemicals go, soaking in plain water or water with a little leave-in fiber wash will remove most of the chemicals and products that can weigh down fibers allowing a revitalization of those processed fibers. Even organic fibers processed without chemicals can do with a bit of a wash to remove any remaining vegetable or animal matter. Special care should be taken to use the appropriate water temperature and amount of agitation for your fabric.

Remember, your handmade fabrics need the same care as your store-bought fabrics. Hot water will not work well with delicate silks and scrubbing and wringing out wooly fabrics will lead to felting.

Shaping

Through the introduction of moisture, blocking makes your fabrics more pliable overall so it is easier to open them up and shape them. Some fibers can be tight or harsh to work with, but after blocking they relax and the fabric can be manipulated so stitch patterns can be opened up and set into place. Even fabrics made with acrylic yarns can be shaped and blocked into place with the use of a little heated moisture in the form of steam.

Taking the Edge Off

Finally, there is the next-to-skin factor. If a finished project is meant to come in direct contact with our skin, we don't want a fabric that is abrasive or irritating.

As you will see in this section, there are a few different ways to block fabrics, and different fibers benefit from different methods of blocking. Whatever the fiber content and method of blocking used, however, the resulting fabric is often much softer and more desirable for use in next-to-skin projects like wraps, afghans, and garments. Wool softens, linen and cotton drape more beautifully, and fabrics made with acrylic yarns are dramatically improved by the introduction of a little heated moisture in the form of steaming.

The Benefits of Blocking are Obvious

Blocking is a necessary step in both the beginning (swatching)
and the end (finishing) of your making process.

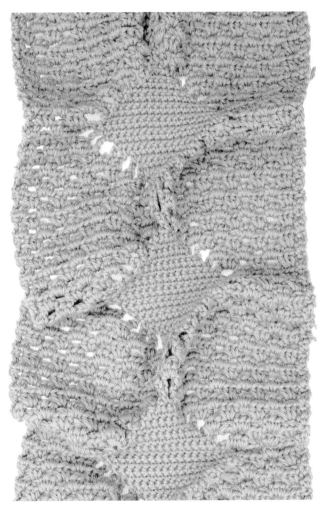

lace collar from the Signature Vests pattern *before* blocking

lace collar from the Signature Vests pattern *after* blocking

Your Blocking Kit

There are many products on the market that help you with blocking. Your basic blocking kit should include:

Fingers

Not all fabrics need to be pinned out. Some just need gentle encouragement to open up and move into shape. For these, your fingers will work just fine.

Blocking Wires

These thin, rustproof wires are a crocheter's best friend for lining up the straight edges of long pieces of fabric. Some are even thin enough to work around curves, perfect for shaping armholes, necklines, and even large shawls and home decor pieces.

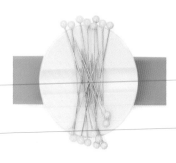

Blocking Pins

When fingers alone just won't do the job done, you will need pins to hold your fabrics in place. T-pins, U-pins, and those pins with the colorful round heads work equally well, but we find the more colorful the head of the pin, the easier they are to find when they go flying to the floor.

Unwaxed Kitchen String

When blocking wires just won't fit the curve, unwaxed kitchen string can be run through the edges of your pieces and pinned into place. The pins hold the shape as you pull the string tight around them, pulling the curve of your armhole or a large circular lace piece into shape. After tightening, the pins can be adjusted for an even more precise curve.

Bowl

These hold water. Got it? Any clean vessel that will hold water AND your fabric will do. In our studio this has included large mixing bowls, a clean sink, and even a large cooler (when there might have been dishes in the sink).

Spray Bottle

Speaking of spritzing: sometimes your fabrics need to have moisture added a little at a time without completely soaking them. In those cases, use a spray bottle with plain water or the leave-in wash of your choice.

Blocking Mats

You need something to poke those pins into. In a pinch, we've used the mattress on our bed or even a piece of cardboard wrapped with a towel when we are working on the road (just make sure to remove all the pins from your towels before the hotel folks come in and get a surprise). There are a number of commercially produced blocking boards and mats on the market. We have also used the sturdy foam mats that are made for garage, gym, and playroom floors. These mats hold the pins securely and lock together to make a customizable work surface on which to block any size of project.

Steamer

Using a simple garment or drapery steamer to introduce moisture into your fabrics is fast and allows you to introduce moisture in controlled amounts. Rather than immediately soaking your fabric, gently steaming while increasing the amount of moisture in small increments lets you gradually put moisture into your fabric until it feels right to you. Please keep in mind that not all fabrics are steaming candidates. While the element of heat that comes with using steam can help wool and even acrylic relax and expand, heat on silk and, yes, acrylic again, can melt those fibers or cause them to stretch grossly out of shape. It is best to do a small test swatch with your fabric to see if it will respond well to steaming, or if soaking or spritzing are more appropriate.

Leave-in Wash

Yes, we said leave-in wash. These are special products made to gently clean your fabrics without harsh chemicals and detergents. They are perfect if you have skin sensitivities to strong soaps, and the best part is that you don't have to rinse them out. This means you can use them with wools that would felt with too much agitation, or with delicate fibers and lace fabrics that would not stand up well to being rinsed out. It is important, when choosing a leave-in wash, that the product explicitly states that it is either no rinse or leave in.

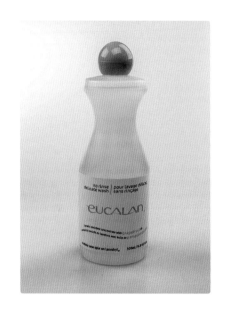

Towel

Before you manipulate your fabrics into their final glorious shapes, you will need to remove as much of the moisture as possible. Folding them into or rolling them up in a thick towel, and then pressing on the towel, will wick away enough water to allow you to handle and pin your fabric.

Fan

Because some of us live in places with high humidity, or because some of us are simply impatient and REALY REALLY REALLY want to feel the finished fabric of our project (Who? Me?!?), a gently blowing fan will help expedite the drying process.

STEP 1: Introducing Water into Your Fabrics

It is important to choose the best method of introducing moisture for the fibers you are using to make your fabric. Look at the care instructions on the yarn ball band for an indication of how to introduce water to your fabric (*see Ball Bands, page 36*). Once you have determined the appropriate method, proceed immediately to your work area and begin the finishing process of your FAB fabrics.

Soaking

Soaking involves submerging your fabrics in a container of water, allowing them to completely absorb water. A leave-in fiber wash will take away most of the chemicals and the smells associated with some fibers. This method is good for most fibers, and is great for cottons and wools that might need to stay in the water longer in order to expand and fill out.

Spraying/Spritzing

You can use a spray bottle with plain water or with water and a leave-in wash as a more gradual method of introducing moisture into your crochet fabrics. Some fibers do not react well to being completely soaked all the way through, so this allows you to give them just enough water to make them happy and pliable. This is also a smart method to use when you are working with a yarn for the first time and aren't sure how much moisture is the right amount for your fabric. Make a small test swatch and give it a spritz until the fibers become pliable and give you the fabric you need.

Steaming

Steaming is also a good technique for gradually introducing moisture into your fabrics, and it comes with the added benefit of warmth. While soaking and spritzing are fine, a little gentle warmth works well to relax some fibers and encourages them to open up, making your final fabric more pliable and easier to work with. Since you are not soaking the fibers completely through, steaming can also dry faster than soaking or spritzing—a definite bonus if you have a lot of projects to block or a large project on your blocking mats.

Steam blocking works for a wide variety of fibers, but since there is heat involved, make sure to check your ball band, and always test a swatch to see how your fabric will react. Acrylic is one fiber for which steam is the only method for blocking that will make the finished fabric stay in place. Because of the chemical makeup of acrylic, you can soak it with as much water as you want and it will just dry out and snap right back into its original shape. While this is an extremely desirable characteristic if your fabrics are going to be used for projects that will see a lot of wear and tear (outerwear, kid's clothes and toys, and home decor that will be used and abused by humans and animals, for example), you need the heat that comes with the steam to set these fabrics into shape—and they will usually retain that shape.

Beware of using an iron to steam your projects! We recommend using a handheld garment steamer, or an iron with a silicone guard in place to keep the heating element from coming in direct contact with your fabrics. Touch your steam iron to wool and it can singe the fibers. Allowing a hot iron to come too close to most fibers will "kill" the fabric, flattening out the stitches and making the fabric unusable.

As you can see, there are many options for introducing moisture into your fabrics. With such a vast array of fibers on the market, and with new blends being created all the time, it is best to test a small swatch of your fabric to see how it will react to moisture before making your final choice.

STEP 2: Shaping the Fabric

Here is where you will check the written pattern or the schematic for the finished measurements of your project, and then shape your fabric to fit those measurements. If you are testing a swatch of a stitch pattern and don't have a measurement to shape to, use your own judgement to shape the stitches so they look good, and so the resulting fabric is what you need for your project. As always: find the right fabric for the right project!

Blocking Mats

Simply put, you can't put pins through your dining room table. Blocking mats provide a surface where you can pin your fabric into place. While there are a number of commercially produced blocking mats on the market, here are a few options we use in our studio.

Interlocking floor mats for garages, playrooms, and gyms

These mats are durable, and they interlock to create a space for blocking just about any type of project. They can be found at hardware stores, auto parts stores, and usually where gym equipment or children's play area equipment is sold. Beware of mats with colorful patterns (letters, numbers, pictures) on them, as these colors could bleed onto your wet fabrics and ruin a project.

Mattress

More than once, we have thrown the sheets off of our bed and used the mattress as a blocking mat. We have found that U-pins, designed for use in upholstery, work best on a mattress, since they are designed to stay in place within the loose filling of a mattress.

Floor with a towel

Have a really big project and can't use the bed? Find a large spot of carpeted floor, lay down a towel or two, and get to pinning! Oh . . . and be sure the block the area off to keep it free of children, cats, dogs, and unsuspecting spouses and roommates.

Sofa cushion with a towel

Are you getting the picture here? Anything you can stick a pin into to hold your fabric in place while drying is fair game for use as a blocking surface. While we favor our interlocking mats, we have used any one of these methods for blocking a project when we needed to get the job done, either in our studio or on the road. As long as the surface is clean, will hold a pin, and is free of family members of all types, you are good to go!

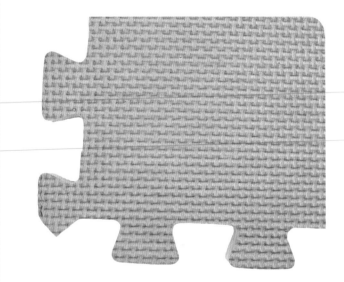

Fingers, Pins, Wires, and String

Fingers

No matter which type of blocking method you use, always start from the center and work your way out, gently shaping the fabric into place. Grabbing the edges and aggressively pulling and yanking will only stretch your stitches out of shape so your finished fabric looks stressed and messy. There are some rare cases where you won't need to do much to shape your fabric—you can simply use your fingers to smooth out your fabric and gently open up the stitches until you are happy with the finished look. In most cases, however, you will notice that the fabric will tend to tighten up again during drying, so you will need to pin the fabric into place.

Pins

There are a bazillion types of pins out there, but we find the ball-headed pins to work just fine, and they come hundreds to a package. Other than the previously mentioned upholstery U-pins for blocking on soft fabric surfaces, any sturdy pin you can get your hands on will work great. The purpose of the pins is to hold the fabric into place, to prevent the stitches from tightening up during drying. You will find pins are especially needed with post stitches, or with fabrics that tend to spring back or curl when dry. Pins are also exactly what you need to use for blocking out points or for opening up features in lace patterns.

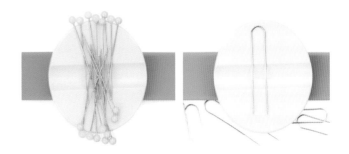

Wires

Blocking wires come in different thicknesses, suitable for blocking everything from delicate lace and curves to heavier fabrics, and provide stability to the edges of your fabric for easier shaping and pinning. Pinning out a large piece of fabric is so much easier when you have wires interlaced through the stitches along the edges of your fabric, rather than using a million pins. Blocking wires keep straight edges true and prevent them from stretching into points where the pins are placed as the fabric dries and contracts.

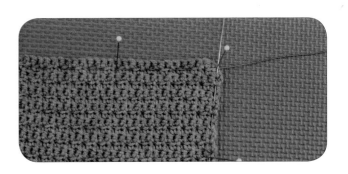

String

Unwaxed kitchen string is the perfect tool for blocking curves.

Here's how:

1. Use a yarn needle to run the string through the stitches along the edges of your fabric.

2. Place pins in blocking surface and wrap one end of the string around one of the pins.

3. Lay the fabric into place, then start pinning at the center point and at two other points along the edge.

4. Place a pin to hold the string at the other end of the curve and hold string across pin.

5. Gently pull on the string, using the pins as guides, until the edge of your fabric follows the curve set out by the other pins.

6. Keep adding pins and gently pulling on the string until the desired curve is set into place. To correct any section of the curve, simply remove a pin, and reset the edge of your curve, then re-pin.

1   2

3   4

5   6

STEP 3: Let Dry

Now that your fabric is shaped correctly, all you need to do is walk away and let the fabric dry. Unless, of course you are impatient, in which case an additional piece of equipment might be called for.

Fan

A fan is a good tool to have if you live in a climate where the humidity does not allow for thorough air drying of your fabrics. Fans are also a good tool for those of us who are impatient and want our fabrics to be dry NOW!

Once the fabric is dry, it should be set. If this is indeed the case, then there should be no spring back or tightening up of the fabric when you remove your pins and wires or string. As we said in the section on swatching (*page 72*), this is the best reason for making a fabric test swatch before you start your project. In the case of some superwash wools, and especially in the case of fabrics made using post stitches, the fabric might tighten up slightly after blocking. If this happens but you are still happy with the finished fabric, then you are good to go. If, however, the fabric tightens up too much and you aren't happy with the stitch definition or the drape of the fabric, you might need to reblock, or to rework the fabric in another yarn or with a different hook size. But since you already figured this out from your fabric test swatch, you are now ready to weave in your ends and put on any finishing touches to your project.

A Special Case: Hang Blocking

Up to this point we have been talking about pinning our fabric to a blocking surface that is lying flat. If, however, you are making a project that consists of large panels of fabric that hang, you should hang block your swatch and fabrics. With larger panels of fabric, the forces of gravity acting upon the weight of the fabric can cause these types of projects to droop and stretch out of shape. Hang blocking should be used for your test swatch when you are making large shawls and wraps, skirts and dresses, and long cardigans and tunics. You need to know right up front if the fabrics for these projects will hold up under wear, or if they will end up a saggy mess. We have heard too many stories about the tunic that becomes a calf-length dress with a sagging neckline and droopy armholes. The good news is that this can be avoided by simply testing your fabric swatch.

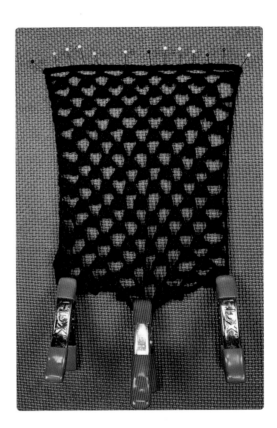

1. Soak, spritz, or steam your swatch, and use blocking wires to stabilize all four sides of your fabric swatch as usual.

2. Pin the top edge of your fabric to a vertical surface such as a wall with a cork board on it, or prop up one of your blocking mats.

3. Add weight to the bottom edge of the swatch. This will require some estimation on your part to determine just how much weight will be involved with the overall piece of fabric. We have used fishing line weights in the past, but our favorite quick fix uses clamps from the hardware store or the office supply store. These clamps come in all sizes. We add them to our swatch, starting with the smallest, then increasing the number of clips until we think the added weight of the clips approximates the weight of the finished piece.

4. Let dry.

Now you are ready to measure your hanging gauge, and you will find out whether your yarn and stitch pattern choices are going to work well together to create a fabric that will hold up to the demands of your finished project.

So now your fabric is clean, dry, and shaped. It's time to weave in those loose ends!

End Cap Finishing Stitch

Sometimes it is the smallest details that make the biggest difference. The End Cap Finishing Stitch is certainly one of those details.

As you finish the last stitch and the instructions read to "fasten off," you will have a length of yarn for weaving in. Make this small detail stitch to make that final stitch a seamless part of the fabric.

(Technique is shown using double crochet stitch.)

Work the last stitch of the row and cut yarn, leaving about a 6"-10"/15–25 cm tail.

1. Draw the last loop still on the hook all the way through the last stitch made, until the tail passes through the stitch. Thread the tail through a yarn needle.
2. Insert the hook from front to back under the two side loops at the bottom of the last stitch made.
3. Gently pull the yarn snug to match the tension of the other stitches.
4. Insert the yarn needle into the center of the stitch where the tail originally came from (last stitch made).
5. Gently pull the yarn snug to create a tidy corner, being careful to match the tension of the last stitch made.
6. Weave in remaining tail.

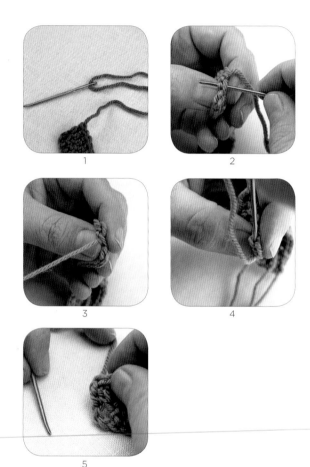

1

2

3

4

5

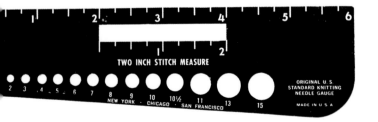

Join with Duplicate Stitch

Joining a round or finishing the top of a sewn seam is where the Duplicate Stitch finishing technique really comes in handy. This finishing stitch creates a duplicate head on the stitch immediately following the last stitch you made before cutting your working yarn, and it makes a nearly invisible join, which is particularly useful along the top of a sock, at the bottom of a top–down hat, or on the final stitches of a motif.

Work the last stitch of the round and cut yarn, leaving about a 6"-10"/15-25 cm tail.

1. Draw the last loop still on the hook all the way through the last stitch made, until the tail passes through the stitch. Thread the tail through a yarn needle.

2. Skip the next stitch (first stitch of round). With the yarn needle, run the end of the tail under both loops of the next stitch and pull the yarn through.

3. Insert the needle back through where the tail originally came from (last stitch made) and behind your work.

4. Snug the yarn to cover the skipped stitch with duplicate stitch just made, matching the tension of the other stitches.

5. Working from the back of the stitches, bring the yarn up through the center of the duplicate stitch just made AND the underlying stitch.

6. Skip the next stitch. Run the end of the tail under both loops of the next stitch and pull the yarn through.

7. Insert the yarn needle back through where the tail originally came from (duplicate stitch AND underlying stitch).

8. Snug the yarn to cover the skipped stitch with duplicate stitch just made, matching the tension of the other stitches.

9. Weave in tail.

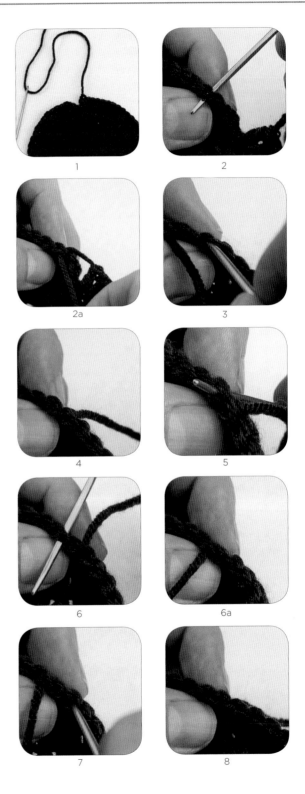

1

2

2a

3

4

5

6

6a

7

8

Weaving In Ends

An important part of weaving in your ends is making sure that they don't come back out again. For this reason, you should leave at least an 8"-10" tail at the beginning and the end of your work and each time you change yarns, to ensure that you have a long enough tail to weave in, and that those tails won't come undone over time. There are a couple of different methods to use when weaving in your ends, and you will probably end up using a little of each, to ensure that your tails are properly and solidly secured.

Follow that Stitch!

Use a yarn needle to follow the natural wraps and loops of the stitches in your fabric to hide and secure your tail.

1. After threading the tail through your yarn needle, use the point of the needle to work down through the centers of the stitches and under the bases of the stitches until the yarn is secured. It is important to go in more than one direction in order to secure the yarn tail more firmly.

yarn needle

Cover as You Go

This is the same method we showed in the Colorwork section, where you carry the unworked yarn along the heads of the row you are working into, covering the yarn tail with the stitches you are making (*see Jacquard, page 200*). We will warn you again that you must be judicious in your use of this method with lighter-weight yarns, or with certain stitch patterns, where working over the tail and the previous row of stitches could cause a noticeable thickening of the fabric, or the tail could show through.

Before You Sew

Before you set needle or hook to task joining your fabric panels, use locking stitch markers or pins to secure the seams you are about to sew. This will stabilize the fabric to make seaming easier, and will ensure that you are staying on track and lining up your rows by giving you guide points along the seams. If you are working on a garment, you can place the pinned-together piece on a dress form for appraisal, or try it on to see if there are any last-minute alterations you need to make before you sew your seams.

Straight Seams

Pinning is easy in the case of straight seams, because all you do is place pins along the seam to match the rows of the two pieces. We cannot stress enough how important this is. If you are using the same stitch pattern and the same yarn on two seamed panels of fabric, the rows of your stitches must match up exactly or your finished piece will have jogs between the panels and will look unprofessional and generally wonky.

Seaming Two Different Fabrics

If you are sewing two pieces of fabric that have been made from different yarns or different stitch patterns, you still need to ensure that you have an even seam. This process is similar to setting in a sleeve or a collar.

1. Lay the two pieces side by side, with WS facing you.

2. Line up the two ends and use locking stitch markers or pins to secure the top and bottom edges of your fabric.

3. Pin the middle of the two fabric panels together.

4. Pin at two points halfway between the first three pins.

5. Continue pinning at points halfway between each set of pins until the panels are pinned together securely along the seam.

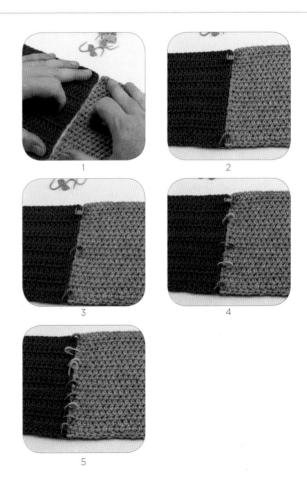

Curved or Non-Linear Seams

There are times when you will need to sew a collar or a sleeve cap into a place where the lines are not all straight. In these cases, you will use the same technique used for seaming two different fabrics to ensure a smooth, even seam.

Setting in a Sleeve

With WS facing:

Fold sleeve in half lengthwise.

1. Pin center of sleeve (at fold) to shoulder seam.
2. Pin bottom corners of sleeve to underarm seam.
3. Pin sleeve to armhole at points halfway between the first three pins.
4. Continue pinning at points halfway between each set of pins until the sleeves are pinned securely in place around the armhole.

After all pins are secured, use Locking Mattress Stitch (*see page 257*) to sew the sleeve in place.

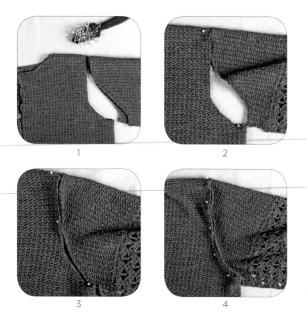

Setting in a Collar

With WS facing:

1. Fold collar in half from end to end.
2. Pin center of collar (at fold) to center back neckline.
3. Pin bottom corners of collar to bottom edges of garment.
4. Pin collar to fronts and neckline at points halfway between the first three pins.
5. Continue pinning at points halfway between each set of pins until the collar is pinned securely in place around the fronts and neckline.

After all pins are secured, use the Locking Mattress Stitch (*see page 257*) to sew the collar in place.

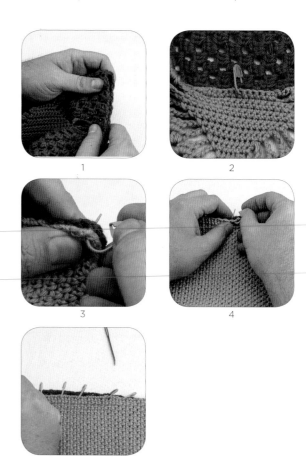

SEAMS OR NO SEAMS?

While making garments with no seams is a perfectly acceptable method of construction, just like any other stitch or technique we have talked about so far in this book, seamless construction is not appropriate for every garment and every fabric.

As we've said before, you must evaluate your project and make the choice as to which techniques to use based on the fabric you need for your project.

Keep in mind that seams are put into garments for support. While a top-down seamless construction might be fine for some garments and some fabrics, others need the added support of seams to ensure that panels of fabric don't sag and stretch out of shape in the course of normal wear.

Seams and Joins

Now that you have the components of your project stitched and blocked, the ends are woven in, and the seams are pinned, you are ready to start sewing them together!

There are many ways to join panels of crochet fabric together, depending on whether you want your seam to be visible and decorative or invisible with a seamless look. We will give you both types of seams here so you are well equipped and ready to experiment to see which method works best for your fabric and your project.

Regardless of whether you choose to make a hand-sewn seam, or if you use a joining stitch with your hook, you need to be mindful of maintaining the tension in your stitches and the drape of your overall fabric. Make your seam too tight, and the fabric will gather and bunch up; too loose and the seam will have gaps and sag. For this reason, it is important that you check your seams as you are making them, to ensure that you are keeping this tension correct. Don't be afraid to take out a few stitches of your seam if you need to adjust it. It is definitely worth taking the time to make a beautiful seam that just melts into your finished project without being noticed. Remember what we said earlier: the biggest compliment a crocheter can receive about their finishing is no compliment at all.

To practice your seams, start by making two swatches in the same stitch, with the same number of rows. After you have your seaming techniques down, practice seaming swatches with different stitches but the same length, and seaming the sides of swatches to the tops of swatches of the same length. This will prepare you for any seaming situations you might come up against in your future projects, or you can always reference this book later when you have a seaming conundrum.

Sewn Seams

These are hand-sewn seams using a yarn or tapestry needle and a length of the same yarn you crocheted your project with.

Locking Mattress Stitch

The Locking Mattress Stitch is, by far, the most secure of all the hand-sewn seams you can use. Because it uses only one loop from each side of the panels you are sewing together, the Locking Mattress Stitch seam is completely invisible from the front side, and leaves only a trace of a seam on the inside of the fabric. The "locking" part of this technique is the key. When we teach the Locking Mattress Stitch in our live classes, the chant of "up one, back where you came from, up one, back where you came from" can be heard as students learn and work this seam.

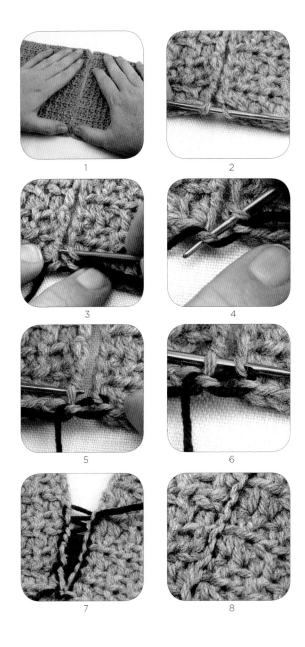

1. Begin by laying work with RS down and edges to be sewn side by side. Stitches will be worked through the top loop only of each side.

2. Insert the needle from left to right through the first stitches of both panels at the bottom of your work to begin joining the two panels.

3. Moving up the seam, insert the needle from right to left through the next loop on the right pane . . . (up one).

4. Continue by inse.rting the needle through the last loop worked of the left panel (back where you came from).

5. Again moving up the seam, insert the needle from left to right through the next loop on the left panel . . . (up one).

6. . . . and continue by inserting the needle through the last loop worked of the right panel (back where you came from).

7. Repeat Steps 3–6 for several rows.

8. Gently pull the yarn snug as you go to close the seam, being careful to match the fabric gauge so as to not create a puckered seam.

9. The photo on the opposite page is what your seam should look like from the front side of the fabric.

10. Weave in ends.

Alternate Hold Locking Mattress Stitch

If working this seam with the pieces lying side by side seems awkward to you, you can try picking them up and holding them with RS together.

1. Hold the two pieces with RS together and your index finger separating the seam to be sewn and work Locking Mattress Stitch as usual, being mindful to run needle through the outside stitches of your seams, as follows: moving up the seam, insert the needle from one side to the other, picking up only the outside loops (up one). Go back where you came from, working your needle under only the outside loops.

2. Continue working Locking Mattress Stitch as usual. When you are finished, you should see the same beautiful seam on the front side of the fabric.

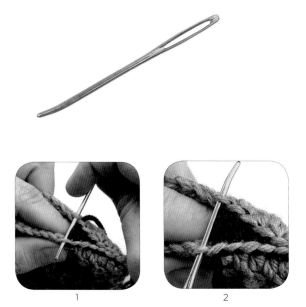

1   2

Other Hand-Sewn Stitches

There are many hand sewing stitches, some decorative and some invisible, that you can use to finish off your projects. Here we offer you the three most commonly used hand sewing stitches appropriate for crochet fabrics.

Running Stitch

The Running Stitch is a visible stitch that works well as a temporary hold for fabric, or for making a gather or ruching. This stitch comes in handy for initially testing placement when sewing on pockets or patches, and when setting in a zipper.

1. Insert threaded needle from back to front of the fabric layers.

2. Following a straight line, insert the needle from front to back into the fabric layers, ¼" to ½" from your first stitch.

3. Pull the yarn snug.

4. Insert the needle from back to front of the fabric layers, the same distance from the second stitch as the first (¼" to ½").

5. Pull the yarn snug, be careful not to bunch or gather your fabric.

6. Repeat Steps 2–5 for the length of the seam.

1   2

3   4

5   6

Back Stitch

The Back Stitch is also a visible stitch and can be used interchangeably with the Running Stitch. The Back Stitch is a more secure stitch, and is used for adding support to seams that are showing signs of drooping, and for the final stage of sewing on patches or pockets and setting in zippers.

1. Insert threaded needle from back to front of the fabric layers.

2. Following a straight line, insert the needle from front to back into the fabric layers, ¼" to ½" from your first stitch, and pull the yarn snug.

3. Insert the needle from back to front of the fabric layers, the same distance from the second stitch as the first (¼" to ½") and pull the yarn snug, being careful not to bunch or gather your fabric.

4. Working backward along your sewing line, insert your needle from front to back of the fabric layers, in the same place where your last stitch went into the fabric.

5. Pull the yarn snug, be careful not to bunch or gather your fabric .

6. Repeat Steps 3–5 for the length of the seam.

Whip Stitch

The Whip Stitch is invisible when worked through single loops on the WS of the fabric. This stitch can be used when sewing seams, but is not as secure as the Locking Mattress Stitch, and makes a bulkier seam overall.

1. Hold the two pieces with RS together and insert the needle from back to front and through adjoining loops on both layers of fabric.

2. Following the seam, insert the needle again from back to front and through adjoining loops.

3. Repeat Step 2 for the length of the seam.

NOTE: the distance you move the needle forward along the seam to make this next stitch will depend on the fabric for your project—the key is to find the next set of loops along the seam you are sewing. If you skip loops, you might end up with a hole in your seam.

Head-to-Head Seam

The Head-to-Head Seam is a zigzag stitch in which the needle is inserted under the inside loops that make up the heads of the stitches (the bump) rather than the outside loops (*see Parts of a Stitch, page 41*). This makes the seam invisible from either side of the fabric, and is ideal for projects in which both sides or your work will show. This seaming technique is ideal for joining motifs in which the outside round consists entirely of the heads of stitches, and is most easily worked using a bent or curved needle.

1. Hold the two motifs with sides facing each other and the adjacent heads of the stitches facing you.

2. Insert the needle into the head and under the bump of the first stitch on the first motif and pull through.

3. Insert the needle into the head and under the bump of the corresponding first stitch of the second motif and pull through.

4. Going to the next unworked stitch on the first motif, insert the needle into the head and under the bump of that stitch and pull through.

5. Working across to the next unworked stitch on the second motif, insert the needle into the head and under the bump of that stitch and pull through.

6. Repeat Steps 4–5 for the length of the seam, gently pulling the yarn snug as you go to close the seam, being careful to match the fabric gauge so as to not create a puckered seam.

1

2

3

4

5

6

Hooked Seams

Simply put, these seams are made using your hook rather than a needle. Hooked seams add one more layer of stitches to your work, so they are more bulky and more visible than hand-sewn seams. These seams are more appropriate for joining afghan pieces, rugs, and other home decor pieces, rather than for joining garments or projects using lightweight yarns. That said, if you have a garment for which you want a raised decorative seam, one of these might be appropriate to use.

Slip Stitch Seam

1. Hold the two pieces of fabric with RS together.
2. Insert hook through adjoining stitches. Shown here, we are working through only one loop from each side.
3. Yarn over and draw through both layers of fabric and loop on hook.
4. Repeat Steps 2–3 for the length of the seam.

Single Crochet Seam

1. Hold both pieces of fabric with RS together.
2. Insert hook through adjoining stitches. Shown here, we are working through only one loop from each side.
3. Yarn over and draw through both layers of fabric (2 loops on hook).
4. Yarn over and draw through both loops on hook.
5. Repeat Steps 2–4 for the length of the seam.

Join-As-You-Go Seams

As the name implies, Join-As-You-Go seams are made as you are working your fabric, rather than after the fabric panels are made. This gives you a finished join without getting out a needle, and there are no ends to weave in.

Chain Joins

Chain Joins work very well for joining motifs by connecting adjoining chain stitches. They are also great for attaching the chain section of a motif or lace panel to the stitches of another panel of lace or solid fabric. As long as you can insert your hook into a panel of fabric, these joins will work perfectly.

> **Joining Chain**
> Insert hook from front to back through the corresponding chain space or stitch of a neighboring motif or fabric panel, yo and draw up a through the motif or fabric panel AND the lp on hook.

Chain 3 Join

> Chain 3 join (ch-3 join): Ch 1; keeping yarn on hook and holding yarn to back of work, insert hook into corresponding ch-3 sp, work sl st in corresponding ch-3 sp, ch 1.

1. Chain 1; keep yarn on hook and hold yarn to back of work.
2. Insert hook in corresponding chain 3 space.
3. Yarn over and draw through chain 3 space AND loop on hook.
4. Chain 1.

In order for your Chain Joins to be balanced, you will always work them with an odd number of stitches. The important point to remember is that the middle chain is the joining chain that is worked into the adjacent chain, chain space, or stitch. This same technique works the same for chain 5 joins, chain 7 joins, etc.

1

2

3

4

5

Top-Linked Stitches

Top-Linked stitches can be used anywhere you are joining the tops of the stitches to any other fabric. They work equally well for motifs or for flat fabrics. The key feature of this technique is that you are joining the head of the stitch you are making to an adjacent chain, chain space, or stitch. Top-Linked joins can be made with any height of stitch—as long as it has a head to use to make the join, you are good to go!

Top-Linked Double Crochet:

Remove loop from hook, insert hook from front to back through corresponding stitch of second fabric panel, return loop to hook, yo, insert hook in indicated stitch of first fabric panel, yo and draw up a loop, yo and draw through 2 loops on hook, yo and draw through 2 loops on hook and through stitch of second fabric panel.

1. Remove loop from hook.
2. Insert hook from front to back through the corresponding stitch of the second fabric panel.
3. Return loop to hook.
4. Yarn over and insert hook into the next stitch of the first fabric panel.
5. Yarn over and draw up a loop.
6. Yarn over and draw through 2 loops on hook.
7. Yarn over and draw through 2 loops on hook AND through the stitch of the second fabric panel.
8. Repeat Steps 1–7 along stitches to be joined.

This type of join creates a seam that can definitely be seen on one side of the work but is hardly noticeable on the other. In fact, the resulting seam has a twist to it, where the loop is removed and placed under the head of the stitch it is joined to.

NOTE: This same join can be worked without the first step of removing the loop from the hook. Try this technique again, working only Steps 2–6. The result is a thicker seam, with the loop from the first panel sitting on top of the stitch head from the second panel.

Finally, try this join again, working the head of your double crochet into the chain space of one of your swatches, and without first removing the loop from your hook. This creates a beautiful join that is similar to a Chain Join.

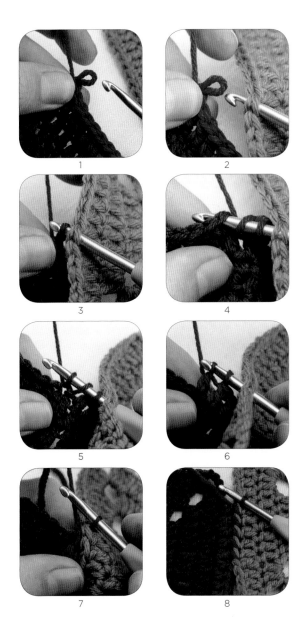

1 2

3 4

5 6

7 8

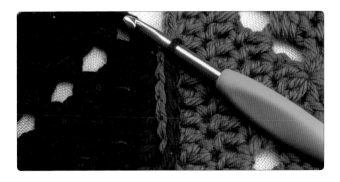

Buttonholes

Buttons and similar closures such as toggles come in a vast array of shapes and sizes. We have spent large portions of our creative time staring at different buttons and toggles, trying to decide which one is the perfect one for our designs. We expect no less of a creative dilemma from you. Once you have settled on the style, size, shape, and color of button that perfectly complements your project, all that's left is to make sure it will fit through the buttonhole. Here we offer a few of our favorite buttonholes for you to choose from.

Extending Foundation Stitches Buttonhole

This technique uses extending foundation stitches (*page 111*) to create a buttonhole. The result is a nearly invisible hole that is resistant to sagging and pulling. It can be made with any one of the extending foundation stitches, but here we will demonstrate with the Ext-Fsc stitch.

Note: You can work larger or smaller buttonholes and use any foundation stitch. The principle is to work the number of extending foundation stitches needed, skip the same number of stitches, then rejoin by working into the next stitch as you finish the last extending foundation stitch.

3-Stitch Buttonhole: Make 2 Ext-Fsc, insert hook under 2 lps of last "chain" made, yo and draw up a lp, sk next 3 sts, insert hook into next st, yo and draw up a lp through st AND 1 lp on hook, yo and draw through 2 lps on hook.

4-Stitch Buttonhole: Make 3 Ext-Fsc, insert hook under 2 lps of last "chain" made, yo and draw up a lp, sk next 4 sts, insert hook into next st, yo and draw up a lp through st AND 1 lp on hook, yo and draw through 2 lps on hook.

Here is the breakdown for the 4-Stitch Buttonhole using extending foundation stitches:

1. Make 3 Ext-Fsc, insert hook under 2 loops of last "chain" made, yarn over and draw up a loop.
2. Skip next 4 stitches and insert hook into the next stitch.
3. Yarn over and draw up a loop through the stitch AND 1 loop on hook.
4. Yarn over and draw through 2 loops on hook.

1

2

3

4

finished buttonhole

nearly invisible

Chain and Stitch Back Buttonhole

The Chain and Stitch Back technique for making buttonholes is worked on the outside edge of your fabric and makes the buttonhole in one row. This technique can be worked with any height of stitch, but here we will demonstrate with a half double crochet. The key here is the sc stitches that are worked over the chains.

> **Chain and Stitch Back Buttonhole:** Hdc in each of next 6 sts (6 Buttonhole Hdc made), ch 5, remove lp from hook, insert hook from front to back into head of first Buttonhole Hdc made, place lp back on hook and draw through hdc, sc 7 times in ch-5 sp, sl st in head of sixth Buttonhole Hdc.

1. Hdc in each of next 6 stitches (6 Buttonhole Hdc made), chain 5.
2. Remove loop from hook.
3. Insert hook from front to back into head of first Buttonhole Hdc made.
4. Place loop back on hook.
5. Draw loop through hdc.
6. Sc 7 times in chain 5 space.
7. Slip stitch in head of sixth Buttonhole Hdc.

1

2

3

4

5

6

7

Button Loops

A button loop is a simple loop that is worked either as a chain or as a chain with single crochet stitches worked over it to reinforce the loop and keep it from stretching out with use. These loops can be made in the edge of your fabric or can be set in from the edge, to overlap the buttoned fabric slightly.

You can make these loops from any number of chains and single crochet stitches, to accommodate any button, toggle, or similar closure. The key is to have a large enough opening so you can get your button through the loop without the loop slipping off while the garment is being worn. For demonstration purposes, we are working our reinforced button loop with eight chains, then working ten single crochet stitches to fill the chain.

Chain Button Loop

1. Join yarn in the stitch where you want to place the button loop.

2. Make enough chain stitches to fit over your button.

3. Join chain with slip stitch to next stitch if the loop is to be made on the edge of the fabric, or in the same stitch as the original yarn join if the loop is to be inset from the edge.

1

:2

3

Reinforced Button Loop

1. Work Steps 1–3 of Chain Button Loop, making 8 chain stitches.

2. Turn and work 10 single crochet stitches in chain 8 space.

3. Slip stitch in the base of the chain loop.

1

2

3

4

Sewing On Buttons

Buttons, whether practical or decorative, are just one option for closures you can add to your projects. The technique for sewing on a button is universal and can be applied to any closure you wish to add to your crochet projects.

1. Place button in desired location.
2. Working from back to front, insert needle through fabric and hole of button.
3. Working from front to back, insert needle through second hole in button and through fabric.
4. Repeat Steps 2–3 until button is secured to fabric.
5. If your button has more than 2 holes, repeat Steps 2–4 through remaining holes.
6. Secure ends of thread or yarn by running needle under loops on back of fabric and tie off.

Zippers

Zippers add a dimension of creativity and security to your projects that other closures cannot offer. The process of setting in a zipper is no more complicated than setting in a sleeve or a collar. As long as you take it step by step and practice at least once on your swatches, you will be a pro in no time.

Setting in a Zipper

1. First, with RS of garment facing, weave in two blocking wires on each side of the garment front —one wire woven along the first set of stitches closest to the edge, the other wire woven about 1" away.

2. Next, position the zipper under the opening in the front of the garment. Take care to center the zipper in the opening.

3. Pin first side of the zipper tape into place by pinning between the blocking wires. Your plexiglass or rotary mat will really help here to prevent accidentally pinning and sewing through to the back of the garment. Check that the zipper will open and close without catching the edges of your garment.

4. Leaving the first side blocking wires in, pin the second side of the zipper tape into place; again pinning between the blocking wires. Be sure to use your plexiglass or rotary mat as a guide. Stop and check occasionally that your pinning creates a straight zipper.

5. On the first side of your zipper: Backstitch the zipper from the bottom edge to the top of the zipper catching one or two stitches in each pass. Follow the stitch pattern closely to make your sewing as invisible as possible. You can also use a sewing machine to sew in your zipper. Utilizing a zipper foot, SLOWLY sew on the zipper. Make sure the zipper tape, not your fabric, is in contact with the feed dogs of your machine. Take your time.

6. Unzip the zipper and sew the second side as you did the first side. Again, check here to ensure that your fabric is straight and you can open and close the zipper with ease.

NOTE: Place a thin piece of plexiglass, a quilting ruler, or a self-healing cutting mat inside the garment to protect from pinning through the back of the garment.

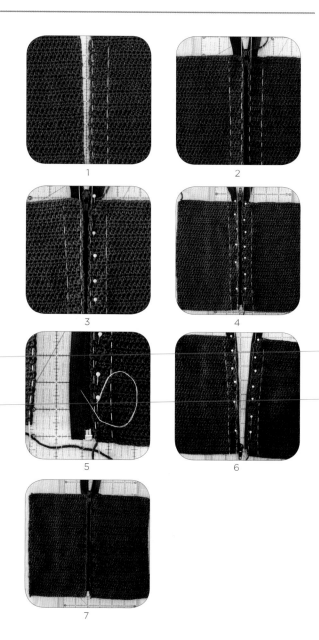

Trimming a Zipper Length

The problem of not being able to find the proper length of zipper for your project is as common as it is frustrating. By using this tutorial, you can buy any zipper of any length (even zipper by the foot) and cut it down to size.

1. First, purchase a zipper that is as close to your required length as possible.

2. Next, measure your zipper from the base up and mark the length you want it to be.

3. Add one inch to that measurement for a second mark.

4. Open your zipper, making sure the separating mechanism is at the bottom.

5. Cut the zipper at the second mark.

6. Using pliers or kitchen shears remove the teeth from each side of the zipper tape down to your first mark . . . this gives you 1 inch of fabric at the top of your zipper to fold the 1 inch of fabric to the back of your zipper and sew it down.

7. Once you have cut your zipper to size, a new zipper stop needs to be installed on both sides of the zipper tape. The stop is the metal or plastic tab at the top of the zipper that keeps the separating mechanism from coming off the top.

   The simplest way to do this is to whip stitch your own stop between two of the top teeth on each side of the zipper tape. Using a sewing needle and thread similarly colored to your zipper, insert your needle from the back of tape through the middle of the zipper tape between one of the last two teeth.

   Sew around the edge of the tape to back side and insert your needle again through the same hole. Continue to sew through this same hole 8–10 times until a thick ridge fully fills the space between the two zipper teeth.

   Secure your sting and cut. Your newly stitched stop should be thick enough to keep the separating mechanism from sliding off the top of your cut zipper.

8. Remember to do this to each side of the zipper tape.

NOTE: Rather than sewing a stop, another option is to purchase a new stop. Zipper repair kits which include new stops are available at most sewing centers. Simply crimp the metal stop between the top two zipper teeth of each side of the zipper tape. Now just sew in your zipper by hand or by machine as if it were always that length. You can now make zippers of any length! Nifty eh?

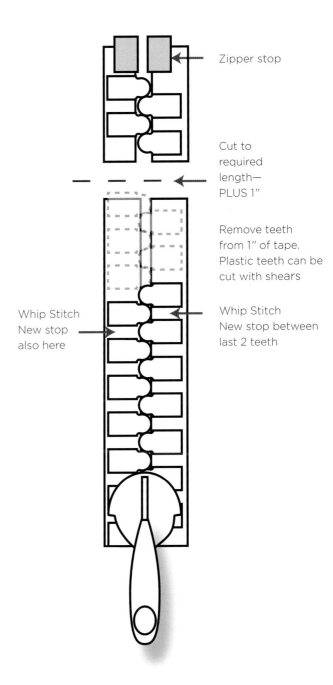

Zipper stop

Cut to required length— PLUS 1"

Remove teeth from 1" of tape. Plastic teeth can be cut with shears

Whip Stitch New stop between last 2 teeth

Whip Stitch New stop also here

THE PROJECTS

My First Cardi

My First Cardi features easy-to-follow instructions, with minimal shaping from the cuffs to the tops of the sleeves. That's it . . . no other shaping! After making your fabric panels, all that's left is simple construction: sewing straight seams on the sides and shoulders, then setting the straight-edged sleeves into the armholes.

You'll love being able to show off your first handmade crochet garment project, and, once you develop into a crochet master, you will love making this easy project that you can whip up in no time.

SKILLS USED

Knotless Starting Chain (*see page 79*)
Foundation Single Crochet (*see page 104*)
Increases (*see page 139*)

Blocking (*see page 240*)
Locking Mattress Stitch (*see page 257*)
Setting in a Sleeve (*see page 254*)

SKILL LEVEL

EASY

SIZES   S (M, L, XL, 2X, 3X, 4X, 5X)
Sample shown in size Medium

FINISHED MEASUREMENTS

To Fit Bust: 32.5 (36, 40, 44, 48.5, 52.5, 56.5, 60.5)"/82.5 (91.5, 101.5, 111.75, 123.25, 133.25, 143.5, 153.75) cm

Finished Bust: 36.5 (40, 44, 48, 52.5, 56.5, 60.5, 64.5)"/92.75 (101.5, 111.75, 122, 133.25, 143.5, 153.75, 163.75) cm

Finished Length from Shoulder: 28 (28, 28, 29, 29, 29, 30, 30)"/71 (71, 71, 73.75, 73.75, 73.75, 76.25, 76.25) cm

MATERIALS AND TOOLS

Sample uses Valley Yarns Valley Superwash Worsted (100% Extra Fine Merino; 1.75 ounces/50g = 97 yards/88.75 m): 21 (22, 24, 26, 28, 29, 32, 33) balls in color Periwinkle #342—2037 (2134, 2328, 2522, 2716, 2813, 3104, 3201) yards/1863.75 (1952.5, 2130, 2307.5, 2485, 2573.75, 2840, 2928.75) m of medium weight yarn

MEDIUM

Crochet hook: 5.00mm (size H-8) or size to obtain gauge

Yarn needle

BLOCKED GAUGES

Single crochet linen stitch: 5.125 sts = 1"/2.5 cm; 41 sts = 8"/20.25 cm; 4.57 rows = 1"/2.5 cm; 32 rows = 7"/17.75 cm

Single crochet ribbing: 4.57 sts = 1"/2.5 cm; 32 sts = 7"/17.75 cm; 5.33 rows = 1"/2.5 cm; 33 rows = 6"/15.25 cm

STITCH GUIDE

Foundation single crochet (Fsc): Ch 2, insert hook into second ch from hook, yo and draw up a lp, yo and draw through 1 lp (first "chain" made), yo and draw through 2 lps on hook (first Fsc made), *insert hook under 2 lps of the "chain" just made, yo and draw up a lp, yo and draw through 1 lp ("chain" made), yo and draw through 2 lps on hook (Fsc made); rep from * for indicated number of foundation sts.

NOTES

▶ When instructed to work in a pattern "as established," work the next row of pattern and ensure that the stitches line up as in previous rows. For the stacked single crochet linen stitch, that means working a sc into every sc and working a ch-1 over every ch-1.

▶ After you have worked increases so there are two additional stitches at the beginning and end of every row, you can then re-establish the stacked single crochet linen stitch by working a ch-1 over the additional sc after the first stitch and before the last stitch of the row.

PATTERN STITCHES

Stacked single crochet linen stitch (stacked sc linen st) (worked over an odd number of sts)

Row 1: Ch 1, sc in first st, *ch 1, sk next st, sc in next st; rep from * to end of row, turn.

Row 2: Ch 1, sc in first st, *ch 1, sk next ch-1 sp, sc in next st; rep from * to end of row, turn. Rep Row 2 for pattern stitch.

Swatch: 41 sts and 32 rows (+ 1 Fsc row)

Foundation Row: Work 41 Fsc, turn.

Row 1: Work Row 1 of stacked sc linen st.

Rows 2–32: Rep Row 2 of stacked sc linen st. Fasten off.

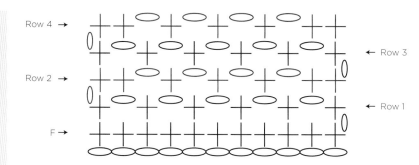

sc linen stitch chart

Single crochet ribbing (sc ribbing) worked over any multiple of sts)

Row 1: Ch 1, sc in first st, sc tbl in next st and in each st to last st, sc in last st, turn. Rep Row 1 for pattern stitch.

Swatch: 32 sts and 32 rows (+ 1 Fsc row)

Foundation Row: Work 32 Fsc, turn.

Rows 1–32: Rep Row 1 of sc ribbing. Fasten off.

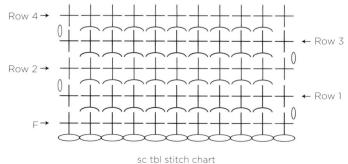

sc tbl stitch chart

INSTRUCTIONS

Back Panel

Foundation Row: Work 93 (103, 113, 123, 135, 145, 155, 165) Fsc, turn.

Rows 1–128 (128, 128, 133, 133, 133, 137, 137): Work in stacked sc linen st.

Cut yarn, leaving tail for weaving in; pull tail through last st made; weave in tail using End Cap Finishing Stitch.

Front Panel (make 2)

Foundation Row: Work 31 (35, 37, 41, 45, 49, 51, 55) Fsc, turn.

Rows 1–128 (128, 128, 133, 133, 133, 137, 137): Work in stacked sc linen st.

Cut yarn, leaving tail for weaving in; pull tail through last st made; weave in tail using End Cap Finishing Stitch.

Sleeve (make 2)

Foundation Row: Work 47 (49, 51, 51, 55, 55, 57, 57) Fsc, turn.

Rows 1–10: Work in stacked sc linen st.

Rows 11–14 (14, 13, 13, 12, 12, 12, 12): Work in stacked sc linen st.

Row 15 (15, 14, 14, 13, 13, 13, 13): Ch 1, sc in first st, sc 2 times in next st, work in stacked sc linen st as established to last 2 sts, sc 2 times in next st, sc in last st, turn – 49 (51, 53, 53, 57, 57, 59, 59) sts.

Sizes M (L, 1X, 2X, 3X, 4X, 5X)

Rows 16 (15, 15, 14, 14, 14, 14)–45 (30, 90, 16, 34, 43, 67): Rep last 5 (4, 4, 3, 3, 3, 3) rows 6 (4, 19, 1, 7, 10, 18) more times – 63 (61, 91, 59, 71, 79, 95) sts.

All Sizes

Rows 16 (46, 31, 91, 17, 35, 44, 68)–20 (50, 34, 94, 19, 37, 46, 70): Work in stacked sc linen st.

Row 21 (51, 35, 95, 20, 38, 47, 71): Ch 1, sc in first st, sc 2 times in next st, work in stacked sc linen st as established to last 2 sts, sc 2 times in next st, sc in last st, turn – 51 (65, 63, 93, 61, 73, 81, 97) sts.

Sizes S (M, L, 2X, 3X, 4X, 5X)

Rows 22 (52, 36, 21, 39, 48)–93 (93, 95, 100, 102, 107, 107): Rep last 6 (6, 5, 4, 4, 4, 4) rows 12 (7, 12, 20, 16, 15, 9) more times – 75 (79, 87, 93, 101, 105, 111, 115) sts.

All Sizes

Rows 94 (94, 96, 96, 101, 103, 108, 108)–103 (103, 105, 105, 110, 112, 117, 117): Work in stacked sc linen st without shaping.

Cut yarn, leaving tail for weaving in; pull tail through last st made; weave in tail using End Cap Finishing Stitch.

Collar

Foundation Row: Work 41 (41, 43, 43, 43, 46, 46, 46) Fsc, turn.

Rows 1–341 (346, 350, 364, 370, 372, 385, 385): Work in sc ribbing.

Cut yarn, leaving tail for weaving in; pull tail through last st made; weave in tail using End Cap Finishing Stitch.

FINISHING

Block all pieces to measurements in schematic.

Attach Front Panels to Back Panel:

1. Line up outside corners of front panels to outside corners of back panel and sew stitch for stitch using Locking Mattress Stitch.

2. Fold Sleeves in half lengthwise. Matching fold to shoulder seam, sew top of Sleeves to Front and Back. Sew sleeve seams.

3. Sew side body seams.

4. Fold Collar in half and pin fold to center back neckline. Set Collar evenly in to front panels and sew into place.

5. Gently steam block seams if needed.

My First Cardi Schematic

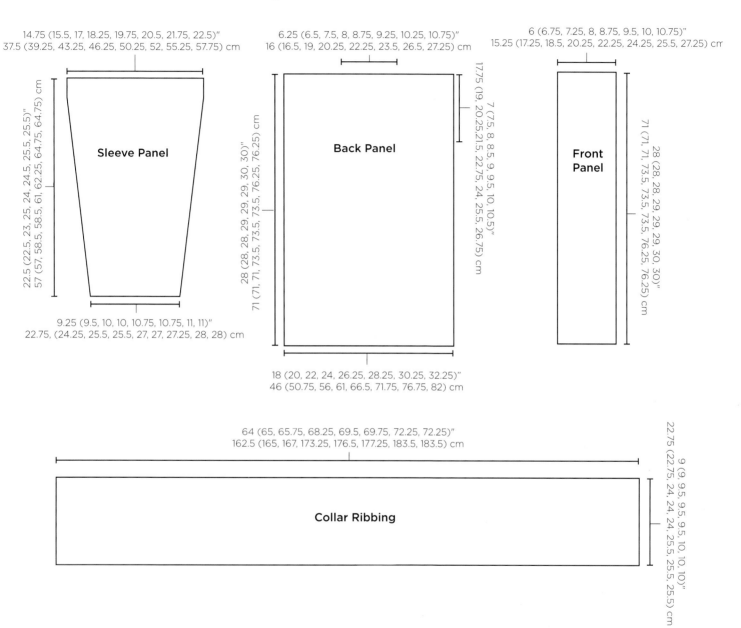

Sleeve Panel

14.75 (15.5, 17, 18.25, 19.75, 20.5, 21.75, 22.5)"
37.5 (39.25, 43.25, 46.25, 50.25, 52, 55.25, 57.75) cm

22.5 (22.5, 23, 25, 24, 24.5, 25.5, 25.5)"
57 (57, 58.5, 58.5, 61, 62.25, 64.75, 64.75) cm

9.25 (9.5, 10, 10, 10.75, 10.75, 11, 11)"
22.75, (24.25, 25.5, 25.5, 27, 27, 27.25, 28, 28) cm

Back Panel

6.25 (6.5, 7.5, 8, 8.75, 9.25, 10.25, 10.75)"
16 (16.5, 19, 20.25, 22.25, 23.5, 26.5, 27.25) cm

17.75 (19, 20.25,21.5, 22.75, 24, 25.5, 26.75) cm
7 (7.5, 8, 8.5, 9, 9.5, 10, 10.5)"

28 (28, 28, 29, 29, 29, 30, 30)"
71 (71, 71, 73.5, 73.5, 73.5, 76.25, 76.25) cm

18 (20, 22, 24, 26.25, 28.25, 30.25, 32.25)"
46 (50.75, 56, 61, 66.5, 71.75, 76.75, 82) cm

Front Panel

6 (6.75, 7.25, 8, 8.75, 9.5, 10, 10.75)"
15.25 (17.25, 18.5, 20.25, 22.25, 24.25, 25.5, 27.25) cm

28 (28, 28, 29, 29, 29, 30, 30)"
71 (71, 71, 73.5, 73.5, 73.5, 76.25, 76.25) cm

Collar Ribbing

64 (65, 65.75, 68.25, 69.5, 69.75, 72.25, 72.25)"
162.5 (165, 167, 173.25, 176.5, 177.25, 183.5, 183.5) cm

9 (9, 9.5, 9.5, 9.5, 10, 10, 10)"
22.75 (22.75, 24, 24, 24, 25.5, 25.5, 25.5) cm

Colorwork Throw

This project combines a simple single crochet stitch pattern with an easy colorwork technique to create a stunning graphic throw that you will be proud to display in your home. After making your squares, follow our assembly diagram to reproduce our pattern or rearrange the blocks to make your own unique design. Personalize your project to fit your personal style by mixing and matching your favorite colors for either a bold, striking visual display or a subtle, calming home décor piece. Up your decorating game by adding blocks to make a larger afghan, or pick just one section of the assembly diagram and make matching pillows. We give you the framework, you make it your own!

SKILLS USED

Foundation Chain (*see page 81*)	Blocking (*see page 240*)
Single Crochet (*see page 84*)	End Cap Finishing Stitch (*see page 250*)
Changing Yarn at the End of a Row (*see page 159*)	Locking Mattress Stitch (*see page 257*)
Changing Yarn in the Middle of a Row (*see page 160*)	Weaving in Ends (*see page 252*)

SKILL LEVEL

EASY

SIZES One Size

FINISHED MEASUREMENTS

48" x 48"/122 x 122 cm

MATERIALS AND TOOLS

Sample uses Lion Brand Wool-Ease (80% Acrylic, 20% Wool; 3 ounces/85g = 197 yards/180 m): 2 balls in color Cranberry (color A) #620-138—394 yards/360 m; 5 balls in color Fisherman (color B) #620-099—985 yards/900 m; 7 balls in color Eggplant (color C) #620-167—1379 yards/1260 m of medium-weight yarn

Crochet hook: 5.00mm (size H-8) or size to obtain gauge

Yarn needle

BLOCKED GAUGE

One block: 4 sts = 1"/2.5 cm; 24 sts = 6"/15.25 cm;
4.5 rows = 1"/2.5 cm; 27 rows = 6"/15.25 cm

Key

- ■ Color A
- □ Color B
- ■ Color C

NOTES

▶ Throw is made of 64 individual blocks that are then sewn together to finished dimensions.

INSTRUCTIONS

Block (make 64)

Following colorwork chart, make block as follows:

Row 1 (RS): Ch 25, sc in second ch from hook and in each ch to end of row, turn – 24 sts.

Rows 2–27: Ch 1, sc in first st and in each st to end of row, turn.

Cut yarn, leaving tail for weaving in; pull tail through last st made; weave in tail using End Cap Finishing Stitch.

FINISHING

Block individual blocks to finished dimensions.

Sew blocks together using Locking Mattress Stitch and following assembly diagram.

Gently steam block seams if needed.

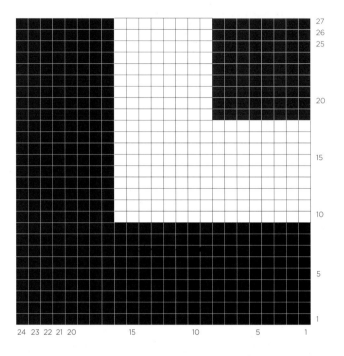

STITCH ON! ➤

Take this project to the next level by making the blocks from a lighter or heavier weight yarn for a dramatically different result!

assembly diagram

finished piece

Rectangle Wrap Vest

It doesn't get much easier than this! Once you learn your first stitches—sc, hdc, dc, and tr—you can put them together in this unique double wave stitch pattern to create a gorgeous fabric for this wrap vest. Side-to-side construction means you can customize the front drape by making more or fewer rows before the armholes. Make more front rows for a more dramatic drape front or make fewer rows for a more subdued effect. The secret (but most FAB part of this project) is that it can be worn with the longer section on top for a cozy wrap look or with the shorter section on top for a fashionable drape-front style. It's up to you!

SKILLS USED

Knotless Starting Chain (*see page 79*)

Foundation Single Crochet (*see page 104*)

Linked First Treble Crochet (*see page 99*)

Foundation Stitches for Extending Rows (*see page 111*)

Blocking (*see page 240*)

End Cap Finishing Stitch (*see page 250*)

SKILL LEVEL

EASY

SIZES S (M, L, XL, 2X, 3X, 4X, 5X)

Sample shown in size Medium

FINISHED MEASUREMENTS

To Fit Bust: 32 (36, 40, 44, 48, 52, 56, 60)"/81.28 (91.5, 101.5, 111.75, 122, 132, 142.25, 152.5) cm

Finished Length from Shoulder: 25.5 (26, 26.5, 27, 27.5, 28, 28.5, 29)"/64.75 (66, 67.3, 68.5, 69.75, 71, 72.3, 73.5) cm

Cross Back Armhole to Armhole: 17 (18.5, 21.25, 24, 25.5, 28.3, 31.20, 32.5"/43 (47, 54, 61, 64.75, 72, 79.25, 82.5)cm

Armhole Depth: 7.5 (8, 8.5, 9, 9.5, 10, 10.5, 11)"/19 (20.3, 21.5, 23, 24, 25.5, 26.5, 28) cm

MATERIALS AND TOOLS

Sample uses Malabrigo Sock (100% Superwash Merino Wool; 3.53 ounces/100g = 440 yards/402 m): 5 (5, 5, 6, 7, 7, 8, 8) balls in color Archangel #SW850—2200 (2200, 2200, 2640, 3080, 3080, 3520, 3520) yards/2010 (2010, 2010, 2412, 2814, 2814, 3216, 3216) m of superfine weight yarn

SUPER FINE

Crochet hook: 3.25mm (size D-3) or size to obtain gauge

Yarn needle

BLOCKED GAUGE

Double wave: 6 sts = 1"/2.5 cm; 57 sts = 9.5"/24 cm; 4.23 rows = 1"/2.5 cm; 37 rows = 8.75"/22.25 cm

STITCH GUIDE

Foundation single crochet (Fsc): Ch 2, insert hook into second ch from hook, yo and draw up a lp, yo and draw through 1 lp (first "chain" made), yo and draw through 2 lps on hook (first Fsc made), *insert hook under 2 lps of the "chain" just made, yo and draw up a lp, yo and draw through 1 lp ("chain" made), yo and draw through 2 lps on hook (Fsc made); rep from * for indicated number of foundation sts.

Extending foundation single crochet (foundation sc as used for extending rows) (Ext-Fsc): Insert hook into last st worked, yo and draw up a lp (first "chain" made), yo and draw through 1 lp, yo and draw through 2 lps on hook (first Ext-Fsc made), *insert hook under 2 lps of the "chain" just made, yo and draw up a lp (first "chain" made), yo and draw through 1 lp, yo and draw through 2 lps on hook (Ext-Fsc made); rep from * for indicated number of extending foundation sc sts.

Linked first treble crochet (Linked first-tr): Ch 2, insert hook into first ch from hook, yo and draw up a lp (2 lps on hook), insert hook into next ch from hook, yo and draw up a lp (3 lps on hook), insert hook into first st, yo and draw up a lp (4 lps on hook), [yo and draw through 2 lps on hook] 3 times.

PATTERN STITCHES

Double wave (worked over a multiple of 14 + 1 sts)

Row 1 (RS): Ch 1, sc in first st, *sc in next st, hdc in each of next 2 sts, dc in each of next 2 sts, tr in each of next 3 sts, dc in each of next 2 sts, hdc in each of next 2 sts, sc in each of next 2 sts; rep from * to end of row, turn.

Row 2 (WS): Rep Row 1.

Row 3: Ch 1, sc in first st and in each st to end of row, turn.

Row 4: Ch 1, work Linked first-tr, *tr in next st, dc in each of next 2 sts, hdc in each of next 2 sts, sc in each of next 3 sts, hdc in each of next 2 sts, dc in each of next 2 sts, tr in each of next 2 sts; rep from * to end of row, turn.

Row 5: Rep Row 4.

Row 6: Rep Row 3.

Rep Rows 1–6 for pattern stitch.

Swatch: 57 sts and 36 rows (+ 1 Fsc row)

Foundation Row: Work 57 Fsc, turn.

Rows 1–36: Rep Rows 1–6 of double wave.

Fasten off.

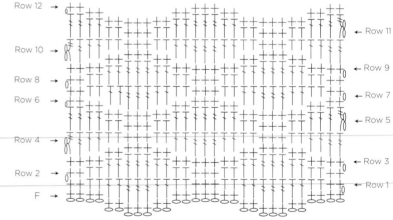

Double wave chart

NOTES

▶ Left Side and Right Side refer to left and right sides as worn.

▶ Garment is made from side to side with openings left for armholes using Extending Foundation Stitches.

▶ When instructed to work in a pattern "as established," work the next row of pattern and ensure that the stitches line up as in previous rows.

INSTRUCTIONS

First side

Foundation Row: Work 197 (197, 197, 197, 221, 221, 221, 221) Fsc, turn.

Rows 1–53 (59, 59, 65, 71, 77, 83, 89): Work in double wave.

Back

First armhole

Note: Row 1 should be a single crochet row to make armhole.

Row 1: Work in double wave as established across first 109 (106, 103, 100, 111, 108, 105, 102) sts, work 45 (48, 51, 54, 57, 60, 63, 66) Ext-Fsc sts, sk next 45 (48, 51, 54, 57, 60, 63, 66) sts, work in double wave as established across last 43 (43, 43, 43, 53, 53, 53, 53) sts, turn.

Rows 2–72 (78, 90, 102, 108, 120, 132, 138): Work in double wave as established.

Second side

Second armhole

Note: Row 1 should be a single crochet row to make armhole.

Row 1: Work in double wave as established across first 109 (106, 103, 100, 111, 108, 105, 102) sts, work 45 (48, 51, 54, 57, 60, 63, 66) Ext-Fsc sts, sk next 45 (48, 51, 54, 57, 60, 63, 66) sts, work in double wave as established across last 43 (43, 43, 43, 53, 53, 53, 53) sts, turn.

Rows 2–55 (61, 61, 67, 73, 79, 85, 91): Work in double wave as established.

Cut yarn, leaving tail for weaving in; pull tail through last st made; weave in tail using End Cap Finishing Stitch.

FINISHING

Block to measurements in schematic.

Weave in ends.

Rectangular Wrap Vest Schematic

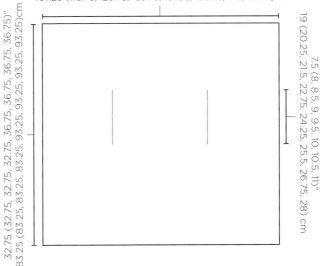

42.25 (46.75, 49.5, 55, 59.5, 65.25, 70.5, 75)"
107.25 (118.75, 125.75, 139.75, 151.25, 165.75, 179, 190.5) cm

32.75 (32.75, 32.75, 32.75, 36.75, 36.75, 36.75, 36.75)"
83.25 (83.25, 83.25, 83.25, 93.25, 93.25, 93.25, 93.25)cm

7.5 (8, 8.5, 9, 9.5, 10, 10.5, 11)"
19 (20.25, 21.5, 22.75, 24.25, 25.5, 26.75, 28) cm

Signature Vests

Throughout this book, we've encouraged you to experiment and play with your crochet stitches and fabrics. Here's a pattern where you can do just that—mix and match—and create a garment that is uniquely you. It's a choose-your-own-adventure pattern!

The side back and front panels of this versatile pattern are worked in single crochet linen stitch. After that, the rest is up to you. Start by customizing your vest with your favorite complimentary colors for a striking, two-toned look like we've done here, or pick a single color for a seamless look. Further personalize your creation by choosing between lace or cables for your center back panel, then finish it all off with a collar made in your choice of lace or single crochet ribbing . . . or maybe no collar at all . . . the choice is up to you!

SKILLS USED

Foundation Single Crochet (*see page 104*)

Single Crochet (*see page 84*)

Half Double Crochet (*see page 92*)

Treble Crochet (*see page 88*)

Front Post Treble Crochet (*see page 125*)

Cables (*see page 174*)

Working Stitch 2 Rows Below (*see page 50*)

Single Crochet through the Back Loop Only (*see page 119*)

Linked First-Half Double Crochet (*see page 98*)

End Cap Finishing Stitch (*see page 250*)

Blocking (*see page 240*)

Locking Mattress Stitch (*see page 257*)

Setting in a Collar (*see page 254*)

Decreases–Single Crochet 2 together (*see page 140*)

SKILL LEVEL

INTERMEDIATE

SIZES S (M, L, XL, 2X, 3X, 4X, 5X)

Lace sample shown in size small
Cable sample shown in size large

FINISHED MEASUREMENTS

To Fit Bust: 32 (36, 40, 44, 49, 52, 58, 61)"/81.25 (91.5, 101.5, 111.75, 124.5, 132, 147.25, 155) cm

Finished Bust: 36 (40, 44, 48, 53, 56, 62, 65)"/91.5 (101.5, 111.75, 124.5, 134.5, 142.25, 157.5, 165) cm

Finished Length From Shoulder: 27.5 (28, 29, 29.25, 29.75, 30.25, 31.5, 32)"/69.75 (71, 73.75, 74.25, 75.5, 76.75, 80, 81.25) cm

MATERIALS AND TOOLS

Sample uses Cascade Yarns Cascade 220 Superwash Sport
(100% Superwash Merino Wool; 3.5 ounces/100g = 306 yards/280 m)

Lace sample shown in color Jasmine Green #240 and color Moss #841

Cable sample shown in color Silver Grey #1946 and color Charcoal #900

Solid Color Lace vest with lace collar: 6 (7, 8, 9, 9, 10, 11, 12) balls; 1320 (1540, 1760, 1980, 1980, 2200, 2400, 2640) yards/1200 (1400, 1600, 1800, 1800, 2000, 2200, 2400) m of lightweight yarn

Solid Color Cable vest with ribbing collar: 7 (8, 8, 9, 10, 11, 12, 12) balls; 1540 (1760, 1760, 1980, 220, 2420, 2640, 2640) yards/1400 (1600, 1600, 1800, 2000, 2200, 2400, 2400) m of lightweight yarn

Solid Color Lace vest with ribbing collar: 7 (8, 9, 9, 10, 11, 12, 13) balls; 1540 (1760, 1980, 1980, 2200, 2400, 2640, 2860) yards/1400 (1600, 1800, 1800, 2000, 2200, 2400, 2600) m of lightweight yarn

Lace vest only: 4 (5, 5, 6, 6, 7, 7, 8) balls; 880 (1100, 1100, 1320, 1320, 1540, 1760) yards/800 (1000, 1000, 1200, 1200, 1400, 1400, 1600) m of lightweight yarn

Cable vest only: 5 (5, 6, 6, 7, 7, 8, 8) balls; 1100 (1100, 1320, 1320, 1540, 1540, 1760) yards/1000 (1000, 1200, 1200, 1400, 1400, 1600) m of lightweight yarn

Ribbing collar only: 3 (3, 3, 3, 3, 3, 4, 4) balls; 660 (660, 660, 660, 660, 660, 880, 880) yards/600 (600, 600, 600, 600, 600, 800, 800) m of lightweight yarn

Lace collar only: 3 (3, 3, 3, 3, 3, 4, 4) balls; 660 (660, 660, 660, 660, 660, 880, 880) yards/600 (600, 600, 600, 600, 600, 800, 800) m of lightweight yarn

Crochet hook: 3.75mm (size F-5) and 4.00mm (size G-6) or size to obtain gauge

Yarn needle

BLOCKED GAUGES

Single Crochet Linen Stitch: 6.38 sts = 1"/2.5 cm; 51 sts = 8"/20.25 cm; 5.57 rows = 1"/2.5 cm; 39 rows = 7"/17.75 cm with 4.00mm (size G-6) hook

Lace pattern: 4.94 sts = 1"/2.5 cm; 42 sts = 8.5"/21.5 cm; 3.4 rows = 1"/2.5 cm; 51 rows = 15"/38 cm with 4.00mm (size G-6) hook

Cable pattern: 5.41 sts = 1"/2.5 cm; 46 sts = 8.5"/21.5 cm; 5.94 rows = 1"/2.5 cm; 92 rows = 15.5"/39.25 cm with 4.00mm (G-6) hook

Single Crochet Ribbing: 5.71 sts = 1"/2.5 cm; 40 sts = 7"/17.75cm; 7.04 rows = 1"/2.5cm; 44 rows = 6.25"/16 cm with 3.75mm (F-5) hook

STITCH GUIDE

Foundation single crochet (Fsc): Ch 2, insert hook into second ch from hook, yo and draw up a lp, yo and draw through 1 lp (first "chain" made), yo and draw through 2 lps on hook (first Fsc made), *insert hook under 2 lps of the "chain" just made, yo and draw up a lp, yo and draw through 1 lp ("chain" made), yo and draw through 2 lps on hook (Fsc made); rep from * for indicated number of foundation sts.

2-over-2 Front Post treble crochet left cross cable (2/2 FPtr LC) (worked over 4 sts): Sk next 2 sts, FPtr around each of next 2 sts 2 rows below; working in front of FPtr just made, FPtr around each of 2 skipped sts 2 rows below.

2-over-2 Front Post treble crochet right cross cable (2/2 FPtr RC) (worked over 4 sts): Sk next 2 sts, FPtr around each of next 2 sts 2 rows below; working behind FPtr just made, FPtr around each of 2 skipped sts 2 rows below.

Linked first half double crochet (Linked first-hdc): Pull lp on hook up to slightly taller than normal lp, ch 1, insert hook into first ch from hook, yo and draw up a lp (2 lps on hook), insert hook into first st, yo and draw up a lp (3 lps on hook), yo and draw through all 3 lps on hook.

PATTERN STITCHES

Single crochet linen stitch (sc linen st) (worked over a multiple of 2 + 1 sts)

Row 1 (RS): Ch 1, sc in first st, *ch 1, sk next st, sc in next st; rep from * to end of row, turn.

Row 2 (WS): Ch 1, sc in first st, sc in next ch-1 sp, *ch 1, sk next st, sc in next ch-1 sp; rep from * to last st, sc in last st, turn.

Row 3: Ch 1, sc in first st, *ch 1, sk next st, sc in next ch-1 sp; rep from * to last 2 sts, ch 1, sk next st, sc in last st, turn.

Rep Rows 2–3 for pattern stitch.

Swatch: 51 sts and 39 rows (+ 1 Fsc row) with 4.0mm (size G-6) hook

Foundation Row: Work 51 Fsc, turn.

Row 1: Work Row 1 of sc linen st.

Rows 2–39: Rep Rows 2–3 of sc linen st. Fasten off.

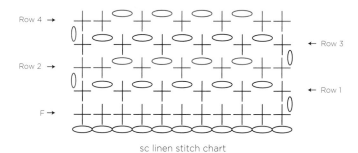

sc linen stitch chart

sc linen swatch

Lace pattern (worked over 42 sts)

Row 1 (RS): (Work Linked first-hdc, hdc) in first st, [ch 1, sk next 2 sts, hdc 3 times in next st] 6 times, ch 5, sk next 4 sts, [hdc 3 times in next st, ch 1, sk next 2 sts] 6 times, hdc 2 times in last st, turn.

Row 2 (WS): Work Linked first-hdc in first st, sk next st, hdc 3 times in next ch-1 sp, [ch 1, sk next 3 hdc, hdc 3 times in next ch-1 sp] 5 times, ch 4, sk next 3 hdc, sc in middle of next ch-5 sp, ch 4, sk next 3 hdc, hdc 3 times in next ch-1 sp, [ch 1, sk next 3 hdc, hdc 3 times in next ch-1 sp] 5 times, sk next st, hdc in last st, turn.

Row 3: (Work Linked first-hdc, hdc) in first st, [ch 1, sk next 3 hdc, hdc 3 times in next ch-1 sp] 5 times, ch 4, sc in next ch-4 sp, sc in next sc, sc in next ch-4 sp, ch 4, sk next 3 hdc, [hdc 3 times in next ch-1 sp, ch 1, sk next 3 hdc] 5 times, hdc 2 times in last st, turn.

Row 4: Work Linked first-hdc in first st, sk next st, hdc 3 times in next ch-1 sp, [ch 1, sk next 3 hdc, hdc 3 times in next ch-1 sp] 4 times, ch 4, sk next 3 hdc, sc in next ch-4 sp, sc in each of next 3 sc, sc in next ch-4 sp, ch 4, sk next 3 hdc, hdc 3 times in next ch-1 sp, [ch 1, sk next 3 hdc, hdc 3 times in next ch-1 sp] 4 times, sk next st, hdc in last st, turn.

Row 5: (Work Linked first-hdc, hdc) in first st, [ch 1, sk next 3 hdc, hdc 3 times in next ch-1 sp] 4 times, ch 4, sk next 3 hdc, sc in next ch-4 sp, sc in each of next 5 sc, sc in next ch-4 sp, ch 4, sk next 3 hdc, [hdc 3 times in next ch-1 sp, ch 1, sk next 3 hdc] 4 times, hdc 2 times in last st, turn.

Row 6: Work Linked first-hdc in first st, sk next st, hdc 3 times in next ch-1 sp, [ch 1, sk next 3 hdc, hdc 3 times in next ch-1 sp] 3 times, ch 4, sk next 3 hdc, sc in next ch-4 sp, sc in each of next 7 sc, sc in next ch-4 sp, ch 4, sk next 3 hdc, hdc 3 times in next ch-1 sp, [ch 1, sk next 3 hdc, hdc 3 times in next ch-1 sp] 3 times, sk next st, hdc in last st, turn.

Row 7: (Work Linked first-hdc, hdc) in first st, [ch 1, sk next 3 hdc, hdc 3 times in next ch-1 sp] 3 times, ch 4, sk next 3 hdc, sc in next ch-4 sp, sc in each of next 9 sc, sc in next ch-4 sp, ch 4, sk next 3 hdc, [hdc 3 times in next ch-1 sp, ch 1, sk next 3 hdc] 3 times, hdc 2 times in last st, turn.

Row 8: Work Linked first-hdc in first st, sk next st, hdc 3 times in next ch-1 sp, [ch 1, sk next 3 hdc, hdc 3 times in next ch-1 sp] 2 times, ch 4, sk next 3 hdc, sc in next ch-4 sp, sc in each of next 11 sc, sc in next ch-4 sp, ch 4, sk next 3 hdc, hdc 3 times in next ch-1 sp, [ch 1, sk next 3 hdc, hdc 3 times in next ch-1 sp] 2 times, sk next st, hdc in last st, turn.

Row 9: (Work Linked first-hdc, hdc) in first st, [ch 1, sk next 3 hdc, hdc 3 times in next ch-1 sp] 2 times, ch 4, sk next 3 hdc, sc in next ch-4 sp, sc in each of next 13 sc, sc in next ch-4 sp, ch 4, sk next 3 hdc, [hdc 3 times in next ch-1 sp, ch 1, sk next 3 hdc] 2 times, hdc 2 times in last st, turn.

Row 10: Work Linked first-hdc in first st, sk next st, hdc 3 times in next ch-1 sp, ch 1, sk next 3 hdc, hdc 3 times in next ch-1 sp, ch 4, sk next 3 hdc, sc in next ch-4 sp, sc in each of next 15 sc, sc in next ch-4 sp, ch 4, sk next 3 hdc, hdc 3 times in next ch-1 sp, ch 1, sk next 3 hdc, hdc 3 times in next ch-1 sp, sk next st, hdc in last st, turn.

Row 11: (Work Linked first-hdc, hdc) in first st, ch 1, sk next 3 hdc, hdc 3 times in next ch-1 sp, ch 4, sk next 3 hdc, sc in next ch-4 sp, sc in each of next 17 sc, sc in next ch-4 sp, ch 4, sk next 3 hdc, hdc 3 times in next ch-1 sp, ch 1, sk next 3 hdc, hdc 2 times in last st, turn.

Row 12: Work Linked first-hdc in first st, sk next st, hdc 3 times in next ch-1 sp, ch 1, sk next 3 hdc, hdc 3 times in next ch-4 sp, ch 4, sk next sc, sc in each of next 17 sc, ch 4, sk next sc, hdc 3 times in next ch-4 sp, ch 1, sk next 3 hdc, hdc 3 times in next ch-1 sp, sk next st, hdc in last st, turn.

Row 13: (Work Linked first-hdc, hdc) in first st, ch 1, sk next 3 hdc, hdc 3 times in next ch-1 sp, ch 1, sk next 3 hdc, hdc 3 times in next ch-4 sp, ch 4, sk next sc, sc in each of next 15 sc, ch 4, sk next sc, hdc 3 times in next ch-4 sp, ch 1, sk next 3 hdc, hdc 3 times in next ch-1 sp, ch 1, sk next 3 hdc, hdc 2 times in last st, turn.

Row 14: Work Linked first-hdc in first st, sk next st, [hdc 3 times in next ch-1 sp, ch 1, sk next 3 hdc] 2 times, hdc 3 times in next ch-4 sp, ch 4, sk next sc, sc in each of next 13 sc, ch 4, sk next sc, hdc 3 times in next ch-4 sp, [ch 1, sk next 3 hdc, hdc 3 times in next ch-1 sp] 2 times, sk next st, hdc in last st, turn.

Row 15: (Work Linked first-hdc, hdc) in first st, [ch 1, sk next 3 hdc, hdc 3 times in next ch-1 sp] 2 times, ch 1, sk next 3 hdc, hdc 3 times in next ch-4 sp, ch 4, sk next sc, sc in each of next 11 sc, ch 4, sk next sc, hdc 3 times in next ch-4 sp, [ch 1, sk next 3 hdc, hdc 3 times in next ch-1 sp] 2 times, ch 1, sk next 3 hdc, hdc 2 times in last st, turn.

Row 16: Work Linked first-hdc in first st, sk next st, [hdc 3 times in next ch-1 sp, ch 1, sk next 3 hdc] 3 times, hdc 3 times in next ch-4 sp, ch 4, sk next sc, sc in each of next 9 sc, ch 4, sk next sc, hdc 3 times in next ch-4 sp, [ch 1, sk next 3 hdc, hdc 3 times in next ch-1 sp] 3 times, sk next st, hdc in last st, turn.

Row 17: (Work Linked first-hdc, hdc) in first st, [ch 1, sk next 3 hdc, hdc 3 times in next ch-1 sp] 3 times, ch 1, sk next 3 hdc, hdc 3 times in next ch-4 sp, ch 4, sk next sc, sc in each of next 7 sc, ch 4, sk next sc, hdc 3 times in next ch-4 sp, [ch 1, sk next 3 hdc, hdc 3 times in next ch-1 sp] 3 times, ch 1, sk next 3 hdc, hdc 2 times in last st, turn.

Lace Back Panel
chart

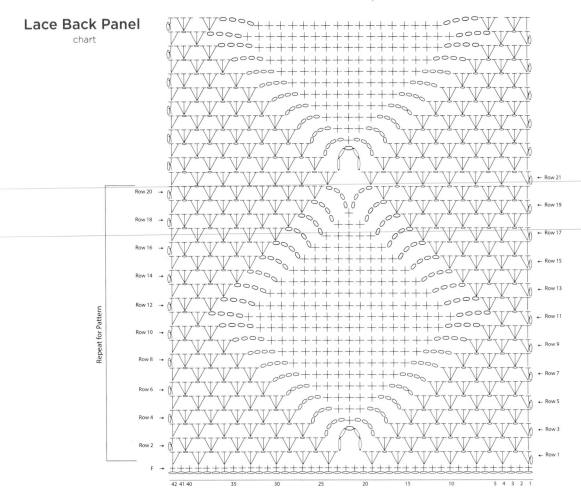

Row 18: Work Linked first-hdc in first st, sk next st, [hdc 3 times in next ch-1 sp, ch 1, sk next 3 hdc] 4 times, hdc 3 times in next ch-4 sp, ch 4, sk next sc, sc in each of next 5 sc, ch 4, sk next sc, hdc 3 times in next ch-4 sp, [ch 1, sk next 3 hdc, hdc 3 times in next ch-1 sp] 4 times, sk next st, hdc in last st, turn.

Row 19: (Work Linked first-hdc, hdc) in first st, [ch 1, sk next 3 hdc, hdc 3 times in next ch-1 sp] 4 times, ch 1, sk next 3 hdc, hdc 3 times in next ch-4 sp, ch 4, sk next sc, sc in each of next 3 sc, ch 4, sk next sc, hdc 3 times in next ch-4 sp, [ch 1, sk next 3 hdc, hdc 3 times in next ch-1 sp] 4 times, ch 1, sk next 3 hdc, hdc 2 times in last st, turn.

Row 20: Work Linked first-hdc in first st, sk next st, [hdc 3 times in next ch-1 sp, ch 1, sk next 3 hdc] 5 times, hdc 3 times in next ch-4 sp, ch 4, sk next sc, sc in next sc, ch 4, sk next sc, hdc 3 times in next ch-4 sp, [ch 1, sk next 3 hdc, hdc 3 times in next ch-1 sp] 5 times, sk next st, hdc in last st, turn.

Row 21: (Work Linked first-hdc, hdc) in first st, [ch 1, sk next 3 hdc, hdc 3 times in next ch-1 sp] 5 times, ch 1, sk next 3 hdc, hdc 3 times in next ch-4 sp, ch 5, sk next sc, hdc 3 times in next ch-4 sp, [ch 1, sk next 3 hdc, hdc 3 times in next ch-1 sp] 5 times, ch 1, sk next 3 hdc, hdc 2 times in last st, turn.

Rep Rows 2–21 for pattern stitch.

Swatch: 42 sts and 52 rows (+ 1 Fsc row) with 4.0mm (size G-6) hook

Foundation Row: Work 42 Fsc, turn.

Row 1: Work Row 1 of lace pattern.

Rows 2–41: Work Rows 2–21 of lace pattern 2 times.

Rows 42–52: Work Rows 2–12 of lace pattern. Fasten off.

Cable pattern (worked over 46 sts)

Rows 1–2: Ch 1, sc in first st and in each st to end of row, turn.

Row 3 (RS): Ch 1, sc in each of first 18 sts, work 2/2 FPtr RC, sc in each of next 24 sts, turn.

Row 4 (and all WS rows): Ch 1, sc in first st and in each st to end of row, turn.

Row 5: Rep Row 3.

Row 7: Rep Row 3.

Row 9: Rep Row 3.

Row 11: Ch 1, sc in each of first 16 sts, [FPtr around next st 2 rows below and 1 st to the left of current st] 2 times, sc in each of next 4 sts, [FPtr around st 2 rows below and 1 st to the right of current st] 2 times, sc in each of next 4 sts, work 2/2 FPtr RC, sc in each of next 14 sts, turn.

Row 13: Ch 1, sc in each of first 14 sts, [FPtr around next st 2 rows below and 1 st to the left of current st] 2 times, sc in each of next 6 sts, work 2/2 FPtr RC, sc in each of next 2 sts, work 2/2 FPtr RC, sc in each of next 14 sts, turn.

Row 15: Ch 1, sc in each of first 16 sts, [FPtr around st 2 rows below and 1 st to the right of current st] 2 times, sc in each of next 4 sts, work 2/2 FPtr RC, sc in each of next 2 sts, work 2/2 FPtr RC, sc in each of next 14 sts, turn.

Row 17: Ch 1, sc in each of first 18 sts, [FPtr around st 2 rows below and 1 st to the right of current st] 2 times, [FPtr around next st 2 rows below and 1 st to the left of current st] 2 times, sc in each of next 6 sts, work 2/2 FPtr RC, sc in each of next 14 sts, turn.

Row 19: Ch 1, sc in each of first 18 sts, work 2/2 FPtr RC, sc in each of next 4 sts, [FPtr around next st 2 rows below and 1 st to the left of current st] 2 times, sc in each of next 4 sts, [FPtr around st 2 rows below and 1 st to the right of current st] 2 times, sc in each of next 12 sts, turn.

Row 21: Ch 1, sc in each of first 18 sts, work 2/2 FPtr RC, sc in each of next 2 sts, [FPtr around next st 2 rows below and 1 st to the left of current st] 2 times, sc in each of next 6 sts, work 2/2 FPtr RC, sc in each of next 10 sts, turn.

Row 23: Ch 1, sc in each of first 18 sts, work 2/2 FPtr RC, sc in each of next 4 sts, [FPtr around st 2 rows below and 1 st to the right of current st] 2 times, sc in each of next 4 sts, work 2/2 FPtr RC, sc in each of next 10 sts, turn.

Row 25: Ch 1, sc in each of first 18 sts, work 2/2 FPtr RC, sc in each of next 6 sts, [FPtr around st 2 rows below and 1 st to the right of current st] 2 times, [FPtr around next st 2 rows below and 1 st to the left of current st] 2 times, sc in each of next 14 sts, turn.

Row 27: Ch 1, sc in each of first 16 sts, [FPtr around next st 2 rows below and 1 st to the left of current st] 2 times, sc in each of next 4 sts, [FPtr around next st 2 rows below and 1 st to the right of current st] 2 times, sc in each of next 4 sts, work 2/2 FPtr RC, sc in each of next 14 sts, turn.

Row 29: Ch 1, sc in each of first 14 sts, work 2/2 FPtr RC, sc in each of next 4 sts, work 2/2 FPtr RC, sc in each of next 2 sts, work 2/2 FPtr RC, sc in each of next 14 sts, turn.

Row 31: Ch 1, sc in each of first 14 sts, work 2/2 FPtr RC, sc in each of next 4 sts, work 2/2 FPtr RC, sc in each of next 20 sts, turn.

Row 33: Ch 1, sc in each of first 12 sts, [FPtr around next st 2 rows below and 1 st to the left of current st] 2 times, sc in each of next 4 sts, [FPtr around next st 2 rows below and 1 st to the right of current st] 2 times, [FPtr around next st 2 rows below and 1 st to the left of current st] 2 times, sc in each of next 4 sts, [FPtr around next st 2 rows below and 1 st to the left of current st] 2 times, sc in each of next 18 sts, turn.

Row 35: Ch 1, sc in each of first 10 sts, [work 2/2 FPtr LC, sc in each of next 4 sts] 2 times, work 2/2 FPtr LC, sc in each of next 16 sts, turn.

Row 37: Ch 1, sc in each of first 10 sts, [work 2/2 FPtr LC, sc in each of next 4 sts] 2 times, work 2/2 FPtr LC, sc in each of next 6 sts, work 2/2 FPtr RC, sc in each of next 6 sts, turn.

Row 39: Ch 1, sc in each of first 8 sts, [FPtr around next st 2 rows below and 1 st to the left of current st] 2 times, [sc in each of next 4 sts, (FPtr around next st 2 rows below and 1 st to the right of current st) 2 times, (FPtr around next st 2 rows below and 1 st to the left of current st) 2 times] 2 times, sc in each of next 4 sts, [FPtr around next st 2 rows below and 1 st to the right of current st] 2 times, sc in each of next 4 sts, work 2/2 FPtr RC, sc in each of next 6 sts, turn.

Row 41: Ch 1, sc in each of first 6 sts, [work 2/2 FPtr RC, sc in each of next 4 sts] 2 times, work 2/2 FPtr RC, sc in each of next 6 sts, [FPtr around next st 2 rows below and 1 st to the right of current st] 2 times, sc in each of next 2 sts, work 2/2 FPtr RC, sc in each of next 6 sts, turn.

Row 43: Ch 1, sc in each of first 6 sts, [work 2/2 FPtr RC, sc in each of next 4 sts] 3 times, [FPtr around next st 2 rows below and 1 st to the left of current st] 2 times, sc in each of next 4 sts, work 2/2 FPtr RC, sc in each of next 6 sts, turn.

Row 45: Ch 1, sc in each of first 4 sts, [FPtr around next st 2 rows below and 1 st to the left of current st] 2 times, [sc in each of next 4 sts, (FPtr around next st 2 rows below and 1 st to the right of current st) 2 times, (FPtr around next st 2 rows below and 1 st to the left of current st) 2 times] 3 times, sc in each of next 4 sts, [FPtr around next st 2 rows below and 1 st to the left of current st] 2 times, sc in each of next 4 sts, [FPtr around next st 2 rows below and 1 st to the right of current st] 2 times, sc in each of next 4 sts, turn.

Row 47: Ch 1, sc in each of first 2 sts, [FPtr around next st 2 rows below and 1 st to the left of current st] 2 times, sc in each of next 6 sts, [work 2/2 FPtr LC, sc in each of next 4 sts] 2 times, work 2/2 FPtr LC, sc in each of next 2 sts, [FPtr around next st 2 rows below and 1 st to the left of current st] 2 times, sc in each of next 6 sts, work 2/2 FPtr RC, sc in each of next 2 sts, turn.

Row 49: Ch 1, sc in each of first 4 sts, [FPtr around next st 2 rows below and 1 st to the right of current st] 2 times, [sc in each of next 4 sts, work 2/2 FPtr LC] 3 times, sc in each of next 4 sts, [FPtr around next st 2 rows below and 1 st to the right of current st] 2 times, sc in each of next 4 sts, work 2/2 FPtr RC, sc in each of next 2 sts, turn.

Row 51: Ch 1, sc in each of first 6 sts, [(FPtr around next st 2 rows below and 1 st to the right of current st) 2 times, (FPtr around next st 2 rows below and 1 st to the left of current st) 2 times, sc in each of next 4 sts]

3 times, [FPtr around next st 2 rows below and 1 st to the right of current st] 2 times, sc in each of next 4 sts, [FPtr around next st 2 rows below and 1 st to the right of current st] 2 times, [FPtr around next st 2 rows below and 1 st to the left of current st] 2 times, sc in each of next 6 sts, turn.

Row 53: Ch 1, sc in each of first 6 sts, [work 2/2 FPtr RC, sc in each of next 4 sts] 2 times, work 2/2 FPtr RC, sc in each of next 6 sts, [FPtr around next st 2 rows below and 1 st to the right of current st] 2 times, sc in each of next 2 sts, work 2/2 FPtr RC, sc in each of next 6 sts, turn.

Row 55: Ch 1, sc in each of first 6 sts, [work 2/2 FPtr RC, sc in each of next 4 sts] 3 times, [FPtr around next st 2 rows below and 1 st to the left of current st] 2 times, sc in each of next 4 sts, work 2/2 FPtr RC, sc in each of next 6 sts, turn.

Row 57: Ch 1, sc in each of first 10 sts, [(FPtr around next st 2 rows below and 1 st to the right of current st) 2 times, (FPtr around next st 2 rows below and 1 st to the left of current st) 2 times, sc in each of next 4 sts] 2 times, [FPtr around next st 2 rows below and 1 st to the right of current st] 2 times, [FPtr around next st 2 rows below and 1 st to the left of current st] 2 times, sc in each of next 6 sts, work 2/2 FPtr RC, sc in each of next 6 sts, turn.

Row 59: Ch 1, sc in each of first 10 sts, [work 2/2 FPtr LC, sc in each of next 4 sts] 2 times, work 2/2 FPtr LC, sc in each of next 6 sts, work 2/2 FPtr RC, sc in each of next 6 sts, turn.

Row 61: Ch 1, sc in each of first 10 sts, [work 2/2 FPtr LC, sc in each of next 4 sts] 2 times, work 2/2 FPtr LC, sc in each of next 16 sts, turn.

Row 63: Ch 1, sc in each of first 14 sts, [FPtr around next st 2 rows below and 1 st to the right of current st] 2 times, [FPtr around next st 2 rows below and 1 st to the left of current st] 2 times, sc in each of next 4 sts, [FPtr around next st 2 rows below and 1 st to the right of current st] 2 times, [FPtr around next st 2 rows below and 1 st to the left of current st] 2 times, sc in each of next 20 sts, turn.

Row 65: Ch 1, sc in each of first 14 sts, work 2/2 FPtr RC, sc in each of next 4 sts, work 2/2 FPtr RC, sc in each of next 20 sts, turn.

Row 67: Ch 1, sc in each of first 14 sts, work 2/2 FPtr RC, sc in each of next 4 sts, work 2/2 FPtr RC, sc in each of next 2 sts, work 2/2 FPtr RC, sc in each of next 14 sts, turn.

Row 69: Ch 1, sc in each of first 18 sts, [FPtr around next st 2 rows below and 1 st to the right of current st] 2 times, [FPtr around next st 2 rows below and 1 st to the left of current st] 2 times, sc in each of next 6 sts, work 2/2 FPtr RC, sc in each of next 14 sts, turn.

Cable Back Panel
chart

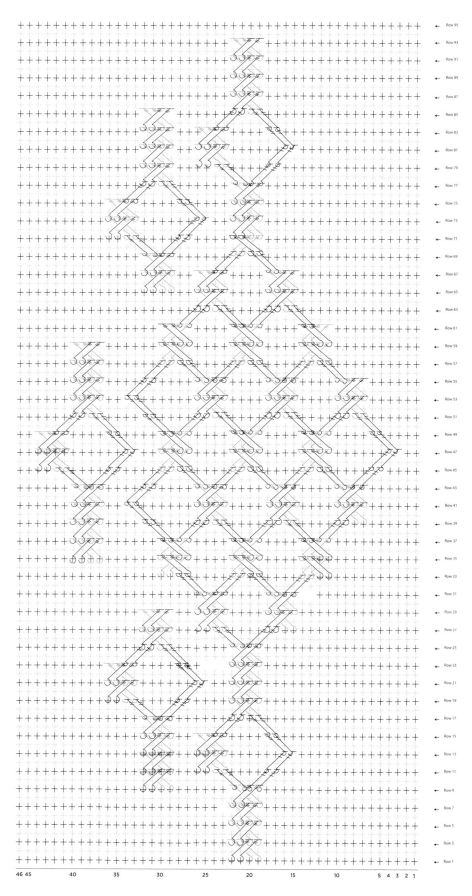

← Row 95
← Row 93
← Row 91
← Row 89
← Row 87
← Row 85
← Row 83
← Row 81
← Row 79
← Row 77
← Row 75
← Row 73
← Row 71
← Row 69
← Row 67
← Row 65
← Row 63
← Row 61
← Row 59
← Row 57
← Row 55
← Row 53
← Row 51
← Row 49
← Row 47
← Row 45
← Row 43
← Row 41
← Row 39
← Row 37
← Row 35
← Row 33
← Row 31
← Row 29
← Row 27
← Row 25
← Row 23
← Row 21
← Row 19
← Row 17
← Row 15
← Row 13
← Row 11
← Row 9
← Row 7
← Row 5
← Row 3
← Row 1

46 45   40   35   30   25   20   15   10   5 4 3 2 1

Row 71: Ch 1, sc in each of first 18 sts, work 2/2 FPtr LC, sc in each of next 4 sts, [FPtr around next st 2 rows below and 1 st to the left of current st] 2 times, sc in each of next 4 sts, [FPtr around next st 2 rows below and 1 st to the right of current st] 2 times, sc in each of next 12 sts, turn.

Row 73: Ch 1, sc in each of first 18 sts, work 2/2 FPtr RC, sc in each of next 2 sts, [FPtr around next st 2 rows below and 1 st to the left of current st] 2 times, sc in each of next 6 sts, work 2/2 FPtr RC, sc in each of next 10 sts, turn.

Row 75: Ch 1, sc in each of first 18 sts, work 2/2 FPtr RC, sc in each of next 4 sts, [FPtr around next st 2 rows below and 1 st to the right of current st] 2 times, sc in each of next 4 sts, work 2/2 FPtr RC, sc in each of next 10 sts, turn.

Row 77: Ch 1, sc in each of first 18 sts, work 2/2 FPtr RC, sc in each of next 6 sts, [FPtr around next st 2 rows below and 1 st to the right of current st] 2 times, [FPtr around next st 2 rows below and 1 st to the left of current st] 2 times, sc in each of next 14 sts, turn.

Row 79: Ch 1, sc in each of first 16 sts, [FPtr around next st 2 rows below and 1 st to the left of current st] 2 times, sc in each of next 4 sts, [FPtr around next st 2 rows below and 1 st to the right of current st] 2 times, sc in each of next 4 sts, work 2/2 FPtr RC, sc in each of next 14 sts, turn.

Row 81: Ch 1, sc in each of first 14 sts, [FPtr around next st 2 rows below and 1 st to the left of current st] 2 times, sc in each of next 6 sts, work 2/2 FPtr RC, sc in each of next 2 sts, work 2/2 FPtr RC, sc in each of next 14 sts, turn.

Row 83: Ch 1, sc in each of first 16 sts, [FPtr around next st 2 rows below and 1 st to the right of current st] 2 times, sc in each of next 4 sts, work 2/2 FPtr RC, sc in each of next 2 sts, work 2/2 FPtr RC, sc in each of next 14 sts, turn.

Row 85: Ch 1, sc in each of first 18 sts, [FPtr around next st 2 rows below and 1 st to the right of current st] 2 times, [FPtr around next st 2 rows below and 1 st to the left of current st] 2 times, sc in each of next 6 sts, work 2/2 FPtr RC, sc in each of next 14 sts, turn.

Rows 87, 89, 91, and 93: Ch 1, sc in each of first 18 sts, work 2/2 FPtr RC, sc in each of next 24 sts, turn.

Row 94: Ch 1, sc in first st and in each st to end of row, turn.

Cable Swatch: 46 sts and 94 rows (+ 1 Fsc row) with 4.0mm (size G-6) hook

Foundation Row: Work 46 Fsc, turn.

Rows 1–94: Work Rows 1–94 of cable pattern.
Fasten off.

Single crochet ribbing (sc ribbing)

Row 1: Ch 1, sc in first st, sc tbl in next st and tbl in each st to last st, sc in last st, turn.
Rep Row 1 for pattern stitch.

Swatch: 40 sts and 43 rows (+ 1 Fsc row) with 3.75mm (size F-5) hook

Foundation Row: Work 40 Fsc, turn.

Rows 1–43: Rep Row 1 of sc ribbing.
Fasten off.

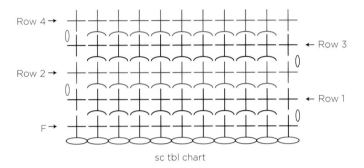

sc tbl chart

sc tbl (sc ribbing)

NOTES

▸ When instructed to work in stitch 2 rows below, insert hook into indicated stitch in the row numbered 2 less than the row you are working. **For example**, if you are working Row 5, a stitch "2 rows below" is worked in Row 3. Row 5 – 2 = Row 3. When working "2 rows below," stitch of current row will remain unworked.

▸ Left Side and Right Side refer to left and right sides as worn.

▸ When instructed to work in a pattern "as established," work the next row of pattern and ensure that the stitches line up as in previous rows.

INSTRUCTIONS

Right Back Side Panel

With larger hook

Foundation Row: Work 31 (37, 43, 49, 57, 63, 71, 77) Fsc, turn.

Rows 1–114 (114, 116, 116, 116, 116, 120, 120): Work in sc linen st.

Begin Armhole Shaping

Row 1 (WS): Work in sc linen st as established to last 6 sts, turn, leaving last 6 sts unworked – 25 (31, 37, 43, 51, 57, 65, 71) sts.

Row 2: Work in sc linen st as established, turn.

Row 3: Work in sc linen st as established to last 6 (9, 9, 9, 9, 9, 9, 9) sts, [sc2tog, sc in next st] 2 (3, 3, 3, 3, 3, 3, 3) times, turn – 23 (28, 34, 40, 48, 54, 62, 68) sts.

Row 4: Rep Row 2.

Row 5: Work in sc linen st as established to last 3 (6, 6, 9, 9, 9, 9, 9) sts, [sc2tog, sc in next st] 1 (2, 2, 3, 3, 3, 3, 3) times, turn – 22 (26, 32, 37, 45, 51, 59, 65) sts.

Row 6: Rep Row 2.

Row 7: Work in sc linen st as established to last 6 sts, [sc2tog, sc in next st] 2 times, turn – 20 (24, 30, 35, 43, 49, 57, 63) sts.

Row 8: Rep Row 2.

Row 9: Work in sc linen st as established to last 3 (3, 3, 6, 6, 6, 6) sts, [sc2tog, sc in next st] 1 (1, 1, 1, 2, 2, 2, 2) times, turn – 19 (23, 29, 34, 41, 47, 55, 61) sts.

Row 10: Rep Row 2.

Sizes L (1X, 2X, 3X, 4X, 5X) Only

Row 11: Work in sc linen st as established to last 3 (3, 9, 9, 9, 9) sts, [sc2tog, sc in next st] 1 (1, 3, 3, 3, 3) times, turn – 28 (33, 38, 44, 52, 58) sts.

Row 12: Rep Row 2.

Row 13: Work in sc linen st as established to last 6 (6, 9, 9, 9, 9) sts, [sc2tog, sc in next st] 2 (2, 3, 3, 3, 3) times, turn – 26 (31, 35, 41, 49, 55) sts.

Row 14: Rep Row 2.

Row 15: Work in sc linen st as established to last 3 (6, 6, 6, 6, 6) sts, [sc2tog, sc in next st] 1 (2, 2, 2, 2, 2) times, turn – 25 (29, 33, 39, 47, 53) sts.

Row 16: Rep Row 2.

Sizes 1X (2X, 3X, 4X, 5X) Only

Row 17: Work in sc linen st as established to last 3 (6, 6, 6, 6) sts, [sc2tog, sc in next st] 1 (2, 2, 2, 2) times, turn – 28 (31, 37, 45, 51) sts.

Row 18: Rep Row 2.

Row 19: Work in sc linen st as established to last 3 (3, 3, 9, 9) sts, [sc2tog, sc in next st] 1 (1, 1, 3, 3) times, turn – 27 (30, 36, 42, 48) sts.

Row 20: Rep Row 2.

Sizes 3X (4X, 5X) Only

Row 21: Work in sc linen st as established to last 3 (9, 9) sts, [sc2tog, sc in next st] 1 (3, 3) times, turn – 35 (39, 45) sts.

Row 22: Rep Row 2.

Row 23: Work in sc linen st as established to last 6 sts, [sc2tog, sc in next st] 2 times, turn – 33 (37, 43) sts.

Row 24: Rep Row 2.

Row 25: Work in sc linen st as established to last 6 sts, [sc2tog, sc in next st] 2 times, turn – 31 (35, 41) sts.

Row 26: Rep Row 2.

Row 27: Work in sc linen st as established to last 3 (3, 6) sts, [sc2tog, sc in next st] 1 (1, 2) times, turn – 30 (34, 39) sts.

Row 28: Rep Row 2.

Sizes 4X (5X) Only

Row 29: Work in sc linen st as established to last 3 (9) sts, [sc2tog, sc in next st] 1 (3) times, turn – 33 (36) sts.

Row 30: Rep Row 2.

Size 5X Only

Row 31: Work in sc linen st as established to last 6 sts, [sc2tog, sc in next st] 2 times, turn – 34 sts.

Row 32: Rep Row 2.

Row 33: Work in sc linen st as established to last 3 sts, sc2tog, sc in next st, turn – 33 sts.

Row 34: Rep Row 2.

All Sizes

Rows 11 (11, 17, 21, 21, 29, 31, 35)–39 (42, 45, 47, 50, 53, 56, 58): Work in sc linen st as established without shaping.

Cut yarn, leaving tail for weaving in; pull tail through last st made; weave in tail using End Cap Finishing Stitch.

Left Back Side Panel

With larger hook

Foundation Row: Work 31 (37, 43, 49, 57, 63, 71, 77) Fsc, turn.

Row 1–114 (114, 116, 116, 116, 116, 120, 120): Work in sc linen st.

Begin Armhole Shaping

Row 1 (WS): Sl st in each of first 6 sts, ch 1, sc in next st, work in sc linen st as established to end of row, turn. – 25 (31, 37, 43, 51, 57, 65, 71) sts.

Row 2: Work in sc linen st as established, turn.

Row 3: Ch 1, [sc2tog, sc in next st] 2 (3, 3, 3, 3, 3, 3, 3) times, work in sc linen st as established to end of row, turn – 23 (28, 34, 40, 48, 54, 62, 68) sts.

Row 4: Rep Row 2.

Row 5: Ch 1, [sc2tog, sc in next st] 1 (2, 2, 3, 3, 3, 3, 3) times, work in sc linen st as established to end of row, turn – 22 (26, 32, 37, 45, 51, 59, 65) sts.

Row 6: Rep Row 2.

Row 7: Ch 1, [sc2tog, sc in next st] 2 times, work in sc linen st as established to end of row, turn – 20 (24, 30, 35, 43, 49, 57, 63) sts.

Row 8: Rep Row 2.

Row 9: Ch 1, [sc2tog, sc in next st] 1 (1, 1, 1, 2, 2, 2, 2) times, work in sc linen st as established to end of row, turn – 19 (23, 29, 34, 41, 47, 55, 61) sts.

Row 10: Rep Row 2.

Sizes L (1X, 2X, 3X, 4X, 5X) Only

Row 11: Ch 1, [sc2tog, sc in next st] 1 (1, 3, 3, 3, 3) times, work in sc linen st as established to end of row, turn – 28 (33, 38, 44, 52, 58) sts.

Row 12: Rep Row 2.

Row 13: Ch 1, [sc2tog, sc in next st] 2 (2, 3, 3, 3, 3) times, work in sc linen st as established to end of row, turn – 26 (31, 35, 41, 49, 55) sts.

Row 14: Rep Row 2.

Row 15: Ch 1, [sc2tog, sc in next st] 1 (2, 2, 2, 2, 2) times, work in sc linen st as established to end of row, turn – 25 (29, 33, 39, 47, 53) sts.

Row 16: Rep Row 2.

Sizes 1X (2X, 3X, 4X, 5X) Only

Row 17: Ch 1, [sc2tog, sc in next st] 1 (2, 2, 2, 2) times, work in sc linen st as established to end of row, turn – 28 (31, 37, 45, 51) sts.

Row 18: Rep Row 2.

Row 19: Ch 1, [sc2tog, sc in next st] 1 (1, 1, 3, 3) times, work in sc linen st as established to end of row, turn – 27 (30, 36, 42, 48) sts.

Row 20: Rep Row 2.

Sizes 3X (4X, 5X) Only

Row 21: Ch 1, [sc2tog, sc in next st] 1 (3, 3) times, work in sc linen st as established to end of row, turn – 35 (39, 45) sts.

Row 22: Rep Row 2.

Row 23: Ch 1, [sc2tog, sc in next st] 2 times, work in sc linen st as established to end of row, turn – 33 (37, 43) sts.

Row 24: Rep Row 2.

Row 25: Ch 1, [sc2tog, sc in next st] 2 times, work in sc linen st as established to end of row, turn – 31 (35, 41) sts.

Row 26: Rep Row 2.

Row 27: Ch 1, [sc2tog, sc in next st] 1 (1, 2) times, work in sc linen st as established to end of row, turn – 30 (34, 39) sts.

Row 28: Rep Row 2.

Sizes 4X (5X) Only

Row 29: Ch 1, [sc2tog, sc in next st] 1 (3) times, work in sc linen st as established to end of row, turn – 33 (36) sts.

Row 30: Rep Row 2.

Size 5X Only

Row 31: Ch 1, [sc2tog, sc in next st] 2 times, work in sc linen st as established to end of row, turn – 34 sts.

Row 32: Rep Row 2.

Row 33: Ch 1, sc2tog, sc in next st, work in sc linen st as established to end of row, turn – 33 sts.

Row 34: Rep Row 2.

All Sizes

Row 11 (11, 17, 21, 21, 29, 31, 35)–39 (42, 45, 47, 50, 53, 56, 58): Work in sc linen st as established without shaping.

Cut yarn, leaving tail for weaving in; pull tail through last st made; weave in tail using End Cap Finishing Stitch.

Left Front Panel

With larger hook

Foundation Row: Work 39 (41, 47, 51, 55, 61, 65, 71) Fsc, turn.

Rows 1–114 (114, 116, 116, 116, 116, 120, 120): Work in sc linen st.

Begin Armhole Shaping

Row 1 (WS): Work in sc linen st to last 6 sts, turn, leaving last 6 sts unworked – 33 (35, 41, 45, 49, 55, 59, 65) sts.

Row 2: Work in sc linen st as established, turn.

Row 3: Work in sc linen st as established to last 6 (9, 9, 9, 9, 9, 9, 9) sts, [sc2tog, sc in next st] 2 (3, 3, 3, 3, 3, 3, 3) times, turn – 31 (32, 38, 42, 46, 52, 56, 62) sts.

Row 4: Rep Row 2.

Row 5: Work in sc linen st as established to last 3 (6, 6, 9, 9, 9, 9, 9) sts, [sc2tog, sc in next st] 1 (2, 2, 3, 3, 3, 3, 3) times, turn – 30 (30, 36, 39, 43, 49, 53, 59) sts.

Row 6: Rep Row 2.

Row 7: Work in sc linen st as established to last 6 sts, [sc2tog, sc in next st] 2 times, turn – 28 (28, 34, 37, 41, 47, 51, 57) sts.

Row 8: Rep Row 2.

Row 9: Work in sc linen st as established to last 3 (3, 3, 3, 6, 6, 6, 6) sts, [sc2tog, sc in next st] 1 (1, 1, 1, 2, 2, 2, 2) times, turn – 27 (27, 33, 36, 39, 45, 49, 55) sts.

Row 10: Rep Row 2.

Sizes L (1X, 2X, 3X, 4X, 5X) Only

Row 11: Work in sc linen st as established to last 3 (3, 9, 9, 9, 9) sts, [sc2tog, sc in next st] 1 (1, 3, 3, 3, 3) times, turn – 32 (35, 36, 42, 46, 52) sts.

Row 12: Rep Row 2.

Row 13: Work in sc linen st as established to last 6 (6, 9, 9, 9, 9) sts, [sc2tog, sc in next st] 2 (2, 3, 3, 3, 3) times, turn – 30 (33, 33, 39, 43, 49) sts.

Row 14: Rep Row 2.

Row 15: Work in sc linen st as established to last 3 (6, 6, 6, 6, 6) sts, [sc2tog, sc in next st] 1 (2, 2, 2, 2, 2) times, turn – 29 (31, 31, 37, 41, 47) sts.

Row 16: Rep Row 2.

Sizes 1X (2X, 3X, 4X, 5X) Only

Row 17: Work in sc linen st as established to last 3 (6, 6, 6, 6) sts, [sc2tog, sc in next st] 1 (2, 2, 2, 2) times, turn – 30 (29, 35, 39, 45) sts.

Row 18: Rep Row 2.

Row 19: Work in sc linen st as established to last 3 (3, 3, 9, 9) sts, [sc2tog, sc in next st] 1 (1, 1, 3, 3) times, turn – 29 (28, 34, 36, 42) sts.

Row 20: Rep Row 2.

Sizes 3X (4X, 5X) Only

Row 21: Work in sc linen st as established to last 3 (9, 9) sts, [sc2tog, sc in next st] 1 (3, 3) times, turn – 33 (33, 39) sts.

Row 22: Rep Row 2.

Row 23: Work in sc linen st as established to last 6 sts, [sc2tog, sc in next st] 2 times, turn – 31 (31, 37) sts.

Row 24: Rep Row 2.

Row 25: Work in sc linen st as established to last 6 sts, [sc2tog, sc in next st] 2 times, turn – 29 (29, 35) sts.

Row 26: Rep Row 2.

Row 27: Work in sc linen st as established to last 3 (3, 6) sts, [sc2tog, sc in next st] 1 (1, 2) times, turn – 28 (28, 33) sts.

Row 28: Rep Row 2.

Sizes 4X (5X) Only

Row 29: Work in sc linen st as established to last 3 (9) sts, [sc2tog, sc in next st] 1 (3) times, turn – 27 (30) sts.

Row 30: Rep Row 2.

Size 5X Only

Row 31: Work in sc linen st as established to last 6 sts, [sc2tog, sc in next st] 2 times, turn – 28 sts.

Row 32: Rep Row 2.

Row 33: Work in sc linen st as established to last 3 sts, sc2tog, sc in next st, turn – 27 sts.

Row 34: Rep Row 2.

All Sizes

Rows 11 (11, 17, 21, 21, 29, 31, 35)–39 (42, 45, 47, 50, 53, 56, 58): Work in sc linen st as established without shaping.

Cut yarn, leaving tail for weaving in; pull tail through last st made; weave in tail using End Cap Finishing Stitch.

Right Front Panel

With larger hook

Foundation Row: Work 39 (41, 47, 51, 55, 61, 65, 71) Fsc, turn.

Rows 1–114 (114, 116, 116, 116, 116, 120, 120): Work in sc linen st.

Begin Armhole Shaping

Row 1 (WS): Sl st in each of first 6 sts, ch 1, sc in next st, work in sc linen st as established to end of row, turn. – 33 (35, 41, 45, 49, 55, 59, 65) sts.

Row 2: Work in sc linen st as established, turn.

Row 3: Ch 1, [sc2tog, sc in next st] 2 (3, 3, 3, 3, 3, 3, 3) times, work in sc linen st as established to end of row, turn – 31 (32, 38, 42, 46, 52, 56, 62) sts.

Row 4: Rep Row 2.

Row 5: Ch 1, [sc2tog, sc in next st] 1 (2, 2, 3, 3, 3, 3, 3) times, work in sc linen st as established to end of row, turn – 30 (30, 36, 39, 43, 49, 53, 59) sts.

Row 6: Rep Row 2.

Row 7: Ch 1, [sc2tog, sc in next st] 2 times, work in sc linen st as established to end of row, turn – 28 (28, 34, 37, 41, 47, 51, 57) sts.

Row 8: Rep Row 2.

Row 9: Ch 1, [sc2tog, sc in next st] 1 (1, 1, 1, 2, 2, 2, 2) times, work in sc linen st as established to end of row, turn – 27 (27, 33, 36, 39, 45, 49, 55) sts.

Row 10: Rep Row 2.

Sizes L (1X, 2X, 3X, 4X, 5X) Only

Row 11: Ch 1, [sc2tog, sc in next st] 1 (1, 3, 3, 3, 3) times, work in sc linen st as established to end of row, turn – 32 (35, 36, 42, 46, 52) sts.

Row 12: Rep Row 2.

Row 13: Ch 1, [sc2tog, sc in next st] 2 (2, 3, 3, 3, 3) times, work in sc linen st as established to end of row, turn – 30 (33, 33, 39, 43, 49) sts.

Row 14: Rep Row 2.

Row 15: Ch 1, [sc2tog, sc in next st] 1 (2, 2, 2, 2, 2) times, work in sc linen st as established to end of row, turn – 29 (31, 31, 37, 41, 47) sts.

Row 16: Rep Row 2.

Sizes 1X (2X, 3X, 4X, 5X) Only

Row 17: Ch 1, [sc2tog, sc in next st] 1 (2, 2, 2, 2) times, work in sc linen st as established to end of row, turn – 30 (29, 35, 39, 45) sts.

Row 18: Rep Row 2.

Row 19: Ch 1, [sc2tog, sc in next st] 1 (1, 1, 3, 3) times, work in sc linen st as established to end of row, turn – 29 (28, 34, 36, 42) sts.

Row 20: Rep Row 2.

Sizes 3X (4X, 5X) Only

Row 21: Ch 1, [sc2tog, sc in next st] 1 (3, 3) times, work in sc linen st as established to end of row, turn – 33 (33, 39) sts.

Row 22: Rep Row 2.

Row 23: Ch 1, [sc2tog, sc in next st] 2 times, work in sc linen st as established to end of row, turn – 31 (31, 37) sts.

Row 24: Rep Row 2.

Row 25: Ch 1, [sc2tog, sc in next st] 2 times, work in sc linen st as established to end of row, turn – 29 (29, 35) sts.

Row 26: Rep Row 2.

Row 27: Ch 1, [sc2tog, sc in next st] 1 (1, 2) times, work in sc linen st as established to end of row, turn – 28 (28, 33) sts.

Row 28: Rep Row 2.

Sizes 4X (5X) Only

Row 29: Ch 1, [sc2tog, sc in next st] 1 (3) times, work in sc linen st as established to end of row, turn – 27 (30) sts.

Row 30: Rep Row 2.

Row 31: Ch 1, [sc2tog, sc in next st] 2 times, work in sc linen st as established to end of row, turn – 28 sts.

Row 32: Rep Row 2.

Row 33: Ch 1, sc2tog, sc in next st, work in sc linen st as established to end of row, turn – 27 sts.

Row 34: Rep Row 2.

All Sizes

Rows 11 (11, 17, 21, 21, 29, 31, 35)–39 (42, 45, 47, 50, 53, 56, 58): Work in sc linen st as established without shaping.

Cut yarn, leaving tail for weaving in; pull tail through last st made; weave in tail using End Cap Finishing Stitch.

Back Center Panel

Lace Option

With larger hook

Foundation Row: Work 42 Fsc, turn.

Rows 1–95 (95, 99, 99, 102, 102, 109, 109): Work in lace pattern.

Cut yarn, leaving tail for weaving in; pull tail through last st made; weave in tail using End Cap Finishing Stitch.

Cable Option

With larger hook

Foundation Row: Work 46 Fsc, turn.

Rows 1–47 (47, 53, 53, 59, 59, 71, 71): Ch 1, sc in first st and in each st to end of row, turn.

Begin Cable

Rows 1–94: Work in cable pattern.

Rows 1–25 (25, 26, 26, 25, 26, 25, 25): Ch 1, sc in first st and in each st to end of row, turn.

Cut yarn, leaving tail for weaving in; pull tail through last st made; weave in tail using End Cap Finishing Stitch.

Collar Panel

Lace Option

With larger hook

Foundation Row: Work 42 Fsc, turn.

Rows 1–213 (220, 228, 231, 239, 243, 256, 259): Work in lace pattern.

Cut yarn, leaving tail for weaving in; pull tail through last st made; weave in tail using End Cap Finishing Stitch.

Ribbing Option

With smaller hook

Foundation Row: Work 40 Fsc, turn.

Rows 1–442 (457, 473, 482, 496, 504, 532, 537): Work in sc ribbing.

Cut yarn, leaving tail for weaving in; pull tail through last st made; weave in tail using End Cap Finishing Stitch.

FINISHING

Block all pieces to measurements in schematic.

Sew back side panels to back center panel.

Using Locking Mattress Stitch, attach front panels to assembled back panel by sewing 4.25 (4.25, 4.5, 4.5, 4.5, 4.5, 4.25, 4.25)"/10.75 (10.75, 11.5, 11.5, 11.5, 11.5, 10.75, 10.75) cm shoulder seams.

Sew side body seams.

Pin collar into place and sew evenly to fronts and neckline.

Gently block sewn seams if needed.

Signature Vests Schematic

14.5(16, 16.5, 17.5, 18, 18, 18.5, 18.5)"
36.75 (40.5, 42, 45, 45.75, 45.75, 47, 47) cm

6 (7, 7.5, 8, 9, 9, 10.5, 10.5)"
15.25 (17.75, 19, 20.25, 22.75, 22.75, 26.5, 26.5) cm

3 (3.5, 4, 4.25, 4.75, 4.75, 5, 5)"
7.5 (8.75, 10, 10.75, 12, 12, 12.75, 12.75) cm

17.75 (19, 20.25, 21.5, 22.75, 24, 25.5, 26.5) cm

7 (7.5, 8, 8.5, 9, 9.5, 10, 10.5)"

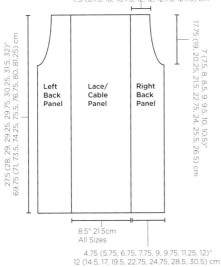

Left Back Panel

Lace/ Cable Panel

Right Back Panel

27.5 (28, 29, 29.25, 29.75, 30.25, 31.5, 32)"
69.75 (71, 73.5, 74.25, 75.5, 76.75, 80, 81.25) cm

8.5" 21.5cm
All Sizes

4.75 (5.75, 6.75, 7.75, 9, 9.75, 11.25, 12)"
12 (14.5, 17, 19.5, 22.75, 24.75, 28.5, 30.5) cm

4.25 (4.25, 4.5, 4.5, 4.5, 4.5, 4.25, 4.25)"
10.75 (10.75, 11.5, 11.5, 11.5, 11.5, 10.75, 10.75) cm

17.75 (19, 20.25, 21.5, 22.75, 24, 25.5, 26.5) cm

7 (7.5, 8, 8.5, 9, 9.5, 10, 10.5)"

Front Panel

27.5 (28, 29, 29.25, 29.75, 30.25, 31.5, 32)"
69.75 (71, 73.5, 74.25, 75.5, 76.75, 80, 81.25) cm

6 (6.5, 7.25, 8, 8.5, 9.5, 10, 11)"
15.25 (16.5, 18.5, 20.25, 21.5, 24, 26, 28.5) cm

Collar Panel

7" All Sizes Ribbed Collar
8.5" All Sizes Lace Collar
17.75cm/21.5 cm

63 (65, 67.25, 68.25, 70.5, 71.75, 75.5, 76.5)"
160 (165, 170.75, 173.25, 179, 182.25, 191.75, 194.25) cm

Drape Front Cardigan

Now that you've worked through a few beginner projects, it's time to strut your stuff with the Drape Front Cardi. The drape front cardigan is the star of the cardi world and our version features the characteristic flowing front panels to create the drama while set-in sleeves and perfectly proportioned shoulder seams and sleeve caps provide a structured fit. Bring all your top crochet skills to the table for this project and you'll have a favorite garment that will show off your crochet prowess time and time again.

SKILLS USED

Knotless Starting Chain (*see page 79*)
Foundation Double Crochet (*see page 106*)
Linked First Double Crochet (*see page 99*)
Increases (*see page 139*)
Decreases (*see page 139*)

Blocking (*see page 240*)
Locking Mattress Stitch (*see page 257*)
Setting In A Sleeve (*see page 254*)
Double Crochet (*see page 86*)
Joining Yarn – Standing Stitches (*see pages 159, 161*)

SKILL LEVEL

INTERMEDIATE

SIZES S (M, L, XL, 2X, 3X, 4X, 5X)

Sample shown in size Small

FINISHED MEASUREMENTS

To Fit Bust: 32 (36, 40, 44, 48, 52, 56, 60)"/81.5 (91.5, 101.5, 112, 122, 132, 142, 152.5) cm

Finished Length from Shoulder: 25.5 (26, 26.5, 27, 27.5, 28, 28.5, 29)"/64.75 (66, 67.25, 68.5, 69.75, 71, 72.5, 73.75) cm

MATERIALS AND TOOLS

Sample uses Lion Brand Yarns LB Collection, Superwash Merino (100% Superwash Merino Wool; 3.5 ounces/100g = 306 yards/280 m): 8 (8, 9, 10, 11, 12, 13, 14) balls in color Wild Berry #486-141—2448 (2448, 2754, 3060, 3366, 3672, 3978, 4284) yards/2240 (2240, 2520, 2800, 3080, 3360, 3640, 3920) m of lightweight yarn

Crochet hook: 4.00mm (size G-6) or size to obtain gauge

Yarn needle

BLOCKED GAUGES

Stacked lace: 4.9 sts = 1"/2.5 cm; 65 sts = 13.25"/33.5 cm; 2.33 rows = 1"/2.5 cm; 21 rows = 9"/22.75 cm

Single crochet through front loop: 5.56 sts = 1"/2.5 cm; 50 sts = 9"/22.75 cm; 5.1 rows = 1"/2.5 cm; 33 rows = 6.5"/16.5 cm

STITCH GUIDE

Foundation Double Crochet (Fdc): Ch 2, insert hook into first ch from hook, yo and draw up a lp, insert hook into next ch, yo and draw up a lp (3 lps on hook), yo and draw through 1 lp (first "chain" made), [yo and draw through 2 lps on hook] 2 times (first Fdc made), *yo, insert hook under 2 lps of the "chain" just made, yo and draw up a lp ("chain" made), yo and draw through 1 lp, [yo and draw through 2 lps on hook] 2 times (Fdc made); rep from * for indicated number of foundation sts.

Linked first double crochet (Linked first-dc): Ch 1, insert hook into first ch from hook, yo and draw up a lp (2 lps on hook), insert hook into first st, yo and draw up a lp (3 lps on hook), [yo and draw through 2 lps on hook] 2 times.

Double crochet v-stitch (dc-v): (Dc, ch 1, dc) in indicated st or space.

3 Double Crochet Shell (3-dc Shell): Dc 3 times in indicated st or space.

Inverted double crochet v-stitch (inverted dc-v): Yo, insert hook into next ch sp, yo and draw up a lp, yo and draw through 2 lps on hook, sk next st, yo, insert hook into next ch sp, yo and draw up a lp, yo and draw through 2 lps on hook, yo and draw through all 3 lps on hook.

NOTES

▸ Left Side and Right Side refer to left and right sides as worn.

▸ When instructed to increase 1 stitch at beginning and end of row, work as follows: Ch 1, sc in first st, sc 2 times in next st, work in pattern as instructed to last 2 sts in row, sc 2 times in next st, sc in last st, turn. This will create one additional stitch at the beginning of the row and one additional stitch at the end of the row.

▸ When instructed to work in a pattern "as established," work the next row of pattern and ensure that the stitches line up as in previous rows.

PATTERN STITCHES

Stacked lace (worked over a multiple of 3 + 2 sts)

Row 1: Work Linked first-dc, sk next st, dc-v in next st, *sk next 2 sts, dc-v in next st; rep from * to last 2 sts, sk next st, dc in last st, turn.

Row 2: Work Linked first-dc, *3-dc shell in ch-1 sp of next dc-v; rep from * to last st, dc in last st, turn.

Row 3: Work Linked first-dc, *ch 1, work dc3tog, ch 1; rep from * to last st, dc in last st, turn.

Row 4: Work Linked first-dc, *ch 1, work inverted dc-v, ch 1; rep from * to last st, dc in last st, turn.

Row 5: Work Linked first-dc, dc in next st and in each st to end of row, turn.

Rep Rows 1–5 for pattern stitch.

Swatch: 65 sts and 20 rows (+ 1 Fsc row)

Foundation Row: Work 65 Fdc, turn.

Rows 1-20: Rep Rows 1-5 of stacked lace. Fasten off.

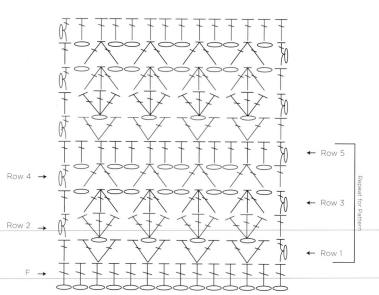

stacked lace chart

stacked lace stitch

Single crochet through front loop pattern (sc tfl pattern) (worked over any multiple of sts)

Row 1: Ch 1, sc in first st, sc tfl in next st and in each st to last st, sc in last st, turn. Rep Row 1 for pattern stitch.

Swatch: 50 sts and 32 rows (+ 1 Fsc row)

Foundation Row: Work 50 Fsc, turn.

Rows 1-32: Rep Row 1 of sc tfl pattern. Fasten off.

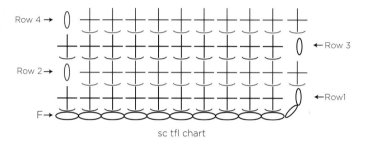

sc tfl chart

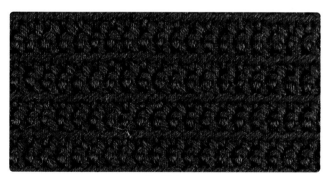

sc tfl stitch

INSTRUCTIONS

Back Panel

Foundation Row: Work 89 (98, 110, 119, 128, 137, 149, 158) Fdc, turn.

Rows 1–40: Work in stacked lace.

Transition Row (RS): Ch 1, sc in each of first 6 (7, 6, 7, 8, 9, 8, 9) sts, [sc 2 times in next st, sc in each of next 6 sts] 11 (12, 14, 15, 16, 17, 19, 20) times, sc 2 times in next st, sc in each of next 5 (6, 5, 6, 7, 8, 7, 8) sts, turn – 101 (111, 125, 135, 145, 155, 169, 179) sts.

Begin armhole shaping

Row 1: Ch 1, sl st in each of first 6 sts, ch 1, sc in next st, sc tfl in next st and in each st to last 7 sts, sc in next st, turn, leaving last 6 sts unworked – 89 (99, 113, 123, 133, 143, 157, 167) sts.

Row 2: Ch 1, sc in first st, sc2tog, work in sc tfl pattern as established to last 3 sts, sc2tog, sc in last st, turn – 87 (97, 111, 121, 131, 141, 155, 165) sts.

Row 3: Ch 1, sc in first st, sc2tog 2 times, work in sc tfl pattern as established to last 5 sts, sc2tog 2 times, sc in last st, turn – 83 (93, 107, 117, 127, 137, 151, 161) sts.

Size S (M) Only

Row 4: Ch 1, sc in first st, sc2tog, work in sc tfl pattern as established to last 3 sts, sc2tog, sc in last st, turn – 81 (91) sts.

Size M Only

Row 5: Ch 1, sc in first st, sc2tog, work in sc tfl pattern as established to last 3 sts, sc2tog, sc in last st, turn – 89 sts.

Sizes L (1X, 2X, 3X, 4X, 5X)

Row 4: Ch 1, sc in first st, sc2tog, [sc in next st, sc2tog] 2 times, work in sc tfl pattern as established to last 9 sts, [sc2tog, sc in next st] 3 times, turn – 101 (111, 121, 131, 145, 155) sts.

Row 5: Ch 1, sc in first st, sc2tog 2 times, work in sc tfl pattern as established to last 5 sts, sc2tog 2 times, sc in last st, turn – 97 (107, 117, 127, 141, 151) sts.

Row 6: Ch 1, sc in first st, sc2tog, work in sc tfl pattern as established to last 3 sts, sc2tog, sc in last st, turn – 95 (105, 115, 125, 139, 149) sts.

Row 7: Ch 1, sc in first st, sc2tog 1 (2, 2, 2, 2, 2) times, work in sc tfl pattern as established to last 3 (5, 5, 5, 5, 5) sts, sc2tog 1 (2, 2, 2, 2, 2) times, sc in last st, turn – 93 (101, 111, 121, 135, 145) sts.

Size 1X Only

Rows 8–9: Ch 1, sc in first st, sc2tog, work in sc tfl pattern as established to last 3 sts, sc2tog, sc in last st, turn – 97 sts after row 9.

Size 2X (3X, 4X, 5X) Only

Row 8: Ch 1, sc in first st, sc2tog, [sc in next st, sc2tog] 2 times, work in sc tfl pattern as established to last 9 sts, [sc2tog, sc in next st] 3 times, turn – 105 (115, 129, 139) sts.

Size 2X Only

Rows 9–10: Ch 1, sc in first st, sc2tog, work in sc tfl pattern as established to last 3 sts, sc2tog, sc in last st, turn – 101 sts after row 10.

Size 3X (4X, 5X) Only

Row 9: Ch 1, sc in first st, sc2tog 2 times, work in sc tfl pattern as established to last 5 sts, sc2tog 2 times, sc in last st, turn – 111 (125, 135) sts.

Row 10: Ch 1, sc in first st, sc2tog, work in sc tfl pattern as established to last 3 sts, sc2tog, sc in last st, turn – 109 (123, 133) sts.

Row 11: Ch 1, sc in first st, sc2tog 2 times, work in sc tfl pattern as established to last 5 sts, sc2tog 2 times, sc in last st, turn – 105 (119, 129) sts.

Size 3X Only

Rows 12–13: Ch 1, sc in first st, sc2tog, work in sc tfl pattern as established to last 3 sts, sc2tog, sc in last st, turn – 101 sts after row 13.

Sizes 4X (5X) Only

Row 12: Ch 1, sc in first st, sc2tog, [sc in next st, sc2tog] 2 times, work in sc tfl pattern as established to last 9 sts, [sc2tog, sc in next st] 3 times, turn – 113 (123) sts.

Row 13: Ch 1, sc in first st, sc2tog 2 times, work in sc tfl pattern as established to last 5 sts, sc2tog 2 times, sc in last st, turn – 109 (119) sts.

Row 14: Ch 1, sc in first st, sc2tog, work in sc tfl pattern as established to last 3 sts, sc2tog, sc in last st, turn – 107 (117) sts.

Size 4X Only

Rows 15–16: Ch 1, sc in first st, sc2tog, work in sc tfl pattern as established to last 3 sts, sc2tog, sc in last st, turn – 103 sts after row 16.

Size 5X Only

Row 15: Ch 1, sc in first st, sc2tog 2 times, work in sc tfl pattern as established to last 5 sts, sc2tog 2 times, sc in last st, turn – 113 sts.

Row 16: Ch 1, sc in first st, sc2tog, [sc in next st, sc2tog] 2 times, work in sc tfl pattern as established to last 9 sts, [sc2tog, sc in next st] 3 times, turn – 107 sts.

Rows 17–18: Ch 1, sc in first st, sc2tog, work in sc tfl pattern as established to last 3 sts, sc2tog, sc in last st, turn – 103 sts after row 18.

All Sizes

End armhole shaping

Rows 5 (6, 8, 10, 11, 14, 17, 19)–38 (41, 43, 46, 49, 51, 54, 56): Ch 1, sc in first st, work in sc tfl pattern as established to last st, sc in last st, turn.

Cut yarn, leaving tail for weaving in; pull tail through last st made; weave in tail using End Cap Finishing Stitch.

First Front

Work as for back to armhole shaping.

Begin armhole shaping

Row 1: Ch 1, sl st in each of first 6 sts, ch 1, sc in next st, work in sc tfl pattern as established to last st, sc in last st, turn – 95 (105, 119, 129, 139, 149, 163, 173) sts.

Row 2: Ch 1, sc in first st, work in sc tfl pattern as established to last 3 sts, sc2tog, sc in last st, turn – 94 (104, 118, 128, 138, 148, 162, 172) sts.

Row 3: Ch 1, sc in first st, sc2tog 2 times, work in sc tfl pattern as established to last st, sc in last st, turn – 92 (102, 116, 126, 136, 146, 160, 170) sts.

Size S (M) Only

Row 4: Ch 1, sc in first st, work in sc tfl pattern as established to last 3 sts, sc2tog, sc in last st, turn – 91 (101) sts.

Size M Only

Row 5: Ch 1, sc in first st, sc2tog, work in sc tfl pattern as established to last st, sc in last st, turn – 100 sts.

Sizes L (1X, 2X, 3X, 4X, 5X)

Row 4: Ch 1, sc in first st, work in sc tfl pattern as established to last 9 sts, [sc2tog, sc in next st] 3 times, turn – 113 (123, 133, 143, 157, 167) sts.

Row 5: Ch 1, sc in first st, sc2tog 2 times, work in sc tfl pattern as established to last st, sc in last st, turn – 111 (121, 131, 141, 155, 165) sts.

Row 6: Ch 1, sc in first st, work in sc tfl pattern as established to last 3 sts, sc2tog, sc in last st, turn – 110 (120, 130, 140, 154, 164) sts.

Row 7: Ch 1, sc in first st sc2tog 1 (2, 2, 2, 2, 2) times, work in sc tfl pattern as established to last st, sc in last st, turn – 109 (118, 128, 138, 152, 162) sts.

Size 1X Only

Row 8: Ch 1, sc in first st, work in sc tfl pattern as established to last 3 sts, sc2tog, sc in last st, turn – 117 sts.

Row 9: Ch 1, sc in first st, sc2tog, work in sc tfl pattern as established to last st, sc in last st, turn – 116 sts.

Size 2X (3X, 4X, 5X) Only

Row 8: Ch 1, sc in first st, work in sc tfl pattern as established to last 9 sts, [sc2tog, sc in next st] 3 times, turn – 125 (135, 149, 159) sts.

Size 2X Only

Row 9: Ch 1, sc in first st, sc2tog, work in sc tfl pattern as established to last st, sc in last st, turn – 124 sts.

Row 10: Ch 1, sc in first st, work in sc tfl pattern as established to last 3 sts, sc2tog, sc in last st, turn – 123 sts.

Size 3X (4X, 5X) Only

Row 9: Ch 1, sc in first st, sc2tog 2 times, work in sc tfl pattern as established to last st, sc in last st, turn – 133 (147, 157) sts.

Row 10: Ch 1, sc in first st, work in sc tfl pattern as established to last 3 sts, sc2tog, sc in last st, turn – 132 (146, 156) sts.

Row 11: Ch 1, sc in first st, sc2tog 2 times, work in sc tfl pattern as established to last st, sc in last st, turn – 130 (144, 154) sts.

Size 3X Only

Row 12: Ch 1, sc in first st, work in sc tfl pattern as established to last 3 sts, sc2tog, sc in last st, turn – 129 sts.

Row 13: Ch 1, sc in first st, sc2tog, work in sc tfl pattern as established to last st, sc in last st, turn – 128 sts.

Sizes 4X (5X) Only

Row 12: Ch 1, sc in first st, work in sc tfl pattern as established to last 9 sts, [sc2tog, sc in next st] 3 times, turn – 141 (151) sts.

Row 13: Ch 1, sc in first st, sc2tog 2 times, work in sc tfl pattern as established to last st, sc in last st, turn – 139 (149) sts.

Row 14: Ch 1, sc in first st, work in sc tfl pattern as established to last 3 sts, sc2tog, sc in last st, turn – 138 (148) sts.

Size 4X Only

Row 15: Ch 1, sc in first st, sc2tog, work in sc tfl pattern as established to last st, sc in last st, turn – 137 sts.

Row 16: Ch 1, sc in first st, work in sc tfl pattern as established to last 3 sts, sc2tog, sc in last st, turn – 136 sts

Size 5X Only

Row 15: Ch 1, sc in first st, sc2tog 2 times, work in sc tfl pattern as established to last st, sc in last st, turn – 146 sts.

Row 16: Ch 1, sc in first st, work in sc tfl pattern as established to last 9 sts, [sc2tog, sc in next st] 3 times, turn – 143 sts.

Row 17: Ch 1, sc in first st, sc2tog, work in sc tfl pattern as established to last st, sc in last st, turn – 142 sts.

Row 18: Ch 1, sc in first st, work in sc tfl pattern as established to last 5 sts, sc2tog, sc in last st, turn – 141 sts.

All Sizes

End armhole shaping

Rows 5 (6, 8, 10, 11, 14, 17, 19)–38 (41, 43, 46, 49, 51, 54, 56): Ch 1, sc in first st, work in sc tfl pattern as established to last st, sc in last st, turn.

Cut yarn, leaving tail for weaving in; pull tail through last st made; weave in tail using End Cap Finishing Stitch.

Second Front

Work as for back to armhole shaping.

Begin armhole shaping

Row 1: Ch 1, sc in first st, work in sc tfl pattern as established to last 7 sts, sc in next st, turn, leaving last 6 sts unworked – 95 (105, 119, 129, 139, 149, 163, 173) sts.

Row 2: Ch 1, sc in first st, sc2tog, work in sc tfl pattern as established to last st, sc in last st, turn – 94 (104, 118, 128, 138, 148, 162, 172) sts.

Row 3: Ch 1, sc in first st, work in sc tfl pattern as established to last 5 sts, sc2tog 2 times, sc in last st, turn – 92 (102, 116, 126, 136, 146, 160, 170) sts.

Size S (M) Only

Row 4: Ch 1, sc in first st, sc2tog, work in sc tfl pattern as established to last st, sc in last st, turn – 91 (101) sts.

Size M Only

Row 5: Ch 1, sc in first st, work in sc tfl pattern as established to last 3 sts, sc2tog, sc in last st, turn – 100 sts.

Sizes L (1X, 2X, 3X, 4X, 5X)

Row 4: Ch 1, sc in first st, sc2tog, [sc in next st, sc2tog] 2 times, work in sc tfl pattern as established to last st, sc in last st, turn – 113 (123, 133, 143, 157, 167) sts.

Row 5: Ch 1, sc in first st, work in sc tfl pattern as established to last 5 sts, sc2tog 2 times, sc in last st, turn – 111 (121, 131, 141, 155, 165) sts.

Row 6: Ch 1, sc in first st, sc2tog, work in sc tfl pattern as established to last st, sc in last st, turn – 110 (120, 130, 140, 154, 164) sts.

Row 7: Ch 1, sc in first st, work in sc tfl pattern as established to last 3 (5, 5, 5, 5, 5) sts, sc2tog 1 (2, 2, 2, 2, 2) times, sc in last st, turn – 109 (118, 128, 138, 152, 162) sts.

Row 8: Ch 1, sc in first st, sc2tog, work in sc tfl pattern as established to last st, sc in last st, turn – 117 sts.

Row 9: Ch 1, sc in first st, work in sc tfl pattern as established to last 3 sts, sc2tog, sc in last st, turn – 116 sts.

Size 2X (3X, 4X, 5X) Only

Row 8: Ch 1, sc in first st, sc2tog, [sc in next st, sc2tog] 2 times, work in sc tfl pattern as established to last st, sc in last st, turn – 125 (135, 149, 159) sts.

Size 2X Only

Row 9: Ch 1, sc in first st, work in sc tfl pattern as established to last 3 sts, sc2tog, sc in last st, turn – 124 sts.

Row 10: Ch 1, sc in first st, sc2tog, work in sc tfl pattern as established to last st, sc in last st, turn – 123 sts.

Size 3X (4X, 5X) Only

Row 9: Ch 1, sc in first st, work in sc tfl pattern as established to last 5 sts, sc2tog 2 times, sc in last st, turn – 133 (147, 157) sts.

Row 10: Ch 1, sc in first st, sc2tog, work in sc tfl pattern as established to last st, sc in last st, turn – 132 (146, 156) sts.

Row 11: Ch 1, sc in first st, work in sc tfl pattern as established to last 5 sts, sc2tog 2 times, sc in last st, turn – 130 (144, 154) sts.

Size 3X Only

Row 12: Ch 1, sc in first st, sc2tog, work in sc tfl pattern as established to last st, sc in last st, turn – 129 sts.

Row 13: Ch 1, sc in first st, work in sc tfl pattern as established to last 3 sts, sc2tog, sc in last st, turn – 128 sts.

Sizes 4X (5X) Only

Row 12: Ch 1, sc in first st, sc2tog, [sc in next st, sc2tog] 2 times, work in sc tfl pattern as established to last st, sc in last st, turn – 141 (151) sts.

Row 13: Ch 1, sc in first st, work in sc tfl pattern as established to last 5 sts, sc2tog 2 times, sc in last st, turn – 139 (149) sts.

Row 14: Ch 1, sc in first st, sc2tog, work in sc tfl pattern as established to last st, sc in last st, turn – 138 (148) sts.

Size 4X Only

Row 15: Ch 1, sc in first st, work in sc tfl pattern as established to last 3 sts, sc2tog, sc in last st, turn – 137 sts.

Row 16: Ch 1, sc in first st, sc2tog, work in sc tfl pattern as established to last st, sc in last st, turn – 136 sts.

Size 5X Only

Row 15: Ch 1, sc in first st, work in sc tfl pattern as established to last 5 sts, sc2tog 2 times, sc in last st, turn – 146 sts.

Row 16: Ch 1, sc in first st, sc2tog, [sc in next st, sc2tog] 2 times, work in sc tfl pattern as established to last st, sc in last st, turn – 143 sts.

Row 17: Ch 1, sc in first st, work in sc tfl pattern as established to last 3 sts, sc2tog, sc in last st, turn – 142 sts.

Row 18: Ch 1, sc in first st, sc2tog 2 times, work in sc tfl pattern as established to last st, sc in last st, turn – 141 sts.

All Sizes

End armhole shaping

Rows 5 (6, 8, 10, 11, 14, 17, 19)–38 (41, 43, 46, 49, 51, 54, 56): Ch 1, sc in first st, work in sc tfl pattern as established to last st, sc in last st, turn.

Cut yarn, leaving tail for weaving in; pull tail through last st made; weave in tail using End Cap Finishing Stitch.

Sleeve (make 2)

Foundation Row: Work 44 (44, 47, 47, 50, 50, 53, 53) Fdc, turn.

Rows 1-4: Work in stacked lace.

Transition Row: Ch 1, sc in each of first 7 (7, 6, 6, 4, 4, 5, 5) sts, [sc 2 times in next st, sc in each of next 5 (5, 6, 6, 5, 5, 5, 5) sts] 5 (5, 5, 5, 7, 7, 7, 7) times, sc 2 times in next st, sc in each of next 6 (6, 5, 5, 3, 3, 5, 5) sts, turn – 50 (50, 53, 53, 58, 58, 61, 61) sts.

Begin sleeve shaping

Row 1: Ch 1, sc in first st, sc 2 times in next st, sc tfl in next st and in each st to last 2 sts, sc 2 times in next st, sc in last st, turn – 52 (52, 55, 55, 60, 60, 63, 63) sts.

Rows 2-5 (4, 4, 3, 3, 3, 3, 3): Ch 1, sc in first st, work in sc tfl pattern as established to last st, sc in last st, turn.

Rows 6 (5, 5, 4, 4, 4, 4, 4)–85 (48, 72, 21, 33, 63, 63, 99): Rep Rows 1-5(4, 4, 3, 3, 3, 3, 3) – 84 (74, 89, 67, 80, 100, 103, 127) sts.

Row 86 (49, 73, 22, 34, 64, 64, 100): Ch 1, sc in first st, sc 2 times in next st, work in sc tfl pattern as established to last 2 sts, sc 2 times in next st, sc in last st, turn – 86 (76, 91, 69, 82, 102, 105, 129) sts.

Rows 87 (50, 74, 23, 35, 65, 65, 101)–91 (53, 77, 25, 37, 67, 67, 103): Ch 1, sc in first st, work in sc tfl pattern as established to last st, sc in last st, turn.

Sizes M (L, 1X, 2X, 3X, 4X, 5X) Only

Row 54 (78, 26, 38, 68, 68, 104)–93 (97, 97, 101, 103, 107, 107): Rep Rows 49 (73, 22, 34, 64, 64, 100) 53 (77, 25, 37, 67, 67, 103) – 92 (99, 105, 114, 120, 125, 131) sts.

All Sizes

Begin sleeve cap shaping

Row 1: Ch 1, sl st in each of first 6 sts, ch 1, sc in next st, work in sc tfl pattern as established to last 7 sts, sc in next st, turn, leaving last 6 sts unworked – 74 (80, 87, 93, 102, 108, 113, 119) sts.

Rows 2–13 (11, 20, 18, 24, 21, 20, 18): Ch 1, sc in first st, sc2tog, work in sc tfl pattern as established to last 2 sts, sc2tog, sc in last st, turn – 50 (60, 49, 59, 56, 68, 75, 85) sts.

Rows 14 (12, 21, 19, 25, 22, 21, 19)–18 (18, 24, 24, 29, 29, 29, 29): Ch 1, sc in first st, sc2tog 2 times, work in sc tfl pattern as established to last 5 sts, sc2tog 2 times, sc in last st, turn – 30 (32, 33, 35, 36, 36, 39, 41) sts.

Rows 19 (19, 25, 25, 30, 30, 30, 30)–20 (20, 26, 26, 31, 31, 31, 31): Ch 1, sc in first st, sc2tog, [sc in next st, sc2tog] 2 times, work in sc tfl pattern as established to last 9 sts, [sc2tog, sc in next st] 3 times, turn – 18 (20, 21, 23, 24, 24, 27, 29) sts.

Cut yarn, leaving tail for weaving in; pull tail through last st made; weave in tail using End Cap Finishing Stitch.

FINISHING

Block all pieces to measurements in schematic.

Using Locking Mattress Stitch, attach Front Panels to Back Panel by sewing 24 (25, 26, 26, 26, 25, 23, 23) sts [4.25 (4.5, 4.75, 4.75, 4.75, 4.5, 4.25, 4.25)"/10.75 (11.5, 12, 12, 12, 11.5, 10.75, 10.75) cm] shoulder seams in preparation for making Top Lace Border.

Top Lace Border

With WS facing, join yarn in top corner st of Left Front panel. First st of transition row is worked in same st where yarn is joined.

Transition row: Ch 1, sc in each of first 3 (8, 8, 8, 10, 17, 37, 42) sts, [sc 2 times in next st, sc in each of next 6 (8, 11, 10, 13, 15, 34, 41) sts] 23 (19, 16, 19, 16, 14, 6, 5) times, sc 2 times in next st, sc in each of next 2 (9, 6, 7, 8, 15, 35, 40) sts, turn – 191 (209, 224, 245, 260, 272, 290, 299) sts.

Rows 1–15: Work in stacked lace.

Cut yarn, leaving tail for weaving in; pull tail through last st made; weave in tail using End Cap Finishing Stitch.

With WS facing: Fold Sleeves in half lengthwise. Matching fold to shoulder seam, sew top of Sleeves to Front and Back. Sew sleeve seams.

Sew side body seams.

Gently steam block seams if needed.

Drape Front Cardigan Schematic

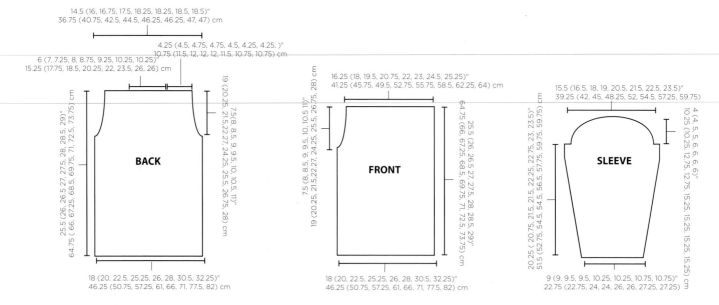

BACK

14.5 (16, 16.75, 17.5, 18.25, 18.25, 18.5, 18.5)"
36.75 (40.75, 42.5, 44.5, 46.25, 46.25, 47, 47) cm

4.25 (4.5, 4.75, 4.75, 4.5, 4.25, 4.25,)"
10.75 (11.5, 12, 12, 12, 11.5, 10.75, 10.75) cm

6 (7, 7.25, 8, 8.75, 9.25, 10.25, 10.25)"
15.25 (17.75, 18.5, 20.25, 22, 23.5, 26, 26) cm

19 (20.25, 21.5, 22.27, 24.25, 25.5, 26.75, 28) cm

7.5 (8, 8.5, 9, 9.5, 10, 10.5, 11)"

25.5 (26, 26.5, 27, 27.5, 28, 28.5, 29)"
64.75 (66, 67.25, 68.5, 69.75, 71, 72.5, 73.75) cm

18 (20, 22.5, 25.25, 26, 28, 30.5, 32.25)"
46.25 (50.75, 57.25, 61, 66, 71, 77.5, 82) cm

FRONT

16.25 (18, 19.5, 20.75, 22, 23, 24.5, 25.25)"
41.25 (45.75, 49.5, 52.75, 55.75, 58.5, 62.25, 64) cm

7.5 (8, 8.5, 9, 9.5, 10, 10.5, 11)"
19 (20.25, 21.5, 22.27, 24.25, 25.5, 26.75, 28) cm

25.5 (26, 26.5, 27, 27.5, 28, 28.5, 29)"
64.75 (66, 67.25, 68.5, 69.75, 71, 72.5, 73.75) cm

18 (20, 22.5, 25.25, 26, 28, 30.5, 32.25)"
46.25 (50.75, 57.25, 61, 66, 71, 77.5, 82) cm

SLEEVE

15.5 (16.5, 18, 19, 20.5, 21.5, 22.5, 23.5)"
39.25 (42, 45, 48.25, 52, 54.5, 57.25, 59.75)

4 (4.5, 5, 6, 6, 6, 6)"
10.25 (10.25, 12.75, 15.25, 15.25, 15.25, 15.25) cm

20.25 (20.75, 21.5, 21.5, 22.25, 22.75, 23, 23.5)"
51.5 (52.75, 54.5, 54.5, 56.5, 57.75, 59.75, 59.75) cm

9 (9, 9.5, 9.5, 10.25, 10.25, 10.75, 10.75)"
22.75 (22.75, 24, 24, 26, 26, 27.25, 27.25) cm

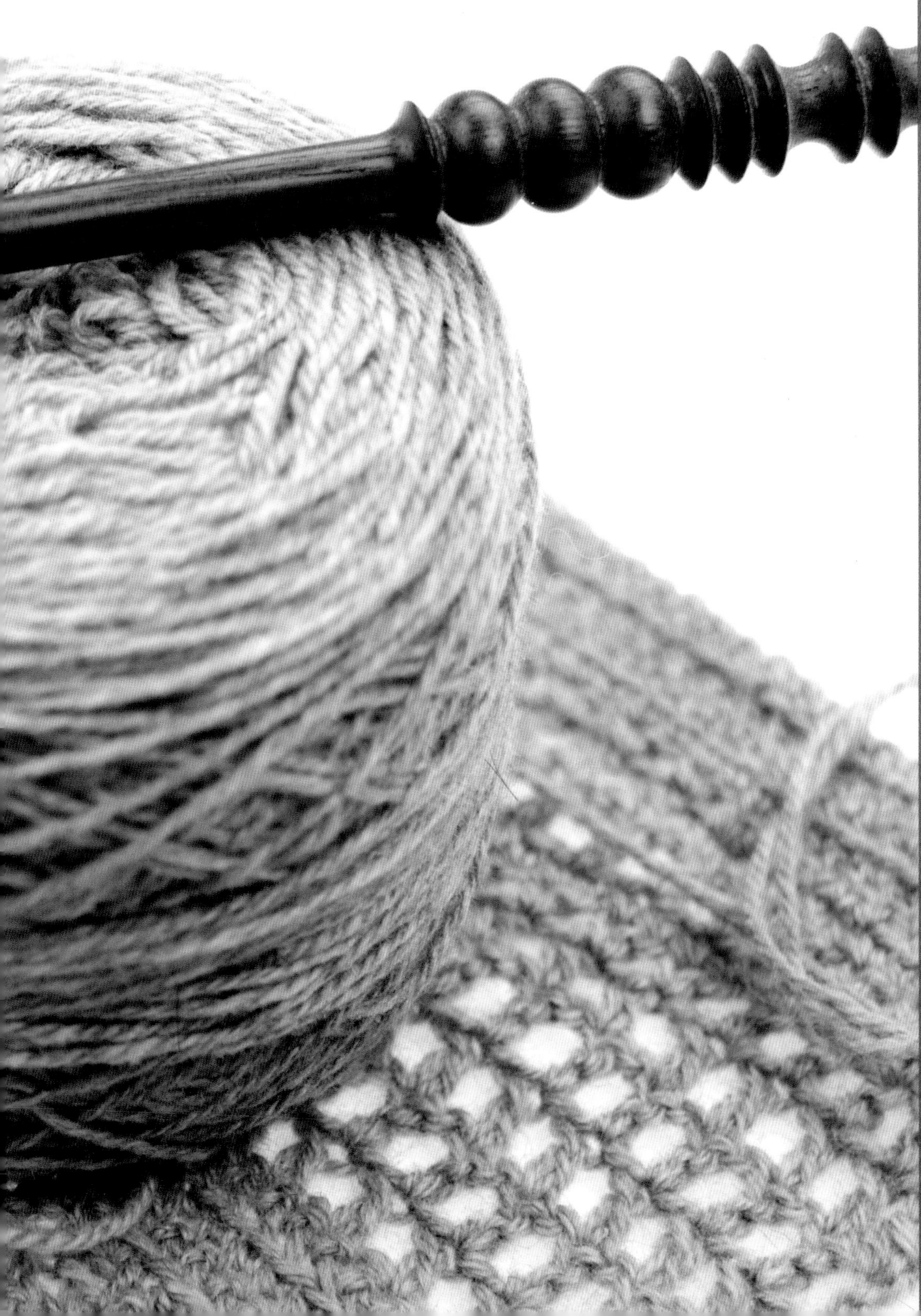

RESOURCES

Stitches and Rows Per Inch Worksheet

Knowing your stitches and rows per inch is a vital part of your swatching and overall making process. The stitches and rows per inch are the gauge the designer gives you so you can duplicate the fabric they have created their design. In general, if you are using the same yarn or a similar yarn as called for in the design, and your stitches and rows per inch match the designer's stitches and rows per inch, then you should be making the same fabric. For more about gauge, see the "Checking Tension and Gauge" section on page 74.

To help you calculate your gauge and evaluate your tension, our step-by-step worksheet (opposite) for figuring your stitches and rows per inch within your fabric.

Stitches and Rows Worksheet

Total Number Rows Ⓑ _____

Total Height Inches Ⓓ _____

Total Number Of Stitches In One Row Ⓐ _____

Total Width Inches Ⓒ _____

Calculations

SWATCH STITCHES PER INCH	
Total Number of Stitches In One Row Ⓐ Divided by Total Swatch Width Inches Ⓒ	_____ _____
Stitches Per Inch	_____

SWATCH ROWS PER INCH	
Total Number of Rows Ⓑ Divided by Total Swatch Height Inches Ⓓ	_____ _____
Rows Per Inch	_____

Stitch Multiples Worksheet

The stitch multiple is the number of stitches needed to work one repeat of a pattern stitch. When working with pattern stitches, you will often see the phrase "worked over a multiple of…" followed by numbers with a plus sign between them, such as 3 + 2, 5 + 2, etc. This information is telling you exactly how many stitches you need in order to work this pattern stitch evenly across a row. For an explanation of stitch multiples, see "Multiple of Stitches for a Pattern Stitch" in the "Shaping" section on page 136 and the "Pattern Stitches" section on page 206.

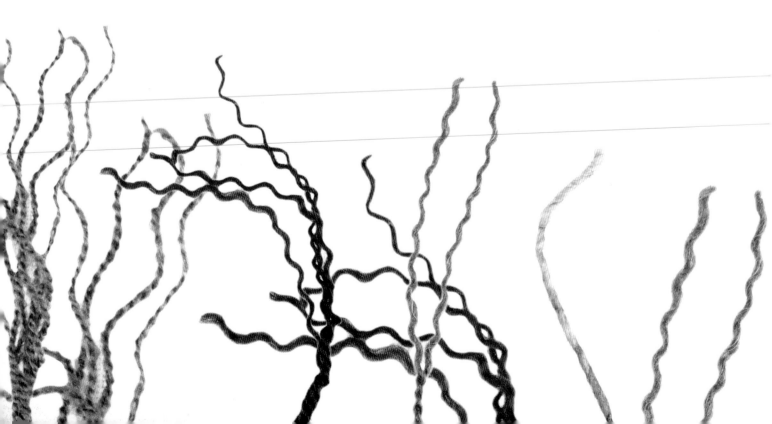

Stitch Multiples Worksheet

> Stitch pattern worked over a multiple of _____ + _____ Stitches
>
> (Y)   (Z)

Total number of Inches   _____

Multipled by   **×**

Stitches per inch   _____

Total Stitches Needed   _____

divided by   **÷**

Stitch Pattern Multiple (Y)   _____

plus   **+**

Add'l stitches for pattern (Z)   _____

equals
Total Stitches to Work   _____

Whole Number of pattern repeats   _____
Rounded Down

Multipled by   **×**

Stitch Pattern Multiple (Y)   _____

Total Stitches Worked In Pattern   _____

plus   **+**

Add'l stitches for pattern (Z)   _____

Total Stitches to Work   _____

Charts and Guides

Skill Level Chart

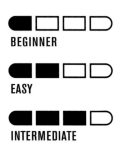

BEGINNER

EASY

INTERMEDIATE

EXPERIENCED

Hook Size Charts

Standard Crochet Hook Sizes

2.25 mm	B-1
2.75 mm	C-2
3.25 mm	D-3
3.5 mm	E-4
3.75 mm	F-5
4 mm	G-6
4.5 mm	7
5 mm	H-8
5.5 mm	I-9
6 mm	J-10
6.5 mm	-10.5
8 mm	L-11
9 mm	M/N-13
10 mm	N/P-15
15 mm	P/Q
16 mm	Q
19 mm	S

Steel Hook Sizes

0.75 mm	14
0.85	13
1 mm	12
1.1 mm	11
1.3 mm	10
1.4 mm	9
1.5 mm	8
1.65 mm	7
1.8 mm	6
1.9 mm	5
2 mm	4
2.1 mm	3
2.25 mm	2
2.75 mm	1
3.25 mm	0
3.5 mm	00

Yarn Weights, Naming Conventions, and Wraps per Inch (WPI)

CYC - 0 Lace	CYC - 1 Super Fine	CYC - 2 Fine	CYC - 3 Light	CYC - 4 Medium	CYC - 5 Bulky	CYC - 6 Super Bulky	CYC - 7 Jumbo
0 LACE	**1** SUPER FINE	**2** FINE	**3** LIGHT	**4** MEDIUM	**5** BULKY	**6** SUPER BULKY	**7** JUMBO
Lace, Light Fingering, #10 Crochet Thread	Sock, Fingering, Baby	Sport, Baby	DK, Light Worsted	Worsted, Afghan, Aran	Chunky, Craft, Rug	Bulky, Roving	Jumbo, Roving
35+ WPI	19–22 WPI	15–18 WPI	12–14 WPI	9–11 WPI	7–8 WPI	5–6 WPI	4 or less WPI

US to UK Conversion Chart

US TERM	UK TERM	CHART SYMBOL
Slip Stitch	Slip	●
Single Crochet	Double Crochet	+
Half Double Crochet	Half Treble Crochet	T
Double Crochet	Treble Crochet	⊤̸
Treble Crochet	Double Treble Crochet	⊤̸
Double Treble Crochet	Triple Treble Crochet	⊤̸

Crochet Abbreviations Master List

[ ]	work instructions within brackets as many times as directed
( )	work instructions within parentheses as many times as directed
*	repeat the instructions following single asterisk
"	inches
alt	alternating
approx.	approximately
beg	begin(ning)
bet	between
bl	back loop
bp	Back Post
BPdc	Back Post double crochet
BPsc	Back Post single crochet
BPtr	Back Post treble crochet
ch	chain
cm	centimeter
cont	continue
dc	double crochet
dc2tog	double crochet 2 together
dc3tog	double crochet 3 together
dec	decrease
dtr	double treble
FP	Front Post
FPdc	Front Post double crochet
FPsc	Front Post single crochet
FPtr	Front Post treble crochet
g	gram

hdc	half double crochet
inc	increase
lp(s)	loop(s)
m	meter
oz	ounce
pm	place marker
prev	previous
rem	remaining
rep	repeat(s)
rnd(s)	round(s)
RS	right side
sc	single crochet
sk	skip
sl st	slip stitch
sp(s)	space(s)
st(s)	stitch(es)
tbl	through the back loop
tfl	through the front loop
tog	together
tr	treble crochet
trtr	triple treble
ws	wrong side
yd(s)	yard(s)
yo	yarn over

PAGE 322   PAGE 324   PAGE 326

1x1 BPdc LC	2-1-2 LC BPdc	3-dc Cluster	4-dc Shell	Adjustable Ring	dc-fan var 1	ext-dc	F Herringbone dc	hdc tbl	Linked First dc	sc-v var 1	Stacked 1st hdc
1x1 BPdc RC	2x2 RC BPdc	3-dc Shell	4-1-4 FPtr LC	BPdc	dc-fan	ext-dtr	F Herringbone hdc	hdc tfl	Linked First hdc	sc-v	Stacked 1st tr
1x1 LC dc	2x2 BPtr RC	3-1-3 FPtr LC	4-1-4 FPtr RC	BPdtr	dc-v var 1	ext-hdc	Fsc	hdc-v var 1	Linked First tr	sc	tr tbl
1x1 RC dc	2x2 FPdc LC	3-1-3 FPtr RC	4x4 FPtr LC	BPhdc	dc-v	ext-sc	Fsl st	hdc-v	Linked hdc	sc2tog	tr tfl
1x1 LC BPdc	2x2 FPdc RC	3x3 FPtr LC	4x4 FPtr RC	BPsc	dc	ext-tr	Ftr	hdc	Linked tr	sl st	
1x1 RC BPdc	2x2 FPtr LC	3x3 tr LC	5-dc Bobble	BPtr	dc2tog	FLdc	FPdc	hdc2tog	Linked tr	Stacked 1st dc	
2-dc Bobble	2x2 FPtr RC	3x3 FPtr LC	5-dc Popcorn	Chain Ring	dc3tog	FLhdc	FPdtr	hdc Herringbone	Picot	tr	
2-dc Cluster	2x2 tr LC	3x3 FPtr RC	5-dc Shell	chain	dtr tbl	FLtr	FPhdc	Herringbone Fdc	Puff	tr2tog	
2-1-2 FPtr LC	2x2 tr RC	3x3 tr LC	7-dc cluster	dc tbl	dtr tfl	Fdc	FPsc	Herringbone Fhdc	sc tbl	tr3tog	
2-1-2 FPtr RC	3-dc Bobble	3x3 tr RC	7-dc Fan	dc tfl	dtr	Fhdc	FPtr	Linked dc	sc tfl	hdc3tog	

PAGE 323   PAGE 325   PAGE 327

Stitch Chart Symbols

PG 322

MASTER KEY

1x1 BPdc LC	2-1-2 LC BPdc	3-dc Cluster	4-dc Shell
1x1 BPdc RC	2x2 RC BPdc	3-dc Shell	4-1-4 FPtr LC
1x1 LC dc	2x2 BPtr RC	3-1-3 FPtr LC	4-1-4 FPtr RC
1x1 RC dc	2x2 FPdc LC	3-1-3 FPtr RC	4x4 FPtr LC
1x1 LC BPdc	2x2 FPdc RC	3x3 FPtr LC	4x4 FPtr RC

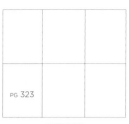

PG 323

MASTER KEY

1x1 RC BPdc	2x2 FPtr LC	3x3 tr LC	5-dc Bobble
2-dc Bobble	2x2 FPtr RC	3x3 FPtr LC	5-dc Popcorn
2-dc Cluster	2x2 tr LC	3x3 FPtr RC	5-dc Shell
2-1-2 FPtr LC	2x2 tr RC	3x3 tr LC	7-dc cluster
2-1-2 FPtr RC	3-dc Bobble	3x3 tr RC	7-dc Fan

Stitch Chart Symbols (continued)

Adjustable Ring	dc-fan var 1	ext-dc	F Herringbone dc
BPdc	dc-fan	ext-dtr	F Herringbone hdc
BPdtr	dc-v var 1	ext-hdc	Fsc
BPhdc	dc-v	ext-sc	Fsl st
BPsc	dc	ext-tr	Ftr

BPtr	dc2tog	FLdc	FPdc
Chain Ring	dc3tog	FLhdc	FPdtr
chain	dtr tbl	FLtr	FPhdc
dc tbl	dtr tfl	Fdc	FPsc
dc tfl	dtr	Fhdc	FPtr

Stitch Chart Symbols *(continued)*

PG 326

MASTER KEY

hdc tbl	 Linked First dc	 sc-v var 1	 Stacked 1st hdc
hdc tfl	 Linked First hdc	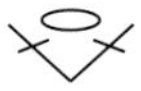 sc-v	 Stacked 1st tr
 hdc-v var 1	 Linked First tr	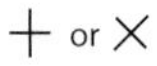 sc	 tr tbl
 hdc-v	 Linked hdc	sc2tog	 tr tfl
hdc	 Linked tr	sl st	

MASTER KEY

PG 327

hdc2tog	Linked tr	Stacked 1st dc
hdc Herringbone	Picot	tr
Herringbone Fdc	Puff	tr2tog
Herringbone Fhdc	⊥ or ✕ sc tbl	tr3tog
Linked dc	⊥ or ✕ sc tfl	hdc3tog

Material Resources

Hooks & Tools

The beautiful hooks and tools photographed were generously provided by:

Clover . . . . clover-usa.com

Stephen Willette . . . . stephenwillette.com

Furls . . . . furlscrochet.com

Yarn

Yarn for the swatches, stepouts, and photography was generously provided by:

Valley Yarns . . . . yarn.com

Cascade Yarns . . . . cascadeyarns.com

Lion Brand Yarns . . . . lionbrand.com

Malabrigo Yarn . . . . malabrigoyarn.com

Anny Blatt . . . . annyblattnorthamerica.com

Buffalo Wool Company . . . . thebuffalowoolco.com

Acknowledgments

CONTRACTORS

Deb

Patrick

Juanita

Lara

Cat

AGENT

Linda Roghaar

YARN & TOOL SUPPORT

Clover

Stephen Willette

Furls

Valley Yarns

Cascade Yarns

Lion Brand Yarns

Malabrigo Yarn

Anny Blatt

Buffalo Wool Company

SPECIAL THANK YOU TO

Barbara Van Elsen
(special envoy to the ICCE)

The Team

While we could fill the entirety of this book with the names of people who helped bring this book to life, there are a few special folks we need to call out by name to show our appreciation:

To our contractors—the FAB stitchers who help us take our patterns and turn them into pieces of art, thank you for all your hard work. You inspire us daily.

To our agent, Linda—who continues to believe in us and in our work, and in turn gets us more work, let's do lunch!

To our studio sponsors—who provide us with yarn, tools, and all the trappings of the trade, thank you for helping us do what we love to do every day.

To our editors and art department folks at Sterling Publishing—who totally rock—thank you for helping us turn our vision into reality.

To Barbara—Thank you for answering the phone.

Index

About the Authors

Shannon and Jason are the DIY duo known as the Shibaguyz, behind the design studio of Shibaguyz Designz and Shibaguyz Photography.

Shannon's award-winning crochet and knit designs have been featured in and on the covers of both US and international publications, and he currently has over 300 published patterns and 10 books credited to his name since his first design was featured on the cover of a magazine in 2010. Shannon has been teaching adults for 20+ years and is a Craft Yarn Council certified instructor. His quirky sense of humor and relatable teaching style have made him a sought-after teacher in national venues like STITCHES! and Vogue Knitting LIVE! He has a wide range of online classes available from Craftsy, Craft University, and Interweave.

Jason is a professional fashion and portrait photographer whose fashion photography can be seen in many of the Shibaguyz' pattern books. Jason also works as a freelance book-packaging designer and photographer for indie knitwear designers, as well as major publishing companies. Jason is known for his candid style of photography in his portrait work, and is sought after in the fiber arts community for his insights into what it takes to show an artist's work at its best. He travels nationally, sharing his photography skills and teaching design classes with Shannon. Jason also has photography videos and workshops available online through Craftsy, Craft University, and Interweave.

Shannon and Jason live in Seattle, Washington with their three Shiba Inu who, more or less, support their ventures as long as enough time is taken for walks and treats.